BEFORE BABEL

The Crystal Tongue

Madeleine Daines

First published in paperback in 2019

Copyright © Madeleine Daines 2019

The right of Madeleine Daines to be identified as the Author of the Work has been asserted by her in accordance with the Copyright, Designs and Patents Act 1988.

All rights reserved. No part of this publication may be reproduced, stored in a retrieval system or transmitted in any form or by any means without the prior written permission of the author, nor be otherwise circulated in any form of binding or cover other than that in which it is published and without a similar condition being imposed on the subsequent purchaser.

ISBN: 978-2-9560459-1-5

All characters in this publication have lived
in some form in a distant past.

HerFairHand

Crystal: Old English cristal 'clear ice; clear, transparent mineral,' from Old French cristal (12c., Modern French crystal), from Latin crystallus 'crystal, ice,' from Greek krystallos, a word of unknown origin.

The dwarf (...) noticed by bringing them close to his eye, that these diamonds, by the manner in which they had been cut, were excellent microscopes. He took a small microscope of 160-foot diameter and applied it to his pupil, while Micromegas took one of 2,500 feet. They were excellent but, at first, nothing could be seen, even with their help; adjustment was needed. Finally, the Saturnian saw something almost imperceptible moving near the surface of the Baltic Sea: it was a whale. Adroitly, he picked it up with his little finger and, placing it on his thumbnail, showed it to the Sirian who started laughing again at the excessive smallness of the inhabitants of our globe. The Saturnian, satisfied that our world was inhabited after all, assumed immediately that its only inhabitants were whales.
Micromégas, Ch.4:3, (1752), Voltaire

Tradition assures us that mankind spoke it before the building of the Tower of Babel, which caused its distortion and, for most people, led to this sacred dialect being completely lost to memory.
The Mystery of the Cathedrals, (1926) Fulcanelli

Sais christ to ypocrites ... yee ar ... al ful wit wickednes, tresun, and bull.
Cursor Mundi, (1300) Author unknown

NAM I-AN

Contents

Preface P.1

1. The Tower of Babel P.3
2. The Enki Heresy P.29
3. Harran P.39
4. Gobekli Tepe P.51
5. The Great Bull and the Flow of Beer P.57
6. Two Horns of the Great Bull P.71
7. The Umbilical Cord and the Flow of Water P.77
8. Springs, Fountains and Waterspouts P.83
9. Cursing Stones of Gods and Bull P.95
10. Signs of the Magician P.103
11. Prometheus P.121
12. The Ancient Clews P.131
13. The Idigna Bird of the Taurus Mountains P.137
14. Bird of Prophecy P.147
15. Shaman and Alchemist P.161
16. Talon, the Metal Robot P.173
17. The Sun, the Lion and the Pyramid P.183
18. Hermes and the Crystal Heresy P.191
19. The Sator Templar Connection P.237
20. Atlantis and the Fish P.269
21. The Sky to Know the End P.279

Notes and References P.297

Index of Symbols P.306

List of Lexical Entries P.309

Annexe: The Story of Sukurru P.310

Preface

The past has been forgotten because we have lost the language of it. Bloodshed isn't mentioned in the story of the Tower of Babel and yet a murder took place in it, the saddest story that we have. Who carried out the crime? This book points out the groundwork. The rest of the mystery is beyond my remit. I have no personal agenda with regard to history other than to find the truth by going back and picking up the thread at the oldest possible source. The result is not the expression of personal opinion or cultural, religious beliefs, but of the consultation of the Sumerian symbols themselves. They have enough to say without forcing and twisting. Coaxing is all it takes.

In 2017, I published a complete re-translation of one of the earliest literary texts known to the modern world under the title *The Instructions of Shuruppak*. It was found on several Mesopotamian clay tablets, the oldest of which firmly dated to around 2600 BC. Using an innovative method, I spent two years discovering the true story inscribed there before giving it the more appropriate title of *The Story of Sukurru*. A copy of that translation is given in an annexe here. This book is not a translation. It's an explanation, a study of the earliest symbols, foundation stones of many if not all later languages, showing how to read and understand them, bypassing the officialised narrative that has built up over past centuries. Making use of conventional sources to resuscitate the original meanings[1], I demonstrate the translation method that refutes the academic understanding of Sumerian texts. The conclusions are all grounded in substantiated findings based on the forms of the old pictograms, their given and their forgotten meanings in context.

What the symbols disclose is a truth very different from everything we have been taught to believe about the origin of the languages spoken today and the manner in which they evolved; a truth so different that the task of recovery appears herculean. But it must be told. It must begin. That the sounds associated with symbols covering clay tablets in the 4th millennium BC became an integral part of the Phoenician alphabet[2] while retaining the essence of their original meanings, and thus that the language of ancient Greece is, in truth, a direct descendant of Sumer. Not only that. The entirety of Greek mythology is considerably older than we have been given to understand. And it is Sumerian. I make no suggestion as to the origin of that language other than to say I believe it to be far, far older than the tablets on which it was found, and that it was worldwide. There is no competition to be invoked for ownership, no national pride to be hurt. It is older than any of us and it belongs to us all.

Thanks to those symbols, it becomes possible to bypass the entirety of history, with its truths and falsehoods, between 3000 BC and the present day. The first stepping-stone was *The Story of Sukurru*. This book is the second. That re-translation demonstrated two fundamental points about Sumerian that had been missed. It is not an isolated language. It has children, many children. And it was a monosyllabic language articulated in a way that has as much affinity with riddles as with modern grammar. It cannot fully reveal its secrets through our alphabet alone.

What the symbols disclose is a myriad of clues about the places, the names, the words that present themselves as blank walls with no doors, no rusted handles. We have to return to the earliest forms, those images that appeared on clay tablets dated to the period between 3350 and 3000 BC, and to stop believing that they were the product of a primitive mindset. The knowledge has been hermetic to us for that reason. If you are prepared to look more closely at each one, the gate is still there, leading back to places beyond time where we can begin to perceive the age-old magic that underlies every word we speak. We might even trace the forgotten hand of Hermes Trismegistus whose revered memory has lingered on for millennia, a figure associated with the highest form of Egyptian magic, and for whom even an approximate age cannot be safely given. The earliest copies of texts known collectively as the Corpus Hermeticum and said to emanate from the great wisdom teacher were written down in Arabic and Greek during the first millennium AD, copied again, this time in Latin, and rediscovered yet again with great excitement at the start of the Renaissance. There is no way to prove that any of those writings date back beyond the earliest years of our era, but what of the Great Magician himself? The old Sumerian symbols, still warm from his touch, are waiting to explain themselves.

How many stepping-stones will it take? How wide is the river? Those essential places, those places of the essence are all still there murmuring to us. Will we succeed in remembering? Would you like to try?

1

The Tower of Babel

An infant's first breath is followed by frantic screams and a search for the maternal breast, for milk, for the food of life. There can be no doubt of the importance given to the matriarchal figure in the most ancient times, born of the boundless, unconditional love that a mother has for her child, shown in the breaking waters at child birth as metaphor for the life-giving rivers and ocean, and in the vision of the Milky Way as gateway to the matriarchal womb.

The cosmic Matriarch is beyond our current understanding of the feminine. Today, because the original stories have been lost, we see the images that remain of her as deformed, with her odd shaped head, massive buttocks and breasts. They make us laugh, but there was a different mindset once. Those images englobe the celestial realm which is her multi-tasking form[3].

An infant sucks at the mother's breasts for some months if all goes well, alternating between the two, but there comes a time, an inevitable time when the weaning must begin, when dependence on milk is replaced by the need for water. From the nipples of the Matriarch flow the rivers and streams, all the way to the tap. Turn it on… Turn it off…

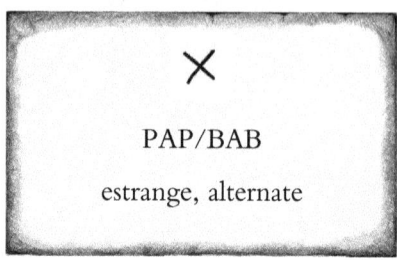

PAP/BAB

estrange, alternate

PAP/BAB is given as 'different', 'to estrange' and 'to alternate' along with other meanings 86 times[1]. There is more than one form to this symbol on the oldest tablets but the above is the most obvious expression of the maternal nipple, found in the lists of 'primitive' forms in *L'Ecriture Cunéiforme*[1]. X marks the spot where life gets a kick start.

> *Pap: 'nipple of a woman's breast,' c. 1200, first attested in Northern and Midlands writing, probably from a Scandinavian source (not recorded in Old Norse, but compare dialectal Swedish pappe), from PIE imitative root *pap- 'to swell' (source also of Latin papilla 'nipple,' papula 'a swelling, pimple;' Lithuanian papas 'nipple').*[1]

Tablets from the earliest Uruk IV period, around 3350 to 3200 BC, pictured on the CDLI site[1] show symbol PAP with a different form, still two strokes but more evocative of a valve or a switch than the cross that marks the nipple.

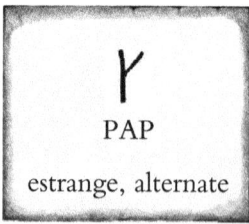

PAP

estrange, alternate

The above shows that nothing is known of the origin of the English word 'pap', its commonly accepted etymology being the nebulous PIE or proto-

Indo-European root.[5] The truth is that it came into being on clay at a period in our history which must be either during the second half of the 4th millennium BC or earlier, even considerably earlier. It looks simple enough but there is always more to the story in matters of Sumerian symbols.

The translation of *The Story of Sukurru*[6] finds PAP on line 27 in a context involving circumcision, an act that can be linked to weaning, but this time a manmade rite of passage from one stage of life to the next. In this context, it's also the alternation of sounds or the gap left between notes. The three symbols, TAR-PAP-RA, translate to an alternating signal played on a horn as people attempt to pass through the gates of a great city; what we might call border control. Let him in… Leave him out…

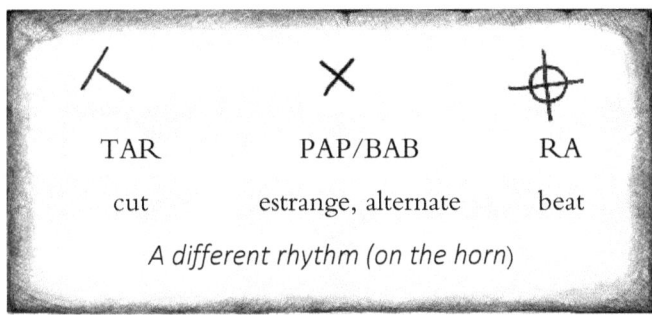

PAP functioned as a valve in more situations than one. The sound varies between a P, a B, or a V, this last not considered in the alphabetical forms of Sumerian. Does symbol PAP/BAB have its origin in the use of water, manually controlled through an instrument opening or closing access to the vital source, some form of tap? Is symbol PAP in the form of an X to be first and foremost linked to the nipple and the act of breast-feeding? Which came first? I would have to side with the Matriarch. You must decide for yourself. But, whatever the truth, those are the only questions we need to ask about the etymology of modern-day 'pap', the nipple.

The story of the Tower as told in Genesis, where God prevents people from collaborating by confusing their language, doesn't include mention of the name. Neither Babel nor Babylon have given up their origins. In etymological dictionaries, Babel is generally linked to the Akkadian language, which was expressed in the well-known cuneiform signs, directly inherited from the original Sumerian symbols. The most commonly held explanation of the sound 'Bab' with 'el' or 'yl' goes as follows:

>   Akkadian Babu-ilu from Sumerian KA_2-AN.

Whoever found that equivalence did so by working backwards from an Akkadian inscription and checking with the old lexical lists[4]. Below are the pictographic forms of the two Sumerian symbols commonly thought to be at the origin of the name.

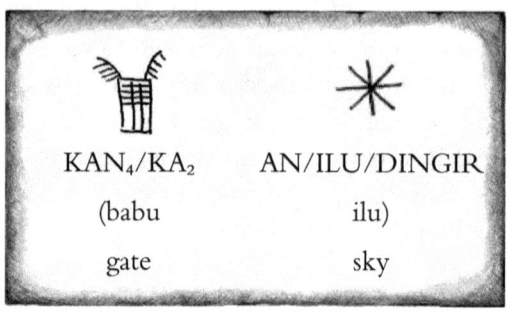

Shown here as it appeared on clay in the earliest Uruk IV period of 3350 to 3200 BC, symbol KAN_4/KA_2 is given as 'gate' 13 times on the ePSD website[1]. It appears to be made up of E_2, symbol for a 'house' or 'temple' with the addition of two or more feather or reed-like forms sprouting above it. Other versions have three or four unadorned lines in their place. It has several phonetic values as do most of the Sumerian symbols, a fact which is both confusing and useful.

Our understanding of the sounds that accompany all of the symbols comes from a category of clay tablets known as the 'lexical lists'. These were etymological dictionaries, tracing back from the Assyrian to their Sumerian source with equivalences given between them along the way. It's thanks to those tablets that we have a method by which to rediscover something of the original meanings and sounds. The small number to the right of the phonetic form indicates that this is the fourth symbol found to have the sound KAN and the second with the sound KA, a philological classification that does not necessarily reflect an original ordering. In the same way, AN can be read out loud as ILU or DINGIR. Whether referred to as AN or ILU or DINGIR, the picture will be that of the eight-pointed star. For my translations, I have almost always used the same phonetic form to refer to a symbol. Thus, the eight-pointed star of 'sky' is always AN. Academic translations have a different approach, sometimes multiplying the phonetic forms of one symbol within the same text.

Opposite KAN₄/KA₂ in the lexical entries appear its two founding symbols, KA-AN, both of which can be traced back to the Uruk IV period, ca. 3350 to 3200 BC:

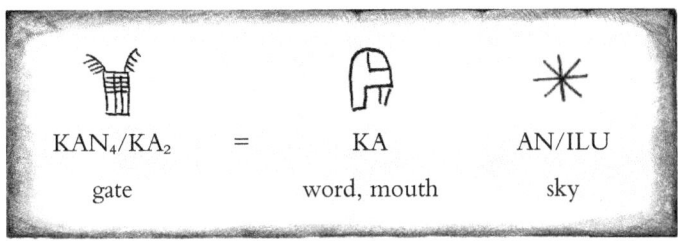

KA

KA is given as 'word' 57 times at the earliest period. KA has an important role in monosyllabic Sumerian. Used for words involving speech and the mouth, it is also apparent in spiritual themes and crops up constantly in the texts. KA as pictogram has a strangely flat profile, with what appears to be a huge closed eye, no nose or mouth, and two strokes emerging from the region of the chin. No doubt it originated with the more naturalistic drawing of a head and all versions still retain traces of the beard below the chin to distinguish KA from another symbol pronounced SAG, 'head'.

An extraordinary and unique Egyptian style head with a goatee beard figures on a Sumerian tablet from the Uruk III period of 3200 to 3000 BC, shown here on the left[7]:

On the right is a simplified profile of the well-known death mask of Egyptian pharaoh Tutankhamun on display at the Egyptian Museum of Cairo. The tablet image has been classified as a 'seal' with 'no linguistic content', but images of this kind not relating to language are uncommon on inscribed tablets and it fits the template for later KA symbols. Inscribed on clay no later than 3000 BC, it corresponds approximately to the Naqada III period of Egyptian history and age of the Narmer palette, another Egyptian artefact with intriguing imagery.

A close relative of KA is BU_3, displaying a more recognisable beard. One has cross hatching which might infer plaiting, and also has the given meaning of 'mouth'. But it might also be said that the form below the chin is that of a ladder. Three examples from the Uruk III, 3200–3000 BC period, are shown below[8]:

 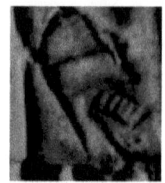 

Sumerian clay tablets are said to represent the very beginning of writing because the evidence for anything earlier is missing. That absence isn't proof. The pictograms are described as primitive. The Egyptian head on one of the earliest tablets shows that to not always be true. It's unlikely that it was derived from the abstract KA rather than the other way around, or that they are unconnected. At the same time and as will be seen here, a strong bond with Egyptian themes is evident in other Sumerian symbols and in several sections of *The Story of Sukurru*.

AN

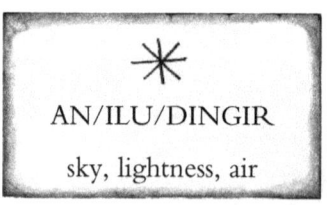

AN/ILU/DINGIR

sky, lightness, air

AN is the eight-pronged star that has the given meanings of 'sky, heaven' 54 times and 'deity, god, goddess' 120 times. This is where God comes into the picture in the classic interpretation of Babel as 'Gate of God'. One important aspect of symbolic Sumerian is the mirroring of sounds. They may be meanings that are opposed. They may be complementary. See KI with IK on

8

page 37. My additions of 'air' and 'lightness' come from the obvious qualities of sky but also a comparison with the inverted phonetic value NA:

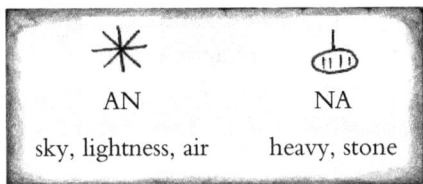

One phonetic form of the eight-pointed star, DINGIR is taken as the prefix signalling the name of a god, and hence the use of 'd' before names which conveniently indicates both deity and DINGIR; for example, ᵈEnki, the popular Enki character who gets short shrift here. See page 29.

Another phonetic value of the AN symbol is ILU carried forward in Akkadian Babu-ilu. The fact that this eight-pronged star turns up relatively frequently in the Sumerian texts perhaps explains why scholars have been convinced that there were many godly figures throughout the millennia BC. Each time the symbol was found in the middle of a line, with the translator's cultural assumption that the meaning was linked to religions, gods and the stories about them, then the one, two or three symbols that followed, too obscure to translate in any other way, would be understood as a name, a new god in a manmade pantheon. There is no way of establishing an accurate time-line for the transformation from AN, the sky and the lightness of air, to AN or DINGIR or ILU, the god. There must have been a time when a heavenly god symbol became a necessity. Without gods, no religion. What better symbol to choose for the role than that of the sky?

ILU

As mentioned earlier, in an effort to avoid the confusion of alternating between different phonetic values for one symbol, this one is always AN in my work. That doesn't negate the usefulness of the other values given to it. On the contrary, it's particularly useful for a study of Babel and Babylon to dissect phonetic ILU according to the lexical entries[4] found opposite it:

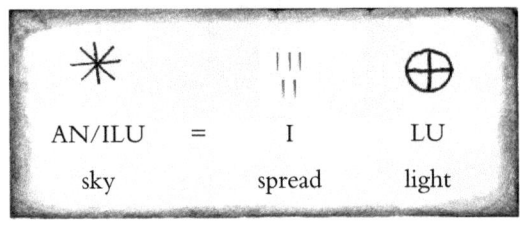

a) I

Represented by five short vertical marks, the meanings of I are 'to spread', 'multiply', and the number 'five'. The Sumerian symbol I is that of the so-called Fibonacci sequence, a system of adding numbers together that mirrors nature. Here the meaning of it is conveyed in the simplest possible way; two vertical strikes that become three, spreading upwards:

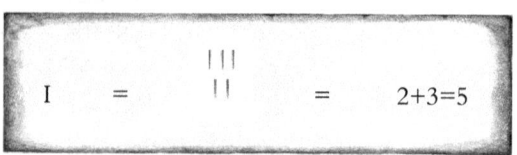

It stands to reason that a symbolic version of the ever-increasing equation would best be found in 2+3=5 rather than 1+1=2 or 3+5=8. Anything smaller or greater would be less obvious or more complicated.

There is just one example of symbol I on CDLI at the earliest Uruk IV period, but it comes in prestigious company with PI. See page 185 for more on PI. Symbol PI has another phonetic form, YA, which appears to be linked to I-A, multiplication of the flow, and is given as 'five'. Unfortunately, the tablet[9] is little more than a fragment and the 'rabbit ears' of PI are damaged:

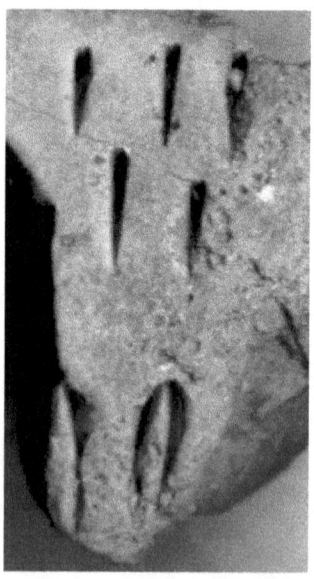

Confirmation of the meanings of I comes from the context; the I-A of Gaia, with the meaning 'multiplying of her waters' are found on line 260 of *The Story of Sukurru*. Symbol A seen at the start of each chapter here, is 'flow' and 'water'. Someone in or before the 4th millennia BC was already aware of the sequencing re-discovered in the 13th century AD. How did Fibonacci come across it?

b) LU

LU

light, sheep

The symbol of LU, also phonetic UDU, is given in Sumerian dictionaries as 'sheep' 1,423 times between 3000 and 2500 BC and 23,724 times after that. That way, there can be no misunderstanding. The numbers have it. The notion of counting sheep in order to sleep is of unknown origin. But with Sumerian LU as the source of 'lunar', the origin becomes obvious. See line 129 of *The Story of Sukurru*. The moon has replaced the sun and the vessel is lulled to sleep.

Sheep are characterised by their meek attitude, the way they crowd together, led by an animal smaller but louder and more ferocious than themselves. No-one can question that trait of character or that the symbol seen here was used on Sumerian clay tablets for the purpose of trading sheep. According to academia, that was the sole reason for the LU/UDU symbol. Nevertheless, it's also given as 'to disturb' and 'to stir up', or 'mix' twice.

Of course, accepting to be herded by a voice louder than one's own is also a human trait. Whether a pontificating leader or bullying voice of a more obvious abuser, the instinct to obey, to fall silent and avoid confrontation is strong. If the herding is done without physical barriers to stop sheep from breaking away and doing their own thing, then whose fault is that? If authoritative voices scoff at my lonely and very different translation of LU into 'light', a vital key on this path to enlightenment, who will be right? I propose that the symbol itself be considered, that the sound of it be assessed, and that the logic of the meanings in context be taken into account. No bullying allowed.

> *Lunar: late 14c. 'the moon,' especially as personified in a Roman goddess answering to Greek Selene; also an alchemical name for 'silver;' from Latin luna 'moon, goddess of the moon,' from PIE root.*
>
> *Luminary: mid-15c., 'lamp, light-giver, source of light,' from Old French luminarie (12c.), 'lamp, lights, (...) from Late Latin luminare 'light, torch, (...),' literally 'that which gives light,' from Latin lumen (genitive luminis) 'light, (...) related to lucere 'to shine,' from suffixed (iterative) form of PIE root.*

LU is the origin of everything 'lunar', representing the light of the moon and even the moon itself through French 'lune'. The majority of entries in etymological dictionaries appear to end with 'from PIE root' or 'unknown source'. I have used Etymonline[1] for the most part because it's a pleasant site to visit and it offers a careful compilation of explanations from different sources. 'From PIE root' is the final entry for most of our words, and it is misleading because it implies a knowledge of the ultimate source when, in fact, PIE (proto-Indo-European) is nothing more than an exercise in comparison of sounds from different related languages. There is no text to back up the results of it, and, when compared to the Sumerian origins offered here, the PIE sounds given are not usually anywhere close to the truth.

Sumerian symbol LU is also the origin of the Templar cross, an emblem that is said to have begun its journey in Babylon. Those two symbols together, I-LU, translate to 'the multiplication, the spreading of light', a description that corresponds well with the composite symbol of the two, the final eight-pointed symbol of AN, the sky. Where else to look for light?

There are many variants to the symbol of the cross found in the context of philosophies or religions around the world, some more distinctive than others. The Sumerian cross can be seen in symbol LU enclosed in a circle, but it also has its place in RA, where the four spokes go beyond the circumference, and again in HER, a symbol discussed in Chapter 18. It may be that the original purpose, the foundation stone so to speak of the cross symbol was to point to the four cardinal directions. The cross is at the heart of the cosmic map, the fundamental starting point leading to all other knowledge and it has its place at the centre of enlightenment. Where did it all begin? Does anyone really know?

Back to Babylon...

> *And the LORD came down to see the city and the tower, which the children of man had built.*
> *And the LORD said, "Behold, they are one people, and they have all one language, and this is only the beginning of what they will do. And nothing that they propose to do will now be impossible for them.*
> *Come, let us go down and there confuse their language, so that they may not understand one another's speech.*[10]

The biblical text makes no bones about it. A culture bound together by a single language was dangerous. It had to be bullied or bulldozed out of existence. Was this the will of an invisible god in the sky or a planned takeover of the public space by a determined group, sufficiently organised to evolve such a plan over generations? That is, of course, the definition of a conspiracy. How old is the story, and to what extent has it been rewritten, distorted? If we are to perceive something of a pragmatic historical account behind this section of Genesis, it might be that a dominant group sought to eliminate a pagan culture. That would have included all memory of it, a re-writing of history. On the other hand, it could be the reworking of an ancient story where a massive natural catastrophe put an end to the adventures of a troublesome ruler, a self-obsessed character who, more than anything, wanted the highest tower as their personal legacy. There have been more than one of those.

Whoever wrote the biblical account of events suggested that the best plan to conquer humanity was not to curse us all to hell or to light a bonfire, but to manipulate our greatest common bond, a sacred language grounded in ancient wisdom. There is an obvious lacuna in the Genesis story. How long did it all take? Destruction of the people and their tower could have been rapid, but not that of a language. It would be impossible to force even a small group of people to stop speaking their mother tongue, to suddenly learn another - particularly true if there were no other languages around to take over. Genesis is clear that there were none but glides over the method employed to create them. I daresay expert linguists could come up with a stream of uncommon words to explain how we ever came to do more than grunt or how to distinguish vocalisation from the written word, but let's not go down that tortuous road. We are left with the sense that the event was sudden and brutal. How could that be? Perhaps another scenario.

A rigorous plan implemented over generations whereby the sacred language was to be gradually imploded, new meanings attributed to old words, old meanings set aside, perhaps vilified or ridiculed out of existence, a project whereby old pictographic forms were violated until they became unrecognizable; that plan might have worked. A controlled language like the Newspeak of George Orwell's novel, 1984, set up in its place, using the familiar sounds for a hidden purpose. Self-imposed constraints through peer pressure, political and religious correctness, adaptation of educational systems to favour new teachings using new references, vilification of dissidents, the burning of manuscripts, the defacing of clay… add one or more global catastrophes into the mix. How long would it have taken, once the common culture had been knocked for six by a mix of cupidity, war, and nature's fury, how long for the ripples of such a plan (perhaps both earthly and cosmic) to spread confusion throughout a planet along with the displaced tribes? How long before a golden age of prosperity, of mutual respect grounded in love was well and truly lost and forgotten? Almost forgotten.

> Language has evolved with the city. The pace has quickened for both. Now, the written word is taught with only speed and accuracy in mind. Elegance has taken second place, and spirituality has no place at all in today's important matters. The old signs, round and awkward to draw quickly, have been upended,
> turned anti-clockwise by 45 degrees and straightened. They have been tamed to suit the times. But more than that, they have been deliberately and radically transformed.
> The Story of Sukurru

This was part of the fictional introduction to my re-translation of The Instructions of Shuruppak, based on evidence that the pictographic forms of early Sumerian were turned in exactly that way at some point during the third millennium BC and made increasingly abstract until no visual interpretations could be made. It didn't happen to a few dozen pictograms. There were many more 'primitive' images. Who knows how many disappeared completely?

But that is not exactly how the story is told today. And it has all been explained. The Sumerians came to the southern region of modern Iraq around 4000 BC and then either left again or merged with another culture further north which, not having a writing system of their own and taking a fancy to the old symbols, re-used them in a new and otherwise unconnected language. The earliest Sumerian language is thus unrelated to anything we know today. It is what they call an isolated language. Job done. Move along. Nothing more to see here.

Given the biblical account where a god destroys a manmade tower, the result from this ongoing dissection of Akkadian babu-ilu leads to a rather different understanding of the damage done. If my theory of an ancient project to forever crush knowledge of mankind's innate spirituality by manipulating the symbolic Sumerian language is correct, then the analysis is profoundly revelatory. All it takes is one symbol, the eight-pointed star of the sky. Proclaiming AN to be first and foremost the epithet of 'god' while LU is forever reduced to the status of 'sheep' is gatekeeping of minds, a door closed on a place of enlightenment.

KAN$_4$/KA$_2$ — AN/ILU
(KA – AN) (I – LU)
(babu) (ilu)

gate sky

Voice of the sky   spreading of light

Babel, Babylon

Gate of the sky

Gateway to the light.

Mouth in the sky spreading enlightenment.

Babu

KAN₄/KA₂ is found opposite BA-A-BU on the lexical texts[4]. This is the breakdown of Akkadian 'babu' and should explain why the original symbol was given this additional phonetic form. It's certainly a good enough reason to consider these three symbols in the context of a gateway.

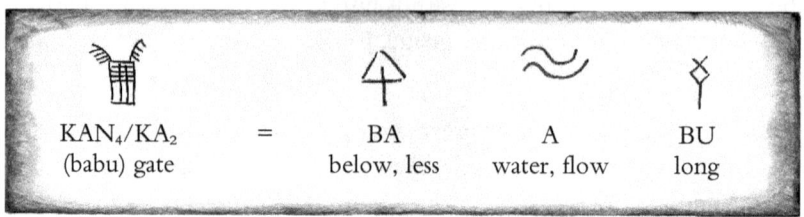

Babu is given in the Manuel d'Epigraphie Akkadienne[1] as both 'gate' and 'weir'. A weir is a barrier that alters the flow of water, and a good fit for the above three symbols where A, the flowing water, is placed between BA, the sign for 'less' or 'below' and BU which I gave in my translation as 'wide'. BU, almost identical to MUŠ, the Sumerian symbol for 'snake', is given 188 times as 'to be long', 'to survey' and 4 times as 'to tear out'. A-BU is likely the origin of Greek 'apo' which tends to confirm the meaning of BU as 'to tear out', synonymous of 'asunder'.

> *Greek apo: 'from, away from; after; in descent from,' in compounds, 'asunder, off; finishing, completing; back again,' of time, 'after,' of origin, 'sprung from, descended from; because of,' from PIE root.*

A-BU is probably also the origin of the Arabian term 'Abu' used to indicate 'father of'. See AB on page 19. If 'babu' refers to regulating the flow of words in the context of Babel, the above analysis makes sense. But that doesn't negate a very real Babylonian gateway, where BA-A-BU is understood as a practical means of controlling the flowing waters, a Mesopotamian weir or the entrance to an underground reservoir. If this is a waterway as a snake, then the symbol is telling us that it's a horned snake which might or might not rule it out as the origin of 'boa'. The two protruding lines above the snake's head can also be understood as two sources of water merging into one reservoir.

It's possible to take the investigation further in that direction by returning to the nipple/valve and looking at a lexical entry[4] for PAP/BAB:

a)

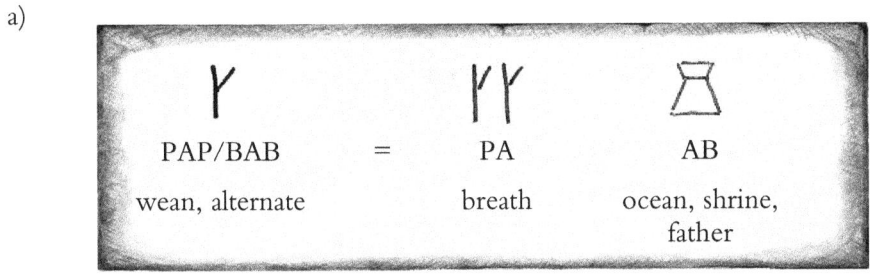

b)

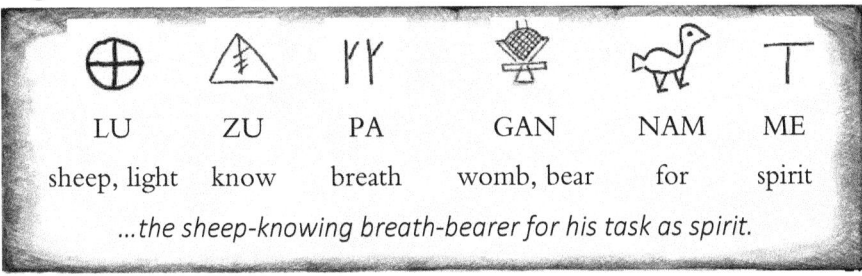

PA

Of the lexical entries opposite PAP, PA is the symbol most often cited with AB. The given meanings of PA at the earliest period include 'overseer' and 'instructor' 390 times, but also 'wing', 'branch' and 'frond' 83 times. From context in *The Story of Sukurru*, I have added what I believe to be its most fundamental meaning which is 'breath'. This is the founding symbol of the pagan god Pan. It's the wind of his windpipes. The meaning is confirmed when PA is associated with AN (see next page) but also by saying PA out loud.

On line 44, PA is collocated with GAN, an association that gives the obvious origin of the word 'pagan':

Suffice to say at this stage that LU-ZU indicates a specialist of sheep, presumably a shepherd but also someone who has 'seen the light', and that ME is an extremely important symbol discussed in its own chapter under the title 'Signs of the Magician' and again in chapter 18, Hermes and the Crystal Heresy. My translation reflects the humour that was used here to describe the original pagan who became Greek Pan. It would have been uninformative and dull to translate this to 'the pagan shepherd'. The two symbols, shown as PA.GAN, are associated under one phonetic value, SAG$_2$, and given as 'to throw down, scatter, disperse, to kill' at a late period on ePSD. My Sumerian explanation of the etymology of pagan – dated here to the 3rd millennium BC – is not reflected in the dictionaries although 'pag' remains unexplained there:

> Pagan: mid-14c., "person of non-Christian or non-Jewish faith," from Late Latin paganus "pagan," in classical Latin "villager, rustic; civilian, non-combatant" noun use of adjective meaning "of the country, of a village," from pagus "country people; province, rural district," originally "district limited by markers," thus related to pangere "to fix, fasten," from PIE root *pag-

On line 130, PA is translated as 'fluttering' in the context of the cosmic ship sailing on the wind:

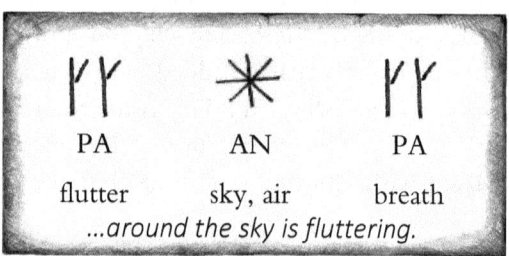

PA	AN	PA
flutter	sky, air	breath

...around the sky is fluttering.

PA-AN is given on ePSD as 'breathing', 'breath', and 'to breath' 7 times at the late period. In this line is found the origin of the great pagan goat's name, Pan, and also the source of the all-inclusive, all-encompassing Greek pan-.

BA

BA, shown in example (b) above, is given as 'to deduct, remove' 41 times. The meanings of 'below, less, without, before' derive from use in context. For example, UD, the sun, with BA is given as 'then', to indicate a past time.

> **Base**: late 14c., 'low, of little height,' from Old French bas 'low, lowly, mean,' from Late Latin bassus 'thick, stumpy, low', possibly from Oscan, or Celtic, or related to Greek basson, comparative of bathys 'deep.'

AB

AB is the father figure in the Matriarchal culture, origin of biblical Abraham. AB/ABA/ABBA is given as 'old person, witness, father, and elder' 5 times at the earliest 3000-2500 BC period on ePSD. Through AB-BA, the inversion of BAB, we find Latin abbas, the 'abbot' derived from Greek abbas, the father, in turn said to come from Aramaic abba. AB is given as 'shrine' 65 times at 3000-2500 BC. AB-BA is discussed again in chapter 21. Ab and abba have retained the meaning 'father' in many Semitic languages. But still nothing about the Sumerian origin in etymological dictionaries:

> Ab- before vowels ap-, word-forming element meaning 'of, from, away from; separate, apart from, free from,' from Greek apo 'from, away from; after; in descent from,' in compounds, 'asunder, off; finishing, completing; back again,' of time, 'after,' of origin, 'sprung from, descended from; because of,' from PIE root.
>
> Abyss: late 14c. in Latin form abyssus, 'depths of the earth or sea; primordial chaos;' early 14c. as abime 'depths of the earth or sea; bottomless pit, Hell' (from Old French; see abysm). Both are from Late Latin abyssus 'bottomless pit,' from Greek abyssos (limne) 'bottomless (pool),'

Together BA-AB give 'the (original) father', 'fatherless', 'below the shrine', 'the ocean below', 'the deep ocean', 'the shrine below', etc. according to context.

> The element bab figures in place-names in the Middle East, such as Bab-el-Mandeb, the strait at the mouth of the Red Sea.[11]

Sumerian BAB/PAP can also be found in the name of Indian stepwells, the vav, or any type of bricked well for the purpose of gathering fresh water – presumably from rain but, in all likelihood, also applied to wells drilled down to aquafers, underground water sources. The letter 'v' is not used in Sumerian dictionaries. There are various names given to stepwells according to the region, but they all incorporate the PA, BA and BAB sounds. The Gujarati name is vav or vaav.

The breath-taking beautiful architecture of the ancient stepwells of India strongly suggests that there was once knowledge there beyond anything we possess today. The original architects of those structures knew about water, not only what the lack of it meant, but how the symmetry and overall harmony of the container would influence every aspect of it. Stepwells gathered water during the rainy season and preserved it for the summer months. The volume of water was carefully measured by the number of steps visible, a way in which the quantities available to the community could be gauged, the distribution made equitable. At the height of summer, the variation from year to year between the position of the sun in the sky and the number of steps visible in the stepwell would have been closely monitored and usage adjusted. But perhaps they also consulted the moon from its position mirrored in the water.

Line 13 of *The Story of Sukurru* conveys something of the importance of water usage in ancient times. AB, who is also Kronos and Father of Time, in his role as gully inspector is a figure of fun, a far cry from what we might expect to read about the patriarchal character. His role in the comedy is surely based on real-life inspectors who had the all-important job of keeping an eye on water consumption and overseeing adjustments to the flow into irrigation canals. Heated arguments with farmers, name-calling and jokes were likely part of the job.

20

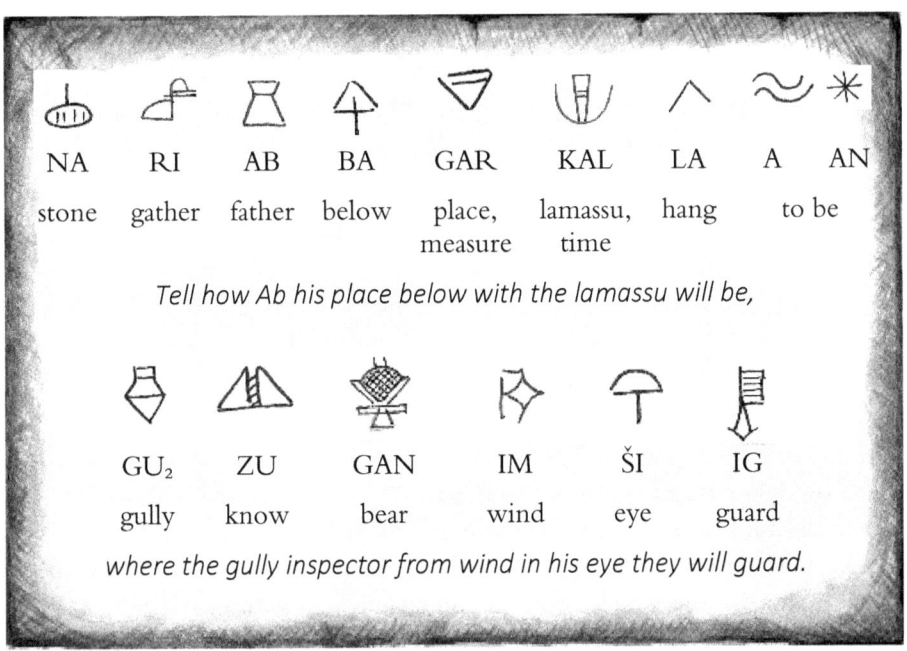

NA, the stone, and RI, the collector bird, are discussed in other chapters here. In the introductory section to *The Story of Sukurru*, they are found together at the beginning of lines 11 and 13 and translated to 'tell' from 'on stone to collect', the written account of events. The symbols in this line are discussed in other parts of the book and can be traced through the index of symbols on page 306.

Line 260 includes another mention of AB in a watery context. AB the Father finds himself relegated to a place 'below' along with a flying stone, the Tree of Consciousness and Knowledge and a rope. This is more than reminiscent of Mesopotamian seals that show a scene fitting that description. It's the cosmic matriarch's decision that AB should spend his time usefully 'multiplying her waters'. The reference to this in a Sumerian text shows that at least some of the seals are meant to be humorous. The combinations of symbols found in line 13 can be interpreted in more than one way, translation always reflecting the surrounding context. For example, see page 164 for IM-ŠI, 'wind in his eye' used as 'clay to see".

ABZU

Those who have read translations of Sumerian stories will have come across the word 'abzu' as referring to an underground kingdom or temple.

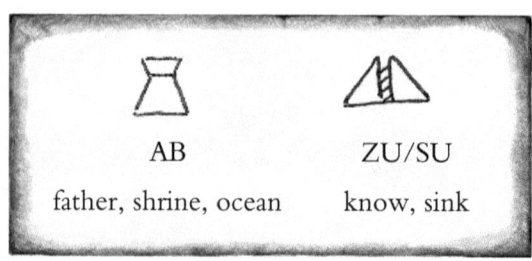

AB
father, shrine, ocean

ZU/SU
know, sink

ABZU or ABSU, a combination of the above two symbols, is given 44 times as '(cosmic) underground water' and 'a ritual water container in a temple'. It's generally understood to be the underground temple of the character called Enki, who will be severely dealt with in the next section. As the symbols appear after E_2, the temple or house, on several lexical entries, ABZU can be understood as more than just a natural aquafer, and as a manmade construction.

ZU, a pyramidal form with a ladder at its centre, is given as 'to know' and 'to learn' 9 times while SU, which is pretty much indistinguishable from ZU, is given as 'skin', 'body', 'flesh' and later as 'to sink' and 'to repay'. ZU equates to knowledge and is part of the title of a person with a specialization; a doctor, a professor. In this context, it indicates knowledge of AB, one who knows about underground waters, or 'an ocean specialist' but it might also be read as 'knowledge of the Father' or 'the Father to know'. Taken as SU, the possibilities include 'the sunken shrine'. With the E_2 temple prefix, it might read 'temple of the underground water expert'. The mysterious water-logged site of Abydos in Egypt comes to mind in that context.

GAN

There are very few pictograms on the oldest tablets recovered from the sand that give us a glimpse of the beautifully executed images of pre-cuneiform times, probably once existing in abundance. One of them is the Egyptian head of KA shown above on page 7. Another is the symbol GAN given as 'to bear young, child-bearing'. It's not what we might expect as an illustration of an internal organ, but then the Sumerian womb was a complex concept, not only earthly but cosmic too. See my less than perfect copy of it here opposite

KAN₄ for the purpose of illustrating how different symbols possessed the same phonetic forms. KAN/GAN, the womb, is another version of a heavenly gateway:

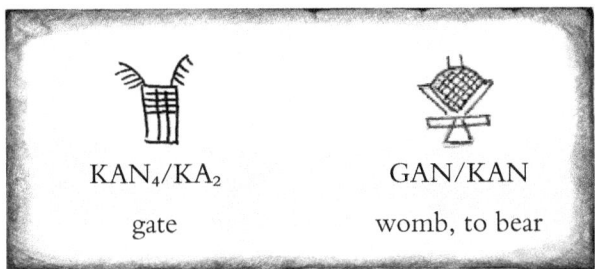

It takes the form of a vessel on a stand with cross-hatching implying that the vessel is full. Without that image, it would be difficult to imagine that the Sumerian notion of the womb was directly linked to alchemy. But it undoubtedly was. This is a crucible, the melting pot; foremost utensil of the most ancient of alchemists. The image is found on a clay tablet dated to the Uruk IV period. See page 165.

Without the lexical entries[4] explaining the source symbols of phonetic GAN, it would be impossible to note that it is, among other things, a reference to the Milky Way, through GA, the milk, and AN, the sky.

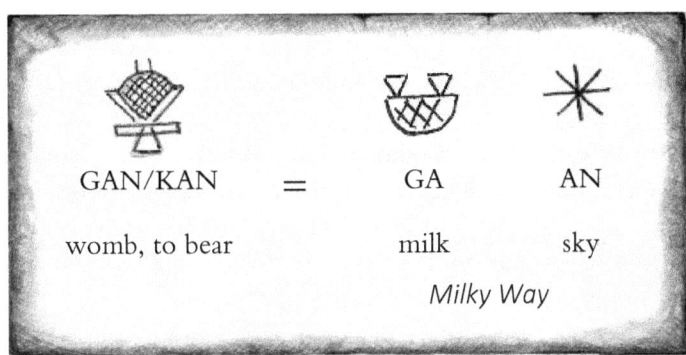

GA is given as 'milk' 155 times, but the two symbols together have never been translated in this way before. GA, source of Gaia, galaxy and the Milky Way, is one possible origin of our verb 'to go'. GA is the sacred cow, the milk and nurturer. For life to exist on Earth, before her milk comes water. GA is I-A, multiplier of the waters. RI-A, gatherer of waters, the waters breaking at the time of birth, the flood, who became Greek Rhea, mother of the gods and goddess of motherhood. She is MA, the land, and Maria, MA-RI-A, the land that collects the waters. The Mother of all things.

> *Gaia: Earth as a goddess, from Greek Gaia, spouse of Uranus, mother of the Titans, personification of gaia 'earth' (as opposed to heaven), 'land' (as opposed to sea), 'a land, country, soil;' it is a collateral form of ge (Dorian ga) 'earth,' which is of unknown origin and perhaps from a pre-Indo-European language of Greece.*
>
> *Go (verb): Old English gan 'to advance, walk; depart, go away; happen, take place; conquer; observe, practice, exercise,' from West Germanic *gaian (source also of Old Saxon, Old Frisian gan, Middle Dutch gaen, Dutch gaan, Old High German gan, German gehen), from PIE root.*

There were two types of gate in Sumerian lore, either of which could be heavenly. In the case of Akkadian Babu-ilu, the so-called 'Gate of God', there is a direct reference to KAN_4/KA_2 as the source symbol. We don't need to stray from it for the officialised origin of the place name. But GAN can also be read as KAN and everything in this language is inter-connected by a multitude of threads between symbols and sounds. The cosmic gateway was an important element in alchemy, and it was the passage through the Milky Way. The reason for adding this symbol into the mix is to demonstrate the fundamental alchemical spirit in which everything, however seemingly mundane, might be read. Spirits come and go through the Milky Way. Substances appear and disappear in the crucible, and alchemy begins in the womb.

Egyptian Babylon

> *Such is the size of the city of Babylon, and it has a magnificence greater than all other cities of which we have knowledge. First there runs around it a deep and broad trench, full of water; then a wall fifty meters in thickness and hundred meters in height [...]. At the top of the wall along the edges they built chambers of one story facing one another; and between the rows of chambers they left space to drive a four-horse chariot. In the circuit of the wall there are set a hundred gates made of bronze.*[12]

Herodotus may or may not have visited Mesopotamian Babylon. It appears that subsequent excavations at the proposed site of that place have given the lie to his one hundred gates. But then again, can we be sure that the Tower of Babel ever existed in physical form, that it was there or anywhere else? Given the analysis of the syllables, the construction would likely have been important both above ground and below.

There is another ancient site called Babylon, this time in Egypt. The origin of the name is not proven one way or another, but there is conjecture that this was a loan name, borrowed from Mesopotamia. That said, there is no way of knowing if one place was named after the other, or which one came first, or even when. Today the ruins of the Babylon Fortress lie in a district of old Cairo and the original fortress is dated to 1900 BC.

Egyptian Babylon was constructed to the east of the Giza plateau where the famed Great Pyramid and Sphinx are situated. The river Nile has always flowed somewhere between them although its course has changed considerably over time. The Babylon Fortress lies on its eastern bank between Giza and the ancient city of Heliopolis with which the fortress is thought to have been associated. Mesopotamian Babylon was situated on the river Euphrates. The presence of a river is significant in both cases. Both names, in Egypt and in Mesopotamia, were grounded in the generic BA-AB symbols. It is probable that they also refer to underground reservoirs from manmade canals accumulating water in their vicinity, essential for comfortable sedentary lifestyles, the bab or vav that were known in all the lands. The Babylon Fortress has also been associated with the Egyptian deity of the Nile, Hapi. It has to be said that I have found no mention of either natural or manmade underground waterways that might once have connected the place to the river Nile.

A form similar to an Indian stepwell did exist along the Nile and an example of a nilometer as they are called can still be seen in Cairo at the southernmost tip of Roda Island, further south than the site of the Babylon Fortress. With steps leading straight down or circling around a narrow shaft, the nilometer is less spectacular than its Indian counterpart but served at least some of the same purpose; the measurement of water levels.

PAD
The following is a symbol with no direct phonetic link to the names Babel and Babylon but is of interest in the subject of water conservation and allocation.

Shown here on a tablet[13] dated to the Uruk III period, the symbol PAD is given 225 times at 3000-2500 BC as 'ration' but also as 'food allocation'. It's another of those rare pictograms inscribed with great care by an attentive scribe some 5,000 years ago. There are two pyramidal forms, separate but complementary. The inverted triangle appears to be symbol GAR which can be translated to 'measure' but also given as 'bread', a picture of a container, probably the reason for its translation to 'food allocation'. It's also apparent that this form is considerably larger than the pyramid above and possible to imagine that the content might flow either upwards or down through the connecting channel to the left. Whichever way the flow, a valve of some kind would be useful.

In the lexical entries[4], PAD is shown several times with the two originating symbols PA-AD:

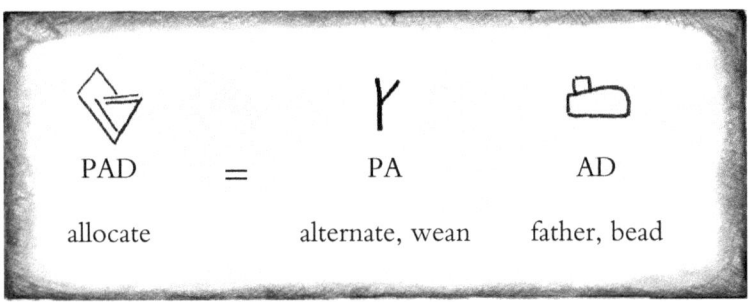

PA has been discussed in the context of breath and the windpipes of Pan. AD is more thoroughly analysed in chapter 20. Suffice to say here that it can be compared to AB as a symbol representing a 'father'. I suggest that it might also be considered in this context of allocation as a 'bead', a round movable part serving to block the flow of water or air. The two symbols might translate to 'alternation of the bead', but this is a suggestion made without evidence of any use in such a context.

A final word on PAP…

The earliest mention of the French word 'soupape', pronounced su-pap, is found in a text dated to 1580[14] where it was given as a valve for a hydraulic pump. The etymology of the word is obscure. There's always a 'soupape' on a pressure cooker to allow the steam to escape. For the 'petite histoire' as the French say, the 'little story', the anecdote; an elderly relative, tired of the hissing coming from the valve of her steam cooker, threw a dishcloth over the top of it. After a while, the cooker took off and flew around the kitchen, crashing into the walls. Fortunately, she had stepped out of the room.

Linked to the Matriarch through PAP, the nipple, to the Patriarch through AB, the shrine and ocean, and to both of them through PA, the breath, valves are all around us and should not be underestimated.

PAP … PAP … PAP …

2

The Enki Heresy

Enki enthusiasts, a group that includes academia as well as the tribe of Zecharia Sitchin fans, might well fear for his fate at my hands. He has featured extensively in Sumerian literary texts; Enki and the World Order, Enki and Ninmah, Enki's Journey to Nibru, etc. The name appears again and again. Enki is too important to die because the quasi-entirety of Mesopotamian myth would collapse around him. Only a magician could survive such an upheaval.

There are around 17 lexical entries showing ᵈEN KI where the small 'd' represents symbol AN for 'god' as mentioned above on page 9. Below is the original Enki shown as he was before his name became completely abstract:

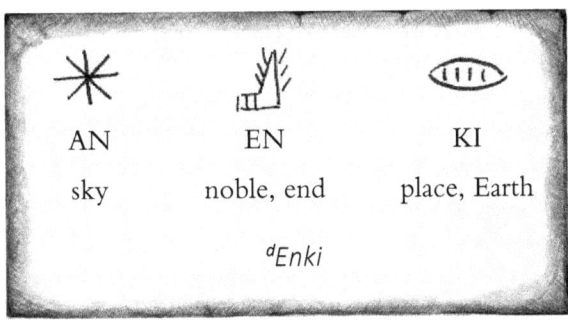

A fair number of Mesopotamian seals show the character who is thought to be Enki. He is sometimes seated, quite a lot bigger than the other characters, has water pouring from either shoulder, and is regularly accompanied by fish that swim upwards. On Enki's head is a pointed hat reminiscent of a medieval wizard except for the addition of spikes or horns on either side of it. On one seal he's holding up a fish, on another a bird and on another, shown here above, a rectangular block, perhaps a stone, perhaps a box, a figure of geometry, a rectangle. Other figures present themselves to him in the manner of people approaching a ruler or benefactor. It's easy to deduce from this plethora of images that Enki, if indeed that's who it is, was a central and revered figure in Sumerian culture at some point in time.

In any text about the period, Enki enjoys the title of Mesopotamian god. He's in good company. I counted 43 names in the list of Mesopotamian gods and goddesses given on the site of the ORACC project[15]. Of course, the list includes a long period of Mesopotamian history. All the texts written down on clay tablets, all the rediscovered temples, the accounts from later times after the original scribes were long gone, have contributed to the list of gods.

Enki and Ea are understood by academia to be one and the same, although Ea has a different set of symbols to his name.

> It is unclear when he was merged with the god Ea, whose name first appears in the 24th century BCE. [16]

Ea is composed of E_2 and A, 'temple' and 'water', perhaps a manmade construction that served to store or regulate water. It was a short trip away from and back to the subject of water management, a matter of great importance to any civilisation. Thanks to the seven lexical entries linking AN-EN-KI, Enki, with E_2-A, the water-distribution building, a strong connection between the two is irrefutable.

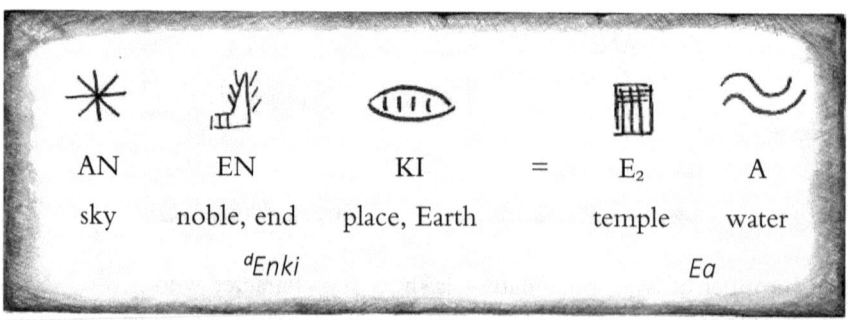

AN	EN	KI	=	E_2	A
sky	noble, end	place, Earth		temple	water
	ᵈEnki			Ea	

Ea is found on line 223 of *The Story of Sukurru*. The combination of AN-EN-KI doesn't appear at all. In context, with the two following symbols adding the humour, this is how the line begins:

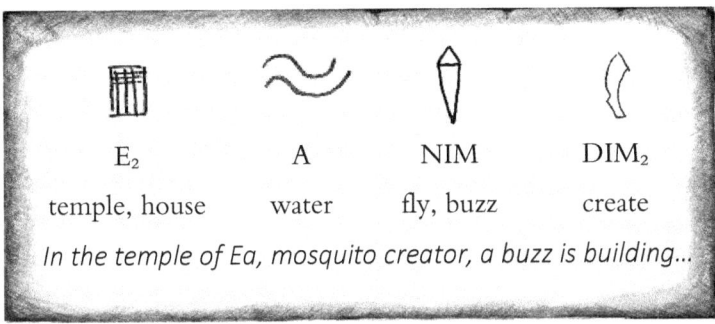

In the temple of Ea, mosquito creator, a buzz is building...

The symbol of the insect combined with the act of creating, NIM-DIM$_2$, were used twice over for the purpose of making the original idea crystal clear. As this line follows on from the section which strongly resembles the biblical account of the nakedness of Noah, it is easy to understand the 'buzz' as gossip aboard. But the story then veers off in another direction, showing the mounting 'buzz' of voices to be part of a ritual. It would have been perfectly acceptable to translate Ea to 'In the water temple' or even 'In the house on the water, a buzz is building...' with the understanding that this was Noah's ark. I chose to integrate the name – perhaps wrongly influenced by the desire to show the modern connection - but that doesn't validate his existence.

Looking again at the images on the old seals where water can be seen flowing from the character's shoulders, it's not difficult to imagine Ea as the personification of a very real and essential element in the lives of any civilisation, a structure from which water flows. The name Ea is more logical than Enki in that it reflects the construction and its use. Contrary to AB and his ocean, Ea doesn't appear to live below ground. It might be that he represents a natural mountain with its waterfalls and rivers where an artificial reservoir would be built. Constructions to retain huge amounts of water, barrages or weirs at strategic points on rivers, are used to generate hydroelectricity. Is it possible that a Mesopotamian watercourse was once harnessed for that purpose?

AN

Symbol AN was discussed in the section on Babel (page 8). where it was considered in the light of the phonetic value, ILU, and the spreading of light, from I-LU, perhaps the source of illumination.

> *Latin illuminare 'to throw into light, make bright, light up;' figuratively, in rhetoric, 'to set off, illustrate,' from assimilated form of in- 'in, into' (from PIE root *en 'in') + lumen (genitive luminis) 'light,' from suffixed form of PIE root.*

The following is a focus on AM_3, collocation of AN with A, the water symbol, not directly relevant to Enki's three symbols but a useful indication of the ways in which it was used:

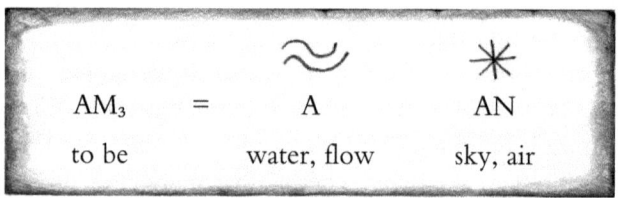

AM_3	=	A	AN
to be		water, flow	sky, air

Water falls from the sky, A from AN. Together, the two symbols are classified as AM_3 in Sumerian dictionaries. This combination is given as 'to be' 5 times, very largely beaten by the symbol ME which is given as 'to be' 1,448 times at 3000-2500 BC. Nevertheless, A-AN is the combination found in numerous lines of *The Story of Sukurru* in the final verbal position and translated as forms of the verb 'to be'. In other words, wherever a line of my translated text ends with a conjugated form of the verb 'to be', the original symbols on the tablet were these two placed close together and given on the transliterated version as AM_3.

> *Am: first person singular present indicative of be (q.v.); Old English eom 'to be, to remain,' (Mercian eam, Northumbrian am), from Proto-Germanic *izm(i)-, from PIE root.*

This is what I wrote in an article for Graham Hancock's website about A with AN, putting the words directly in the mouth of the great King Ashurbanipal[17] who was said to know the secrets of the Sumerian texts; The following is my own interpretation of the reasoning behind A-AN:

> *But, for the beer and the bees to survive, there must be water and air, A and AN. Without them, no beer....as simple, as terrible as that! It is the most evident of origins, don't you see? TO BE is to have water and air, A-AN or AN-A. Which one came first is not important. They are of equal stature. Ana-logia, my friends, ANALOGIA!*

Analogy, the transfer of meaning from one subject to another, is derived from ancient Greek, but has its ultimate source as prefix ana-, result of these two ancient Sumerian symbols; The notion of water and air, or water from the sky, the rain, as analogy for existence and thus the verb 'to be'.

> *Analogy: early 15c., 'correspondence, proportion,' from Old French analogie or directly from Latin analogia, from Greek analogia 'proportion,' from ana 'upon, according to' (see ana-) + logos 'ratio,' also 'word, speech, reckoning,' from PIE root.*

The AN of Enki is the symbol that turned him into a god. My translation of it within this threesome of AN-EN-KI will be 'sky' and not 'god'. Sorry, Enki.

EN

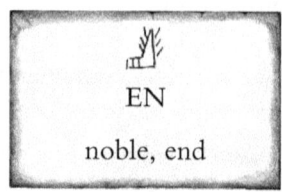

EN has the given meanings of 'lord, master, ruler' 59 times at 3000-2500 BC, and 'priest' 38 times for the same period. I preferred 'noble' which has less of the connotation of religion and power over others. I have also taken the liberty of adding the missing and important meaning 'end'. This last was firmly established during the translation of *The Story of Sukurru*. The opposite of EN, the end, is NE, new, renewal, fire and rebirth. Put EN and NE back to back, and the end will be followed by the beginning, the beginning by the end. The cycle becomes evident and will be mentioned again in chapter 19.

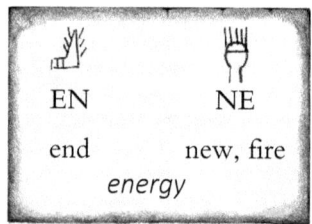

NE is given as 'fire' 44 times at 3000-2500 BC. Line 253 begins and ends with the same symbol, EN, using it three times in all. Comprised of 17 symbols, considerably more than the average 10, it plays on an endless phrase about an endless activity. My version in *The Story of Sukurru* goes as follows:

> The noble who the remote water-churner created, Sis between sky and earth the wall of Gi to establish, her noble heavy hand waves stones from the sky on the master builder of the noble who the remote water-churner created....

It was difficult to pierce the secret of this line of text, and to present a worthy, readable translation. In the introduction, I pointed out that the story is sometimes obscure. Apart from the lost cultural context, the oblique references, the fact that the whole thing presents as a riddle, there are two major reasons for that; breaks in the clay and extra-long lines. Most vary between about 10 to 12 symbols, some with clear grammatical indicators such as an obvious verb in the final position. I chose to use the 'end' meaning at least once as purely grammatical, the indication that the action was circular and never-ending, as I believe it was intended to be used. The final EN is silent because it is also the first... The preceding symbol, KAK, given 518 times as 'to make, to build', (given here as 'created') which takes the form of an inverted pyramid, likely a keystone, is meant as the verb.

The most important result of fathoming what was originally intended by this line is that it confirms the meaning of EN as 'end' and NE as the 'new'. The sound adds to the value of this theory, the origin of the word we use today. The full understanding of this one symbol is fundamental in moving forward to a better overall reading of Sumerian texts.

End: Old English ende 'end, conclusion, boundary, district, species, class,' from Proto-Germanic *andiaz (source also of Old Frisian enda, Old Dutch ende, Dutch einde, Old Norse endir 'end;' Old High German enti 'top, forehead, end,' German Ende, Gothic andeis 'end'), originally 'the opposite side,' from PIE root.

This is not without significance in the context of a noble, a prince, or some character, mythological or not, who is beyond the ordinary: the mythical figure of Enoch, for example. This section tends to demolish Enki as a name and as a god, but that isn't to say that no-one else will be found rising from the ashes at the end of the fire.

KI

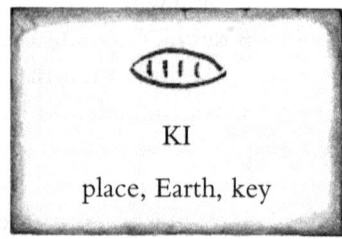

KI

place, Earth, key

KI is given as 'place, ground, earth' (and others) 282 times at 3000-2500 BC. It's recognised as the suffix indicating a place name. Sukurru, SU-KUR-RU in the original symbols of the text, is always followed by KI. It allowed me to re-translate the name Shuruppak (given in The Instructions of Shuruppak) from that of a man to that of a city, radically changing the whole storyline in the first few symbols and, in the process, challenging the translation method of origin. It is quite surprising to note that the same set of symbols, SU-KUR-RU-KI, were translated to the city of Sukurru in the Sumerian King List[18] and yet no-one appears to have challenged the logic of giving the same name to a man in The Instructions of Shuruppak[19] until now. Of course, this also begs the question of why KI was integrated into the name Enki. There are alternatives to the AN-EN-KI phrase:

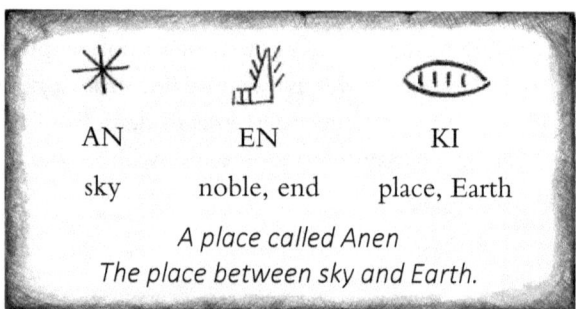

AN   EN   KI

sky   noble, end   place, Earth

A place called Anen
The place between sky and Earth.

Positioning is important in the riddles that constitute the early Sumerian language. Here we find the end in the middle, so to speak. On the left is the sky. On the right is Earth. The meaning of the phrase might be 'In the middle, between the sky and Earth'. Taking into consideration the use of KI as both 'Earth' and indication of a place, we find 'the place where sky and Earth meet' and 'sky-end place' or simply 'Sky-End'. It's interesting to read this phrase as 'a place called ANEN'. Replacing a character called Enki with a place called

Anen in the various long Sumerian texts would imply a massive, unthinkable about-turn and one hell of a lot of re-translation.

Is there or was there ever a place on Earth called Anen? I haven't found any trace. However, Anen is a name given to a character from ancient Egypt, a priestly figure, wearing the skin of a puma or cougar covered in stars. There is an 18th dynasty statue of this hero called Anen, discovered in Egypt and currently residing in the Egizio museum in Turin, Italy. He is not the only Egyptian example of an important figure wearing such a garment. Is it certain that the name applies to a person rather than harking back to the concept of a voyage between Earth and sky, of a heroic figure sailing to Anen? Could this be the EN of Enoch fame? Of course, my questions imply the inheritance of the same stories and of a single original language across Egypt, Mesopotamia and elsewhere, a brilliant and spanking new bridge across the quagmire of our divisive histories.

Babel was the point of departure for this book. Rediscovering the forgotten language that we know as Sumerian has the exciting potential of revealing something of the knowledge that was lost long before the era of Ancient Greece, before Babel or Babylon. There are many who believe or, at least, strongly suspect that there have been other civilisations before ours, possibly highly advanced, with capacities far beyond our own.

My contribution is to find and to reinsert as many of the symbolic keys as possible in that old hermetic door. They might not always take me to an absolute understanding, but I am as curious as anyone to know what it was that the ancients knew.

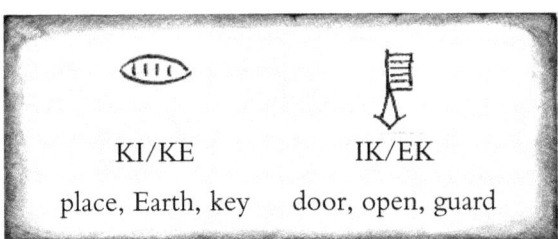

KI/KE
place, Earth, key

IK/EK
door, open, guard

IK is given as 'door' 8 times at 3000-2500 BC and as 'open' just once. There is also mention of 'guard'. See IK/IG in the context of the lion in chapter 17. From there, the added meaning of 'key' for KI/KE becomes evident.

> *Key: 'instrument for opening locks,' Middle English keie, from Old English cæg 'metal piece that works a lock, key' literal and figurative ('solution, explanation, one who or that which opens the way or explains'), a word of unknown origin, abnormal evolution, and no sure cognates other than Old Frisian kei.*

Is it heresy to point out that Enki has no obvious place in any mythology or religion other than Mesopotamian? Is it heresy to question his very existence in the minds of people who once inhabited that region? My attitude to Enki is heretical for those who have never doubted, never questioned that he was once worshipped as a Mesopotamian god, even if that belief is not itself a religion. For those who are outraged by this denial of a seemingly obvious piece of history, I accept the possibility that Enki might have existed under that name at some late point in Assyria. It's not overly important. Although I would not attempt to propose a date for the cover-up, it's another underlying truth that is, in my view, the reason for Enki's existence; he provides the proof that Mesopotamian myths were unique, isolated, not relevant to that of other cultures. Along with certain other uniquely Sumerian or Assyrian characters, he draws attention away from the possibility of a fundamental link with Egyptian or Greek figures. And thus, Enki regally squats the rightful throne of a name that might, even today, be seen to pose a threat to some mainstream dogma.

3
Harran

> *They claim that they worship the seven planets—the sun, the moon, Saturn, Mars, Jupiter, Mercury, Venus—and the twelve zodiacal houses, because they are the ones that create and govern this creation and give good fortune and prosperity in the lower world, and ill fortune and suffering. They said that their prophet in that is Hermes the Sage.* [20]

In Harran, a modest village in southern Turkey, the ruins of a brick tower stand on what is thought to have once been the site of a temple dedicated to the moon. There is little or nothing there today that might be directly linked to pre-Islamic times. Successive invasions have seen to that. The place is best known today for the unusual beehive shape of the local dwellings.

Harran is situated about 40 kilometres from the most exciting and enigmatic of recent archaeological finds, the stone circles of Gobekli Tepe. Safely dated to at least 9000 BC, that site turns conventional teaching about our evolution from primitive hunter-gatherer ancestors on its head. Harran and Gobekli Tepe both lie in the upper reaches of the region known as ancient Mesopotamia. They are situated between but not in the immediate vicinity of the headwaters of the Tigris and Euphrates, two rivers that take their source in the Taurus mountains.

Harran is documented on tablets found in Ebla, Syria, dated to around 2300 BC, where it is mentioned as a crossroads for trade in the Middle East, the implication being that its founding was (perhaps considerably) more ancient. Other documents, from Arabian or Christian sources in the 9th century AD, indicate that it was once a renowned centre for teaching linked to Hermes Trismegistus, who was also said to be Egyptian Thoth. Therein lies the essential attested link between Mesopotamia, particularly the northern region of it, and Ancient Egypt. It is perhaps a tenuous link in that the sources of information are all apparently second-hand and undoubtedly influenced by religious beliefs of their times. However, a study of the Sumerian symbols linked to both the place name and to the name associated with its inhabitants adds some light to the subject.

The people of Harran were reputed as astronomers and they succeeded against all odds in maintaining their isolated culture for many hundreds of years before finally succumbing to a Mongol invasion in the 13th century AD. According to the documents at our disposal, they were called Sabians, 'people of the book' mentioned in the Quran. As such, they were untouchable and succeeded in avoiding the quasi-inevitable absorption into dominant religions.[20] It was said, again in the 1st millennium AD, that the only relevance of that name to the group was as a cover for their pagan activities, implying that the group had somehow cheated their way through the ages and that they had no right to the 'untouchable' status mentioned in the Quran. As this information apparently stems from a second or even third-hand Christian source and as no other group is proposed as the true Sabians, this story is one that I personally choose to disregard in favour of my own findings.

As for the origin of the name, one offering is that Sabian stems from Arabic with the meaning of a 'rising up or out'. This is a popular explanation in that it could apply to the movement of stars and the Sabians were stargazers. However, there is no evidence of this meaning within the Sumerian texts and, Harran being situated in Mesopotamia, it isn't unreasonable to suggest that the origin of 'Sabian' might well be from the language originally spoken throughout that region. Another more likely etymology can be found on line 47 of *The Story of Sukurru*: ŠA₃-BI (pronounced SHA-BI) where it was translated in that context to 'Beer-Heart', the great and pagan lover of beer.

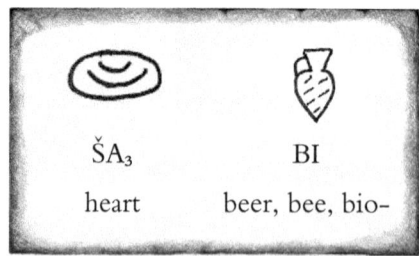

ŠA₃ is given 159 times at 3000-2500 BC as 'inner body, heart' and BI, given 12,226 times at 2500 BC, is easily translated to beer. The form of the symbol is confirmation. I identified ŠA₃-BI as an epithet for a character in *The Story of Sukurru* long before any thought of Harran's beehive houses or the possible connection to Sabians came to mind. BI is also the phonetic source of 'bee'. Without the bees, no beer...and Greek bio- (see page 168) because, without bees and beer, no life at all! An 'inner place of the bee' would be both a reasonable translation of ŠA₃-BI and a description of the dwellings at Harran as we see them today. If that isn't to be brushed off as coincidence, it becomes necessary to consider the possibility of such buildings existing there before 2500 BC. And why not? Another point in favour of my theory: If 'Beer-Heart' is the original nickname of the average Sabian, it fits very well into the idea of the region of Harran and particularly Gobekli Tepe as a place of beer drinkers.

> *Bee: stinging insect of the genus Apis, living in societies under a queen and producing wax and honey, Old English beo "bee," from Proto-Germanic *bion (source also of Old Norse by, Old High German bia, Middle Dutch bie), from PIE root.*
>
> *Beer: alcoholic drink made from grain, generally barley, infused with hops and boiled and fermented, Old English beor "strong drink, beer, mead," cognate with Old Frisian biar, Middle Dutch and Dutch bier, Old High German bior, German Bier; a West Germanic word of much-disputed and ambiguous origin. Probably a 6c. West Germanic monastic borrowing of Vulgar Latin biber "a drink, beverage" (from Latin infinitive bibere "to drink," from PIE root.*

The Old Testament account[21] mentions Harran as the city where Abraham spent time. It's interesting to note that the town of Sanliurfa, formerly Edessa, in the same region is believed by some religions to be his birthplace. Abraham's name originates in AB, the character given in *The Story of Sukurru* as Father of Time and an epithet of Kronos. AB is given as 'father' or 'elder' 5 times at 3000-2500 BC. (See section on Babel.) In Harran, the city of great masters of astronomy, Saturn as Kronos might well have had his place alongside a temple dedicated to the Moon.

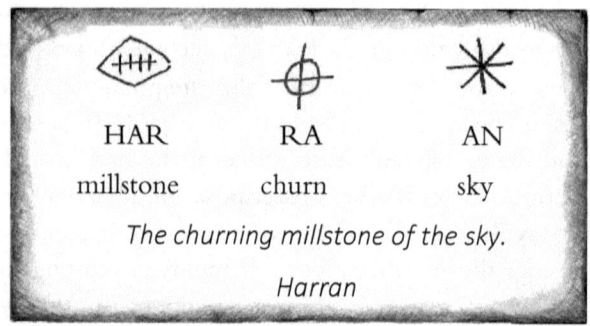

These three symbols together, HAR-RA-AN, are given 5 times as 'route, passage, path', a description that fits with Harran being a major trading centre in northern Mesopotamia during the Assyrian period. The above is the accepted origin of the name Harran. Taken individually and translated through the monosyllabic method, the three symbols tell an interesting story, one that goes a long way to confirming the place as the home of stargazers.

HAR

Symbol HAR given as 'miller' 30 times at 3000-2500 BC but also as 'millstone' and 'to grind', demonstrates how two symbols were used together to combine their meanings into one; phonetic HAR is a composite of $AŠ_2$, the curse or wish, placed inside HI, the sack or hole. This combination has several other phonetic values of which HUR. HAR first appears on a tablet dated to the Uruk IV period, 3350-3200 BC.[22] It appears 6 times on lexical lists dated to 2900-2700 BC and several times in *The Story of Sukurru* at ca.2600 BC. It's also given as 'debt' or 'financial obligation' 10 times; perhaps a link to the commercial negotiations and transactions that took place in the region of Harran.

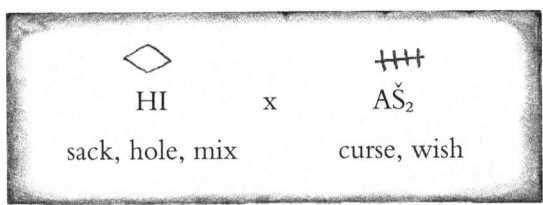

HI, sack, containing AŠ₂ which is given as 'curse' once at 3000-2500 BC together form the image of exposed teeth in a grimacing mouth, an image that sits well with some of the creatures represented in bas and high relief at Gobekli Tepe. They might be the earliest influencers of symbol HAR. Here in the Sanliurfa Museum, one of the stone animal heads baring its teeth:

> *These are the words of him who has the sharp double-edged sword.*[23]

Based on the monosyllabic method, HAR was for the most part translated in *The Story of Sukurru* as an insult, a 'sack of curses'. If HAR, through this combination, is indeed the original symbol of the celestial millstone, the top half, then the Sumerian notion of repeated cursing with long-term consequences that accompanies its grinding movement is validated by the ominous declaration of Celsius, a Greek philosopher of the 2nd century AD:

> *The mills of the gods grind slowly', he says, even 'To children's children, and to those who are born after them.*[24]

But it's also possible to consider the symbol HAR in the light of a myth that has until now been seen as uniquely Nordic. Loki, a mischievous figure in Norse mythology, appears on the Snaptun stone in Denmark, reproduced here below.

His lips have been stitched together to keep him quiet and to prevent him from further annoying the gods. Could it be that the Sumerian symbol HAR reflects the mouth of the original Loki? Luki appears several times in the text of *The Story of Sukurru* through the two symbols of man and Earth, 'man of Earth', and he has the bad idea of goading the 'noble' in line 61:

It might equally have read 'his virile goad'. UŠ is given as 'penis' 42 times at a late period and as 'goad' with other symbols 20 times at the earliest period. In the Nordic poem, the Lokasenna[25], these lines correspond rather well:

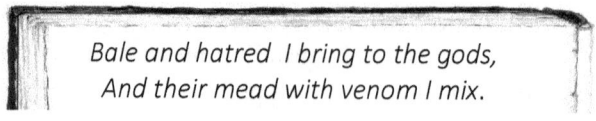

In context on line 133 of *The Story of Sukurru*, HAR is used to infer that the Matriarch carries a noble but unwelcome foetus in her womb.

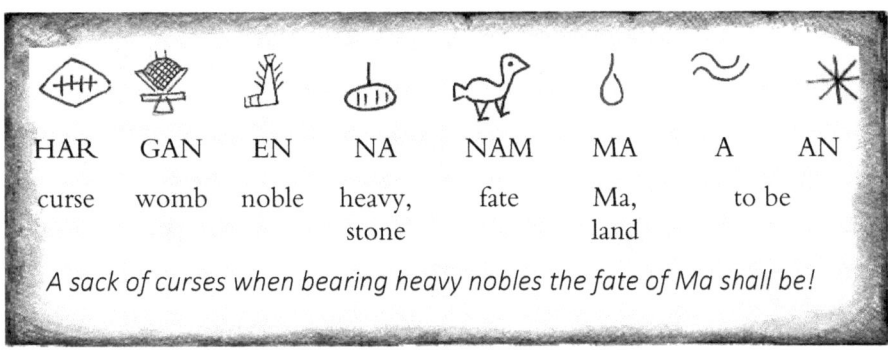

A sack of curses when bearing heavy nobles the fate of Ma shall be!

As always, there are several possibilities for the translation. Attention to context is essential. It would have been possible and correct to write 'the noble womb' for GAN-EN since this is a reference to the cosmic Matriarch. It is also correct to see NA-NAM as 'weight of destiny' or even 'stone of destiny' (see page 158). The curse of HAR has to do with stones, whether the miller's grinding stone in the sky, celestial movements indicating time, or the fate of mankind written on the stone of destiny.

The cursing contained in lines 132 to 142 of *The Story of Sukurru*, a long and vociferous passage, is being done by UD, the sun. It's not difficult to imagine this comedy acted out on stage with much rage and spitting. The sun is the unreasonable spouse of the moon. MA, in this case, should be understood as the entirety of the land, mother of nature and of humanity, a specific role of the Matriarch under that symbol. The sun cursing the land might be indicative of drought and hardship. The lively scene reaches its climax and culminates in a third and final rendition of the refrain translated to 'Native Land', a lamentation. In other words, it ends with a further reference to a catastrophic event. Could this section of the story also be an oblique reference to a ritual performed for many years in Harran; the cruel grinding of a god?

> *But who was Tammuz? The grain god dying with the season, the rural Adonis, would hardly fit into such exalted company. Now it is clear he was astronomical first of all. (...)The cult went on in Harran as late as the 13th century (...).And the lament was mainly over the god who was cruelly killed by being ground between millstones...*[26]

TAM is one of the phonetic values of UD, the sun. To briefly deviate from the name Harran and further investigate the cursing and grinding that are linked to the place, there are several lexical entries that show TAM as TA-AM:

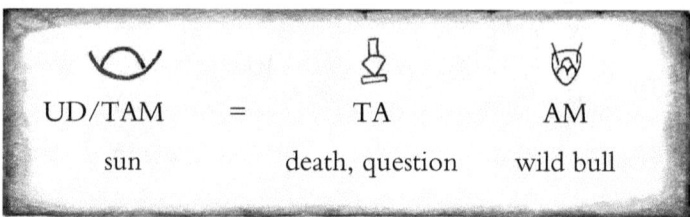

UD/TAM	=	TA	AM
sun		death, question	wild bull

TA is discussed in the analysis of Greek Talon, and AM is found in the context of the bird of destiny with NA-NAM. The death of the wild bull is reminiscent of the well-attested Mesopotamian scenes of a lion bringing down a bull (mentioned on page 282). At the same time, to question the wild bull could be a reference to the bull as oracle, notably in Egyptian lore. See page 154. Or could it be 'death by the wild bull'?

Tammuz is mentioned only once in the biblical texts.

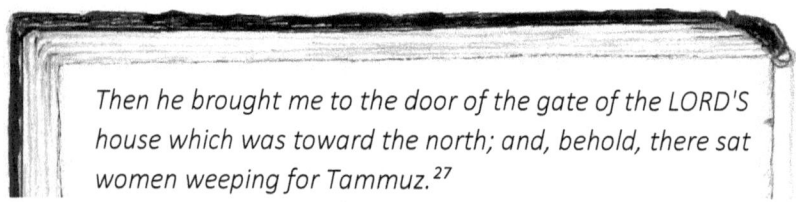

Then he brought me to the door of the gate of the LORD'S house which was toward the north; and, behold, there sat women weeping for Tammuz.[27]

Ezekiel corresponds to a character first found in line 175 of *The Story of Sukurru* as ZA-E, lofty Za, the 'four on high', the 'high noise', and recognised as the biblical figure by his violent discourse and manner of speech.

RA

RA, the second symbol of Harran, is given as 'to beat', 'to crush' and 'to thresh' 16 times at 3000-2500 BC. In the context of the millstone, the meaning is evident. From *The Story of Sukurru*, I add the notion of churning and, another important addition, the musical beat.

One of the other meanings given for RA is 'to kill', not one that was used in *The Story of Sukurru*. Perhaps I am not so different from other translators with a personal agenda; I don't want there to have been bloodshed and so I spent less time considering that meaning than others. Used as a verb, I favoured the 'churning' and 'beating' theme that corresponds well to the movements of the planets but is also involved in harvesting and grinding grain, a rhythmic activity. But it can't be denied that there is an element of death and killing implied in the millstone mythologies. Was it only the death of a season?

There is a line in the story that brings to the fore the possibility that Sumerian RA is linked to the unfortunate pharaoh mentioned in Exodus[28].

> *Then Moses stretched out his hand over the sea. The LORD drove the sea back with a powerful east wind all that night and turned the sea into dry land. (...)*
> *The waters came back and covered the chariots and horsemen, the entire army of Pharaoh, that had gone after them into the sea. None of them survived.*

Any suggestion that *The Story of Sukurru* makes reference to the plight of the biblical pharaoh leads to the obvious necessity to push the accepted timeline of the event considerably further back. The story of the exodus cited here above is commonly estimated to have taken place at around 1440 BC while the latest possible date for *The Story of Sukurru* is ca. 2500 BC. Line 141 is presented here in two parts for clarity:

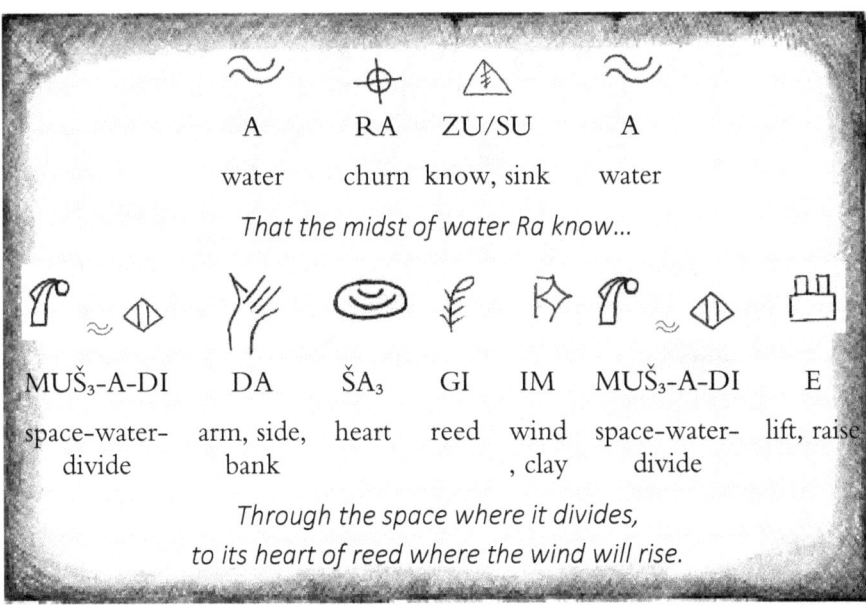

A	RA	ZU/SU	A
water	churn	know, sink	water

That the midst of water Ra know...

MUŠ₃-A-DI	DA	ŠA₃	GI	IM	MUŠ₃-A-DI	E
space-water-divide	arm, side, bank	heart	reed	wind, clay	space-water-divide	lift, raise

Through the space where it divides,
to its heart of reed where the wind will rise.

The first four symbols show RA-ZU (or SU) in the middle of water. That might translate to Ra sinking into and thus having knowledge of the water, a fitting translation in light of the overall humour and style of the text. RA is used twice; as subject and as adjective, as Ra and as the churning motion of the waters. ZU is the symbol of those who have specialist knowledge and RA becomes a specialist of churning waters through force of circumstance. The other possibility is that this section infers an external figure who is acting on the churning water, who is doing the dividing, in which case RA is only the churning. There are other ways to look at it, of course, but the positioning of the surrounding waters is particularly significant in the reading. I favoured a RA floundering in the middle. This is part of the cursing scene. There is a subject and the sun does not wish him well. It's a cosmic cursing scene. But I have since come to understand that RA is one epithet of the sun itself. If that is the case, the two symbols RA with ZU must be read as the 'sun specialist', 'he who knows the sun' which would also fit with the context.

The highlight of the riddle was the combination MUŠ$_3$-A-DI, the most complex combination of symbols that I had come across. This led to several weeks of scrutinizing and agonizing. Don't think that *The Story of Sukurru* gave up its secrets easily. I was pushed around, played with and led in circles in a deep fog for weeks on end. A and DI give the 'division of water', set around four symbols, an arm and a reed with a centre and wind. MUŠ$_3$ is given as 'flat space, a holy area'. There is a compelling resemblance between the combined phonetic values giving MUŠ$_3$-A-DI and the name of the valley in Jordan where the ancient site of Petra is situated. Local legend gives Moses striking a rock to obtain water at Wadi-Musa, said to translate to Valley of Moses. A-DI, to divide the water, to divide for water… It makes the association of this line with two separate events even more intriguing since there is no obvious link between the submerging of Pharaoh's army in the bible and the action of Moses at Wadi-Musa. But there is a reference to the same action at a different location in Numbers 20:11:

> *Then Moses raised his hand and struck the rock twice with his staff, so that a great amount of water gushed out, and the community and their livestock drank.*

The close association of MUŠ$_3$-A-DI with the symbols for 'arm' and 'reed', followed by the verb (in final position) with the meaning of 'rise' lead to the obvious conclusion. GI is given as 'reed' and also as 'cane', an easy leap to reading it as 'staff', the staff of Moses. This time, and in direct (deliberate) contrast to the preceding section of the same line, the water is divided on either side of the central symbols. The evidence of a more ancient Sumerian origin to the biblical stories of Moses dividing but also obtaining water is, I contend, too strong to ignore.

It was the next line 142, also uttered by the sun, that confirmed the drowning scene. All of that said, it's possible that the scene is entirely cosmic, and that Ra's chariot is cosmic too.

> *And a curse divide the basket from the unworldly baggage…*

In conclusion, there is considerably more to be gleaned from the name of Harran than from any material evidence left in the place itself. A friendly squeezing of the old symbols suffices to confirm the veracity of ancient texts' descriptions; the inhabitants, the Sabians were stargazers. They were beer-drinkers too. And pagans. With the understanding that RA refers to the sun, Harran can be read as 'the cursing (HAR) of the sun (RA) in the sky (AN)'.

Sanliurfa, known as Urfa and once called Edessa, is a large and extremely ancient town close to Harran and to Gobekli Tepe. I climbed the hill overlooking the pleasant gardens of Balikli Göl – another name steeped in history - and the sacred pool of Abraham with its impressive number of carp. As already mentioned, local legend has it that Urfa is the birthplace of Abraham and that this is where he was thrown into a fire by Nimrod, a fire that transformed into the waters of the pond. Manmade canals branch off from it and wind around the tree-filled gardens where an equally impressive number of apparently well-nourished cats roam free. I was told that they don't feed on the carp.

I took a path that leads to a quiet place at the summit of the hill next to the ruins of an old fortress and sat on a bench there to catch my breath, gazing down onto the gardens and out over the town to distant hills. The only noise came from the chirping of a great many birds in the trees below. A peaceful, relaxing moment in a hectic week. Then the chant from the mosques began. I don't know who called out first or where, but the sound spread rapidly from one side of the place to the other and, for once, I was struck by the beauty of it. After a minute or two, a deep voice joined the chorus, so much deeper than the others that I turned my head to find its source. He joined in and then abruptly stopped again, long before the other voices faded out. The minutes I spent on that hill in ancient Edessa were made even more unforgettable by the sound. Blending into such an unfamiliar setting, it was abstract, untainted for me by any religious connotation, and strangely exquisite.

In a similar way, the words that sprang from *The Story of Sukurru* brought a sensation of joy each time a new meaning came to light and contact was established with a scribe who had lived at least five thousand years before me. Nothing and no-one came between us to impose a context. Sensing their encouragements as I unravelled the secrets and discovered the humour at the heart of their text were unforgettable moments, simply wonderful.

4
Gobekli Tepe

Sanliurfa, ancient Edessa, is the town to stay in when visiting Gobekli Tepe, a twenty-minute taxi ride away, and it certainly has its own story to tell. It was here that the oldest known statue of a man was dug up, apparently in the Balikli area. He's on display now in the Sanliurfa Museum. The hills just opposite the museum are riddled with caves, many of which have carefully carved entrances, part of a necropolis, an ancient burial place. But perhaps they once served as dwellings for the people who frequented Gobekli Tepe, a place where food was consumed but no signs of homes found. Who can know? The huge pillars of Gobekli Tepe were so deeply integrated into a round hill that the site lay buried for many thousands of years with only the tops of them visible at the surface. German archaeologist, Klaus Schmidt, decided to investigate them in 1995 and his discovery was huge in its implications. Because it had remained underground, it was possible to date the site to around 9600 BC, and to demonstrate beyond doubt that mankind was capable of methodical construction and sophisticated high-relief carving at an age when only roaming primitive hunter-gatherers were purported to be on Earth. 'Strange' comes to mind rather than 'primitive' when you gaze at those pillars. Only a small fraction of its treasures has been presented to the modern world, with about 95 percent still in the ground. Progress seems excruciatingly slow from the outside but at least there is work going on.

Gobekli Tepe takes its name - or so we are told - from its present-day aspect, that of a pot-belly hill. That is the simple and admittedly reasonable explanation. The site of Gobekli Tepe, give or take a few freshly dug-up pillars in stone circles and a spanking new roof, is nothing more in appearance than a round hill. Hence the name.

Turkish 'gobek' translates to 'navel' and 'umbilical'. Although a superficial juxtaposition of 'navel' with 'potbelly' continues to seem reasonable, they don't have quite the same meaning. A navel is that point in the middle of the potbelly. It might be integrated, even deeply so in some cases, but it's not the same thing. And since I'm already nit-picking here, I will add that the umbilical is something else again. It's neither navel nor potbelly. This is the cord between mother and child, between the womb and the navel, the feeding channel, rope of life.

My suggestion is that the Turkish word 'gobek' became synonymous with 'pot-belly' as a result of a pre-existing place name. The 'gobek' of Turkish dictionaries resulted from a more ancient meaning. Gobekli has to do with far more than the superficial visual aspect of that site. This is perhaps a chicken and egg situation, but one where the egg must be considered with its umbilical cord. Chicks have umbilical cords too.

There is another bone of contention surrounding the name 'Gobekli'. It has been claimed that the Turkish word was a direct translation from the real name of the site, which was necessarily an Armenian name. We're told, without precise evidence that I know of, that the place was once called Portasar which also means navel but in Armenian. If that is the only truth, it fundamentally undermines any discussion of phonetic Gobekli in relation to…Gobekli Tepe. But again, I have to insist. I don't doubt that Portasar was an important name in that region and may well have been applied to the site at some point in time, but it's my intention to demonstrate that Gobekli has its origin in deep antiquity. It didn't just appear at a relatively modern date out of a translation. If anything, the Armenian claim reinforces the importance of the 'navel' as a place to begin this study. It is unnecessary, at least in my view, to bow to a distinction made between two modern languages and by people who have a heartfelt reason for making it; to walk away from an analysis when the whole point of this study is to bypass them both and to look for meaning in the original Sumerian language of that region. The Kurdish name for it, Gire Navoki, is also interesting but gives up less information than the GO-BE-KLI sounds and the overall subject of the navel. A study of it will be for another time.

Dictionaries give Turkish 'gobek' opposite Portuguese 'umbigo' for 'navel'. Both have their origin in an unknown (PIE) source. As there is no other word used for the birth cord alone, navel and cord are inseparable. Modern 'gobek' and 'umbigo' do not make that important distinction. 'Navel-string' is an alternative term to 'umbilical cord' used to describe that particular element. It seems to be the best we can do. I repeat. The old meanings of these words had more to do with the ultimate link between mother and child than a simple 'pot-belly' or 'navel' imply:

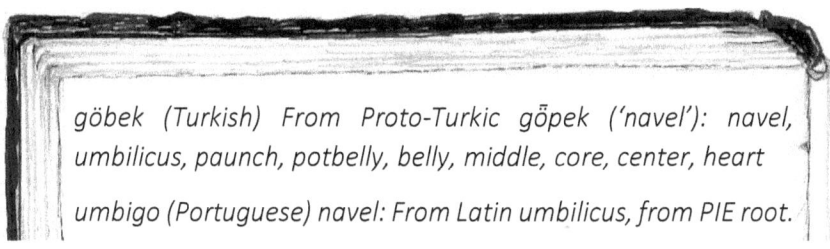

göbek (Turkish) From Proto-Turkic gṓpek ('navel'): navel, umbilicus, paunch, potbelly, belly, middle, core, center, heart

umbigo (Portuguese) navel: From Latin umbilicus, from PIE root.

Going by the indications of the Turkish and Portuguese words, alternation of the syllables is not a problem; GO before BE, BI before GO. Researching generic names for sacred places of extreme antiquity, a superficial search for all forms of BE or BI with GO (Sumerian GU) throws up some but probably not all the names still in existence. In my view, the results don't disappoint:

- Mont Bego in the Alps of southern France, known as the Valley of Marvels, a site with thousands of rock carvings, and reputed for the violence of its thunderstorms. Some petroglyphs are of acrobats and bull-leaping. See page 73.

- Monte Beigua in the Italian Alps, reputed to have once been a sacred mountain to an ancient people called Ligurians, and associated with Mount Bego,

- Beigu Mountain in Zhenjiang, China, overlooking the Yangtze River and famous for the stories of 'The Romance of Three Kingdoms'.

- Gubio, apparently the ancient name of Goa on India's west coast mentioned in the writings of Sumerian King Gudea of Lagash in the third millennium BC. Petroglyphs said to date back as far as 20,000 years have been found there.

- Gubbio in Italy at the foot of Mount Ingino, known as Eugubium in the Middle Ages. Settlements from the Paleolithic era and the Bronze Age have been found there.

- Gobi Desert in Northern China and Mongolia cloaked in mystery and subject of tales about a lost civilisation of great wisdom.

- Gobedra in Ethiopia, place of the carved lion or lioness. This rock carving of unknown origin is situated close to Aksum, where the Ark of the Covenant is said to be kept.[29]

- Bigu. Although not a place name, this is noteworthy. It's the name of the ancient Chinese Daoist practice of grain avoidance, antithesis of the beer-drinking in the text of *The Story of Sukurru*. Chinese GU can be found in the form of a simplified 7-stroke character with the meaning 'valley' or 'gorge'. GU is also the Sumerian sound for 'gorge'.

- Gobekli Tepe.

All the sites of extreme antiquity are the navels of Earth, the spiritual portals of its inhabitants. They speak of an eternal link to the Matriarchal womb from which everything is born. Places where the Mother's waters begin their course carry such tremendous force and have infused the Earth with their energy from such a remote age that mankind will never succeed in cutting the cord or in shaking Her off. Her life blood still flows through our rivers, down through the age-old gullies carved into mountain sides countless years ago, and through us. There is no deal to be done, no covering up of bellybuttons, no final severing possible. Mother knows best.

> *In olden days, when the earth was very young, they say that heaven and earth were very near to one another, because the navel-string of heaven drew the earth very close to it. This navel-string of heaven, resembling flesh, linked a hill near Sumer with heaven. At that time all the subjects of the Siem of Mylliem throughout his kingdom came to one decision: to sever the navel-string from that hill. After they had cut it, the navel-string became short; and, as soon as it shortened, heaven then ascended high. It was since that time that heaven became so high, and it is for that reason that they call that hill which is near Sumer 'U Lum Sohpet Byneng.'* [30]

The Indian myth quoted above cannot ordinarily be linked to Gobekli Tepe, a site in modern Turkey, and yet it seems to describe in detail events that might have led to such a place being deliberately buried - as Gobekli Tepe was sometime after 9600 BC. Bearing in mind my firm belief that all mythologies spring from one worldwide source, the details that led me to seriously consider the possibility of a link were five-fold: the mention of a navel-string, it being associated with a hill, the name 'Sumer', the severing, and the antiquity of the story. The quote refers to a mountain peak and valley in the Ri Bhoi district of Meghalaya, northeast India. There is a place called Sumer, a simple fact that should put an end to my imaginings. Still, it provides an insight into a possible explanation for the burial of Gobekli Tepe. Perhaps there are many similar hills still unexcavated. There is certainly at least one other buried site in Turkey that has the same characteristics as Gobekli Tepe[31], so why not elsewhere?

The name that is associated with navels, umbilical cords and deep antiquity has its source in the earliest Sumerian symbols. The four chapters that follow delve - as deeply as possible at this point in time – into the original reasoning behind its existence.

5

The Great Bull and the Flow of Beer

Hathor, Egyptian goddess, sacred and cosmic cow, stares back at us from the summit of one of her pillars. This photo was taken from a ledge on the exterior of the relatively small temple dedicated to Hathor within the Karnak temple site at Luxor, ancient Thebes, in Egypt. I feel a particular affection for and curiosity about Hathor since visiting her most enigmatic temple at Dendera. There she once looked out in all four directions from each of her many pillars, at a time before her benign face was systematically defaced. There was no other way of escaping her gaze. But who would want to? She is not threatening, however seriously we are expected to take the astronomical teachings that adorn every inch of wall and pillar space there. I post her image here for the pleasure of inviting her into my book and in the hope of one day returning to that most intriguing, mysterious place that is Dendera . But for now, we make our way back to northern Mesopotamia and to the traces of her that are still discernible there.

The story of Gobekli Tepe is that of the bull in all its forms. It's the Great Bull of the Taurus mountains and the Bull that lies across the roof of the Sky, the constellation of Taurus. It's the roaring and force of the wild bull, stampeding down, pulling on the boulders, forming the headwaters and the gullies of the twins, the torrents from which are generated the Tigris and Euphrates rivers. The bull represents the brute force of nature. At the same time, its feminine form is the Matriarchal nurturer, bringing the milk of life to the land. The bull is sacred. Mr Bull and Mrs Bull, the cow, are good.

There are paintings of wild bulls and their ancestor aurochs dating back tens of thousands of years in various places across the world. Perhaps the best and most well-known examples are in the Lascaux caves of southwest France. Clearly, they were given great importance in the earliest known times of mankind's history. They were, no doubt, physically impressive, probably more so than the bulls we know today. To say that the animals were worshipped as gods (in our sense of the word 'god') asserts a connotation given to those ancient paintings in the minds of their authors that may not be correct, that we have no way of proving. But admired and revered? I would say so.

The site at CatalHoyuk situated close to the Euphrates river was inhabited at around 7000 BC by people who painted bulls and placed bullheads on their walls. The bull, its head strangely twisted, is also inscribed on the T-shaped pillars of Gobekli Tepe. And it's the head of the bull that is used for Sumerian symbol GUD. Perhaps not a god, nevertheless the animal had a predominant place in the lore of ancient cultures. Revered as an imposing representation of a force of nature, let's see what more the sacred language can tell us about it.

GUD/GU$_4$

bull, good

Gud is given as 'bull, ox, cattle' 371 times at the earliest period on ePSD. With only a vague frontal shape of head and horns shown, it has the main phonetic values, GU₄ and GUD. In my translations, GUD is used throughout for clarity. No doubt the bulls or aurochs were esteemed for their force and for their usefulness, perhaps painted for the same pleasure that a modern artist would find in that act. But were they seen as gods in the most ancient times? I wouldn't be sure of it even if this is the origin of our word:

> *God: Old English god 'supreme being, deity; the Christian God; image of a god; godlike person,' from Proto-Germanic *guthan (source also of Old Saxon, Old Frisian, Dutch god, Old High German got, German Gott, Old Norse guð, Gothic guþ), which is of uncertain origin; perhaps from PIE root.*
>
> *Good: Old English gōd (with a long 'o') 'excellent, fine; valuable; desirable, favorable, beneficial; full, entire, complete;' of abstractions, actions, etc., 'beneficial, effective; righteous, pious;' of persons or souls, 'righteous, pious, virtuous;' probably originally 'having the right or desirable quality,' from Proto-Germanic *gōda- 'fitting, suitable' (source also of Old Norse goðr, Dutch goed, Old High German guot, German gut, Gothic goþs), a word of uncertain origin, perhaps originally 'fit, adequate, belonging together,' from PIE root.*

Both god and goodness began with the bull. The Proto-Germanic terms of 'fitting' and 'suitable' given here opposite 'good' are awkward synonyms for our modern-day use of the word. It's more likely we would say that something is good when it is pleasing; good food or a good hotel, for example. A child might be good, but a three-piece suit would be a good fit, the word relegated to its adjectival and characterless form.

In *The Story of Sukurru*, there is a line of text which serves to explain where 'good' came from and the fundamental reason behind its interpretation as 'fitting'. Line 94 is of interest on more than one level. It corresponds to the earliest known reference to Noah's Ark and to the instructions whispered from behind a reed façade:

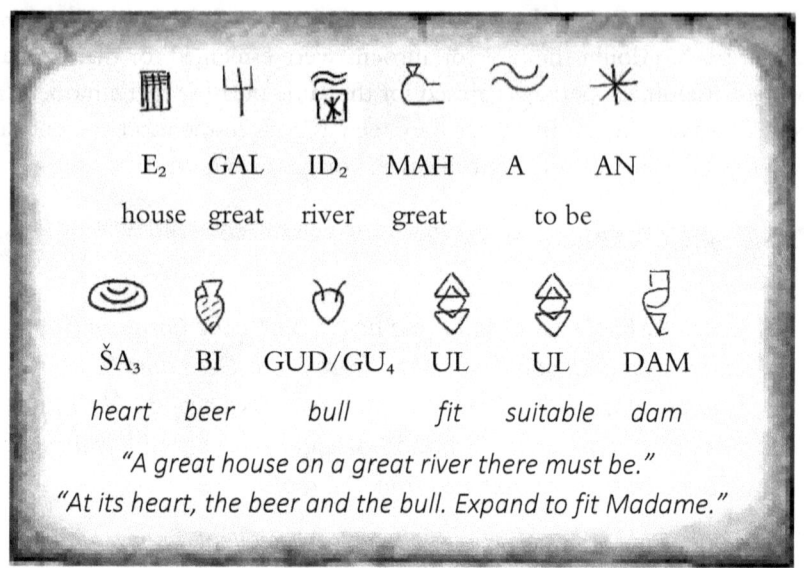

"A great house on a great river there must be."
"At its heart, the beer and the bull. Expand to fit Madame."

The first six symbols are self-explanatory. The great house in question is a river-house, a large boat used as a home on a waterway of some kind. Given the preceding line 93 – *to Beer-Heart a whispering there will be* - and the development of the story, there can be no doubt that this is a reference to the original story of Noah's ark. Of equal interest are the other six symbols associated with the ark in this line. I suggested in chapter 3 that ŠA$_3$-BI, in the overall pagan context, is the origin of the Sabians. Beer-Heart appears for the third time (See lines 19 and 47. See page 40), but the placing inside the ark, at its heart, took precedence over a repetition of 'Beer-Heart' at this point in the translation. Once again, it was a choice made partially in light of the positioning of the symbols and also to convey the overall humour; the beer to be placed in the safest space of the ark with the bull. Also note the collocation of BI with GU$_4$. The line is of the utmost importance, not least because it clearly demonstrates how the sounds we use today and the meanings attributed to them stem from such ancient stories. GUD with UL might even be translated as 'a good fit'. The bull is associated with fitting as both suitable and as a measurement. and, glancing back to the etymology of 'good', becomes good.

Symbol UL is given as 'fitting, suitable' 15 times at the earliest period. The symbol itself, two inverted triangles above and below a central diamond-shaped form, appearing to encase it, is a fitting portrayal of expansion and, I suggest, a founding symbol of sacred geometry. Repetition of UL between the bull and its partner allowed for translation first as 'expand' and then as 'to fit'. But UL-UL must also be understood as an indicator of 'two by two' or 'side by side', the famous phrase that can only bring to mind the popular story of the pairs of animals climbing into Noah's ark. Here we have Mr Bull on the left and his 'dame', Mrs Bull on the right, separated - by two symbols - to avoid quarrelling in the confined space. This notion of 'two by two' is borne out in the next line where the sign GAR, with its meaning 'to place' but also a measurement, surrounds two KU$_4$, a symbol with the given meaning 'to enter'. I left a blank space for KU$_4$ because I didn't find a pictogram of it:

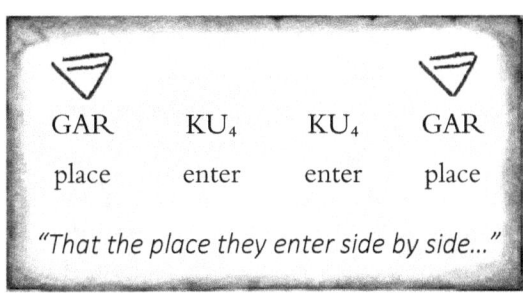

In *The Story of Sukurru*, this line leads on to another amusing section where GAR, is used to 'place' and to name characters in the context of the milk-churning ocean, a reference to the origin of the Hindu myth whereby the ocean is churned to release the nectar of immortality. GAR, as 'measure', extends the reference to the measuring needed to fit everyone into the ark.

Reiteration of GAR three times between lines 95 to 97 gives way to a reiteration of SUM, also with the meaning 'to place', this time the symbol of the reaping of the harvest, the all-important sum of it, as demonstrated by the pictogram of plants laid down:

SUM is repeated five times within this section from line 97 to 101 at which point in the performance a musical handover happens. The double flute is picked up. Thus, the biblical story of Noah's ark blends seamlessly with Indian mythology through the milk-churning ocean while, at the same time, breaking out into a joyful beer-drinking, harvest festival song! Here at the end of line 97 is the popular name of Noah for the first and only time in the text of *The Story of Sukurru*:

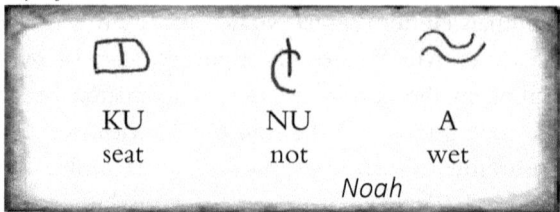

KU	NU	A
seat	not	wet

Noah

Thus did Noah achieve immortality; sitting high and dry. The double flute goes on to play both base notes and shrill, a flirtatious scene, and another obvious reference to the couple inside the ark. The next reiterated symbol will be KA, voice of the Administrator, repeated over six lines: SAYS…SAYS….SAYS…with the instructions for the building of the ark.

The phrase 'Expand to fit Madame' is, of course, a comic reference to the multitude of creatures that were somehow crammed into Noah's ark. How exactly did he manage to fit everyone in? We discover that the question is an old one and still unanswered. But at least we now know how the word 'good' came into being. It was GUD that everyone should fit into the ark, a male and a female, and good that they spend quality time there together thanks to the installation of a reed facade.

> That the place they enter side by side if they agree. If not, by day, between the spouses a thick reed fence place…

'Dam' is still used today to indicate a mother cow and the Latin etymology of 'domus' for 'dame' is unconvincing. There is wordplay with DAM as the final symbol here. I translated this to the verb 'to dam' elsewhere and came to the conclusion that the word 'dame' might well have its origin in sexist jokes made in a distant past. They were perhaps not always lovable people, just immensely human; people who loved their equivalent of our English pantomime. Sumerian DAM is the common source:

> Dam: 'barrier across a stream of water to obstruct its flow and raise its level,' c. 1400 (early 13c. in surnames), probably from Old Norse dammr or Middle Dutch dam, both from Proto-Germanic *dammaz (…), which is of unknown origin.

It seems that Mrs Bull was less than delighted at the installation of the beer in such a central part of the ark and in the heart of her spouse. DAM is both the spouse and the separator that must be put in place to protect Beer-Heart from her rage. But the bull as 'dam' also refers to a reclining bull in the sky who will serve as a roof. See lines 208 and 213. See Hindu Nandi.

GU$_2$

Another symbol of importance in this section and elsewhere comes with the same phonetic value as GUD/GU$_4$:

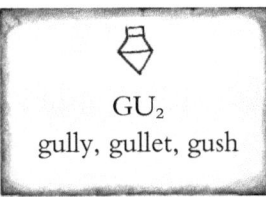

GU$_2$
gully, gullet, gush

Given as 'bank, side, neck' 30 times at the early period, preference is given here to those synonyms deriving directly from the GU sound. 'Neck' is replaced by gullet. These are the water channels that gush and carve their way through mountains; the gorges and the gullies (also written 'gulley'). In the case of GU$_2$, the officialised PIE analysis has done a good job in estimating the phonetic root of words such as 'gush' and 'gullet' and even the channel that is the human gut, simply because the sound has retained its force throughout the millennia. This was the force of the bull, the force of the cascading water digging gullies into the rock. It hasn't been usurped.

> *Gush: c. 1400, 'to rush out suddenly and forcefully' (of blood, water, etc.), probably formed imitatively in English or from Low German, or from or based on Old Norse gusa 'to gush, spurt,' from PIE *gus-, from root *gheu- 'to pour,'*
>
> *Gullet: 'passage from the mouth of an animal to the stomach,' (...) (Modern French gueule), from Latin gula 'throat,' also 'appetite,' from PIE root.*
>
> *Gully: 'channel in earth made by running water,' 1650s, possibly a variant of Middle English golet 'water channel' (see gullet)*

> Gut: Old English *guttas* (plural) 'bowels, entrails,' literally 'a channel,' related to *geotan* 'to pour,' from Proto-Germanic *gut-, from PIE root *gheu- 'to pour.'

GU₂, the gully, with BI, the beer, form the link to Gobekli that is found in the text of *The Story of Sukurru* on line 189. In this line, there are three different symbols that might be represented by phonetic GU:

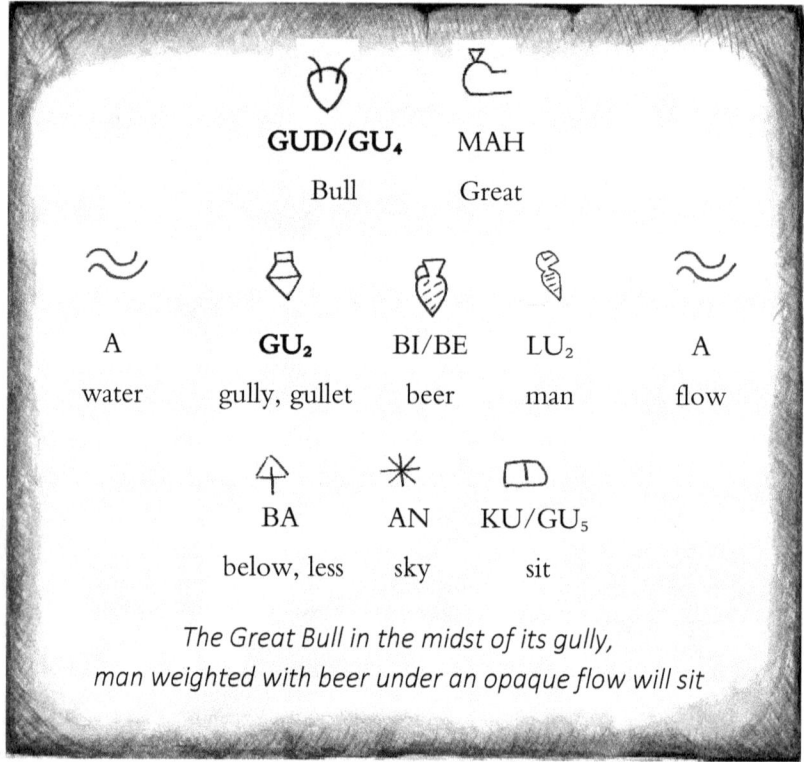

Suggesting that this is a direct, a very real reference to the ancient site of Gobekli Tepe or, at the very least, a site identical to it in a region between two rivers, will cause sceptical eyebrows to shoot up. However, like the Great Bull of the Taurus mountains, the theory has considerable strength. It can be argued on several levels; an analysis of the symbols, their superficial and secondary meanings, and the choice of positioning:

- GUD-MAH, the Great Bull, as a reference to the Taurus mountains and also Taurus, the Bull of Heaven.

- Symbol A, the flowing water, surrounds the central scene. This is not a language that follows rules of grammar as we understand them, and the line has all the hallmarks of a relatively simple Sumerian riddle. As with line 141 shown on page 47, 'in the midst of' is shown rather than spelled out. The line can be read from the middle, fanning out on either side, with the placing of A, the flow, on either side of the gullet of the man and his beer, effectively surrounding and submerging him. Gobekli Tepe is a place between two flows, the twinned headwaters of the rivers Tigris and Euphrates gushing down to lower realms from the nearby Taurus mountains.

- GU_2 is the gully dug by rivers, and it's also the throat or gorge of the drunken man in the story. Another phonetic form TIG gives the origin of 'tiger' and Tigris. See page 141.

- GU_2 with BI, the gully and the beer of life (bios-) placed side by side, are the symbols that gave Gobekli Tepe its enduring name, also origin of the Turkish word for navel, Gobek. This is the navel, positioned at the centre of the phrase, receiving the flow of water (or beer) from the cosmic umbilical cord. BI can also be read as binary, the two gullies carved out by the two principle rivers of the region. GU_2 with BI can be read as 'the two gullies' or the 'life-giving gully' from bios- which takes us rather neatly back to the maternal umbilical cord. It might even be that there are two umbilical cords, as is the case for twins. See UM on page 77.

- BA-AN has the meaning of 'without sky' or 'less light'. With 'sit', it gives 'skyless to sit', which could also be a reference to or an obscured reason for the massive stones of Gobekli Tepe being deliberately buried. They remained underground from around the 10th millennium BC until very recent times. Some of the stones represent people, however strange their appearance. It is the lack of textual evidence that suggests later generations were not aware of such a place and the events there, including the burial. It may be that these were more note-worthy than we have so far imagined. Our thoughts on the subject are deeply influenced by the fact that, until recently, we ourselves were totally unaware of the stone sites.

There are several words that originated with BA-AN. They include 'to ban', a 'ban', 'to banish' with some interesting meanings that we might not think of today. Obsolete English terms for ban include 'to summon, call out', 'to curse' and 'to execrate'. A connotation of threatening and cursing is found in the Old High German bannan, 'to command or forbid under threat of punishment' and bannen 'banish, expel, curse'. It's also of interest to note that Persian 'ban' has the meaning of 'prince, lord, chief, governor'. *The Story of Sukurru* contains a great deal of cursing and some banishing too. The cursing stones mentioned in Chapter 9 might also be linked to this scene.

- KU, 'the seat' and 'seize', is another symbol with the phonetic value GU₅. It's worth adding that this is the closest sound to 'cow' from Old English 'cu'. There are three symbols in line 189 that can be pronounced with the GU sound, of which the first and the last, both of them references to bovines, perhaps the male at one end and the female at the other…? I wouldn't be surprised.

> *Cow: 'female of a bovine animal,' especially the domestic ox, Middle English cu, qu, kowh, from Old English cu 'cow,' (...) from from PIE root *gwou- 'ox, bull, cow.'*

NAR

This is a convenient point at which to mention another character found in *The Story of Sukurru*. A scene in the comedy has GUD, the bull, in the company of LUL, also known as NAR, the fox.

NAR/LUL

fox, musician, singer

Given as 'musician, singer' 52 times at the early period and 'to be false' once at a later date, this is the origin of 'to lull', 'lullaby' and French 'renard'. Line

213 tells the story of how the bull was lulled to sleep and became a roof across the sky, no doubt a scene with astronomical/astrological references. The singing was paid for by the audience (Count your shekels!), who presumably also provided the offerings made in the three rope baskets. See lines 208 to 211. That was my understanding of that particular section of *The Story of Sukurru*, despite some broken patches and the overall obscure nature of the tale. It also reminded me of Indian Nandi, the sacred reclining cow, not least because GUD-NA-AN, bull, stone and sky, occur together on line 212.

I mention it here because the fox and the bull are two of the characters seen on the pillars of Gobekli Tepe and this section ties them both in with the three offering baskets also found there on the now famous pillar 43. I am not suggesting that they constitute proof, especially as my theory incorporates the mind-boggling – and some will say ludicrous - suggestion that this site, built six thousand years before the alleged first invention of a writing system, could have been the subject of that writing. But the fox symbol and its meanings are, nevertheless, extremely thought-provoking in context, as are the three baskets.

There has been much debate on the subject of the three baskets portrayed at the top of pillar 43 at Gobekli Tepe, including discussion of a possible link to the ancient portrayals of a man carrying a bag, the most widely known being those of the Sumerian fish-god and the Mexican feathered serpent, a detail of which below:

In *The Story of Sukurru*, lines 209 to 211, they were offering baskets. I translated the symbols to 'rope baskets'. My understanding was that the rope symbol indicates that the baskets were both woven and possibly hauled up to the top of the pillars by rope. In that comedic account, they were offerings to bring down the cosmic sacred cow. The first contained 'blood and prey', telling us that the people were hunters. The second had 'precious metal and lapis lazuli' indicating that there was trade. The third contained 'yarn and linen' showing that there was some level of sophistication. The wearing of animal skins was understood as a humiliation in *The Story of Sukurru*.

In more than one portrayal of the ancient figure holding a basket, it appears to be in the context of travelling. A quick internet search at 'three baskets' threw up what I would see as a convincing place to begin reflection on their possible original meaning; the Tripitaka or three vessels of knowledge in

Buddhism are referred to as the 'three baskets'. *The Story of Sukurru* shows that the coracle of Noah is also referred to as a 'basket'. My suggestion is that, in the ancient world, the sailing vessel and basket could be synonymous and that a basket perhaps covered a panoply of concepts. This is substantiated by MAL, the basket, given at the start of line 177:

> *But of the hanging basket with the reed paddle....*

and also by symbol AMA, the sky inside a basket, beginning line 155. AMA takes us into the realm of Egyptian Hathor, celestial cow and cosmic container of many boats as the many images on the walls and ceilings of her temple at Dendera attest. Was that understanding of cosmic or earthly ships linked to the carrying of knowledge already ritualised at the site of Gobekli Tepe? Were the baskets in *The Story of Sukurru* destined to be carried up like solar ships into the sky or only their contents? See page 138 and IDIGNA (c) for symbols MAL and AN together. See page 214 for mention of three ships.

All of the above should also be considered in the light of line 190 which follows on from the scene of the drunken man and incorporates KLI into a word with the given meaning of 'river'. In the space of two lines of text, 189 and 190, GO, BE and KILI all appear. There are only six other symbols to separate them. With 280 lines and approximately 2,800 symbols in all, and with no other similar occurrences, this 'coincidence' is noteworthy. If line 189, that of the drunken reveller, does indeed refer to Gobekli Tepe and the activities there, then it should be proven that the place was once very much associated with beer making and drinking. Over 10,000 grinding stones have been found at the site and The Tepe Telegrams website set up by archaeologists in charge of excavating the site comments:

> *Out for a beer at the dawn of agriculture*
> *Finally, the aforementioned insights also provoke new questions relating to the use and consumption of alcohol at Göbekli Tepe, which may have been in the context of religiously motivated feasts and celebrations.*[32]

The movements of the stars and planets in the sky were known as the churning of the top stone of a cosmic mill[33], and there was no shortage of earthly millstones at the Gobekli site. Harran, city of the 'churning millstone in the sky' is situated a short distance from Gobekli Tepe and was, in all probability, a product of the same culture. The milling of grain might have been an arduous task, but subsequent beer-drinking and sky-watching would make a pleasant combination…up to a point.

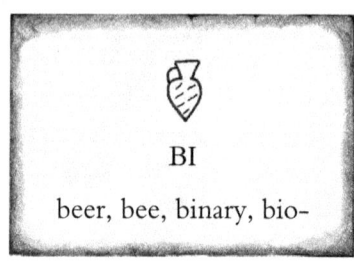

BI

beer, bee, binary, bio-

BI is given as 'beer' or 'alcoholic drink' 61 times at 3000-2500 BC: The other three meanings result from translations and logic. Keeping in mind that the symbol is a vessel presumably containing a fermented and thus a visibly living, bubbling substance, BI must be considered in its alchemical context, (See chapter 15):

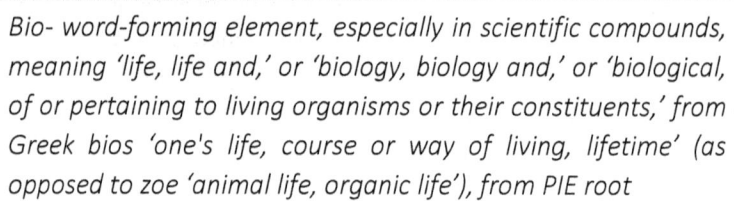

Bio- word-forming element, especially in scientific compounds, meaning 'life, life and,' or 'biology, biology and,' or 'biological, of or pertaining to living organisms or their constituents,' from Greek bios 'one's life, course or way of living, lifetime' (as opposed to zoe 'animal life, organic life'), from PIE root

The Story of Sukurru, its clay dated to around 2600 BC, is the earliest known story of beer drinking and drunkenness in the world. Other translators using different methods and examining different texts have come to the same conclusion about the habit: beer was an important subject in the Mesopotamian world. This said, the investigation of Gobekli as a generic name must move beyond the realm of beer festivals. There is necessarily more to it than that. Otherwise, how would the name have been strong enough to resist the passage of time?

6

The Two Horns of the Great Bull

There were summer festivals in the Landes region of southwest France where holiday makers gathered on warm evenings to watch essentially placid young cows be teased into chasing people around an arena. Acrobats run back and forth, throwing cords and leaping over the increasingly confused, exasperated animals. As I remember it, the show was impressive and the animals, although understandably indignant, physically unhurt by the exercise. Perhaps the act of enraging cows constitutes cruelty – I would say that it does -, but the fact is that they were not physically harmed (or later killed) and the festive atmosphere of the place was pleasing. Until I translated line 45, I had forgotten about those holiday outings and the unique ambience of the mock bull-baiting rings. People change. I don't think I would enjoy it at all today.

And people forget. From reading the old texts and looking into descriptions of this strange age-old tradition of bull-leaping and bull-baiting, the original rationale behind it begins to take shape.

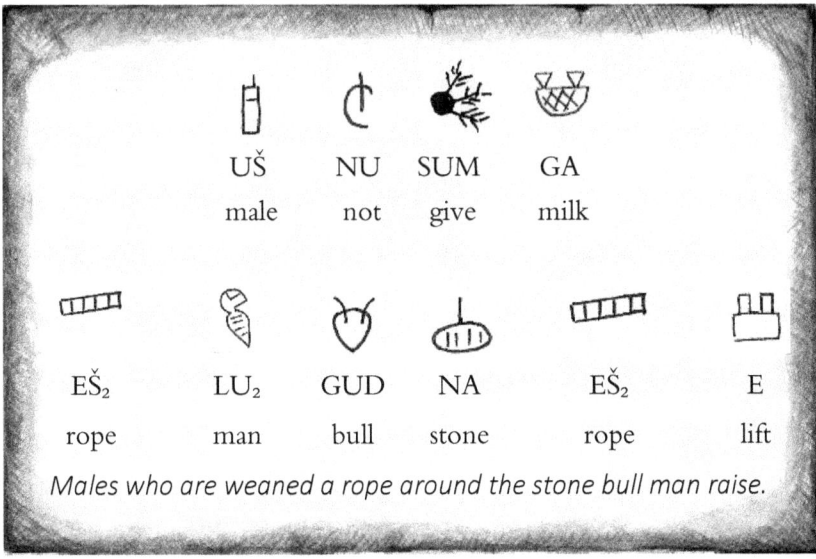

The Story of Sukurru mentions acrobatics as many as four times in different sections. Line 45 shown here is the first. In the space of ten pictograms, it reveals not only the existence of bull-leaping at the 2600 BC mark but also its direct connection to the rituals involved in the weaning from childhood and passage to manhood.

As with line 189, shown on page 64, where water symbols surround the beer-sodden man, the symbol of the rope is given on either side of the stone bull-man. This might also be understood as man and bull between the ropes, but the subject of the phrase, the males through UŠ, symbol of virility, is found at the beginning. The accuracy of the translation of this ritualistic scene is confirmed by the following line 46 which refers to the other kind of male, those who are 'given milk' and thus not weaned.

This doesn't appear to be a living, breathing bull unless the NA symbol serves as 'weighty' rather than 'stone'. That would be a superfluous use of NA in that everyone is aware of the bull's physiognomy. It's my understanding that symbols were not used for stating the obvious. And so, it must have been the poor old stone bull-man of Lamassu fame who was roped in to make himself useful once again. Think about that when you stare up at him next time in a museum. As will I. He might still be annoyed.

Looking for the most ancient scenes of acrobats to use as illustrations for lines 162-166, I came across the well-known Minoan images of bull-leaping acrobats but also mention of an even more ancient tradition on the island of Nias in Indonesia:

> *The purpose of young men jumping over stone hurdles arranged in levels from 2-2.5 meters in height was to develop martial skills (...)*
>
> *This traditional village is a tourist asset of Nias island, wherein one can witness the attraction of stone hurdle jumping (hombo batu) which in former times was part of a series of ceremonies intended for youths who were approaching adulthood.*[34]
>
> *In the past the top of the stone board was covered with spikes and sharp pointed bamboo.*[35]

Going back in time to undatable petroglyphs, I found other compelling images of acrobats but also of two blocks, each mounted by a pair of bull horns and joined by a central ladder. They appear not only among the Neolithic rock carvings of Mont Bego in the Alps of southern France (see the list of sites on pages 53-54) but also at another less well-known site, the caves of Kamyana Mohyla in Ukraine. If the images are to be taken literally, acrobats were flying over manmade vaulting horses (a modern term!) with bull horns sticking up from them at dates so early we cannot integrate them into our current understanding of history. And in more places than one.

The acrobats of Mont Bego can be seen in the following drawings[36]. Notice the scene to the far right where three acrobats figure around two horned shapes with one in the act of passing upside down between the horns. The official descriptions call most of them agricultural scenes but the figures there can be identified with a minimum of imagination as acrobats.

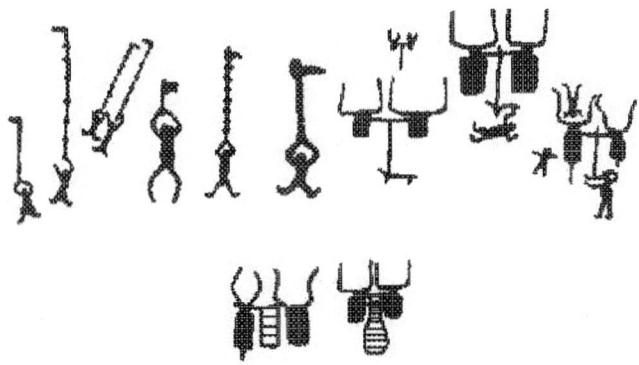

Another petroglyph discovered very far away from the French Alps in the region of Kamyana Mohyla in Ukraine brings confirmation that this was not a localised phenomenon. Shown below, it bears an uncanny resemblance to the pair of bull horns accessed by means of a ladder that appear in the carvings on Mont Bego.

Another probable reference to acrobats occurs between lines 162 and 166, an obscure section about rising and falling. I didn't quite get to the bottom of it. A couple of the Mont Bego petroglyphs are used as the illustration of that page. Was the memory of a sacred ritual, a passage from one stage of life to the next inscribed in petroglyphs? Were the ancient scratches simply signs indicating that this was the place to gather for the next performance?

If it were at all possible to imagine some of the activities that took place at Gobekli Tepe apart from the obvious beer-drinking, would there be the spectacle of young stone-bull leapers and tightrope walkers? The pillars there vary in height, some of them being 5 or 6 metres tall and some with unexplained notches, holes and short channelling which might have served to attach ropes and/or pieces of metal or wood.

Did troops of acrobats and musicians once move between such places? Did they travel from the alps of France to those of Italy, from Bego to Beguia, and then perform again at Gobekli Tepe in Turkey? And did they do the same at Kamyana Moyhla in Ukraine? Were the skills of acrobatics and tight-rope walking intended for more than mere entertainment?

I added tight-rope walking into the mix after discovering that there is an extremely ancient tradition still alive in Dagestan, a remote mountainous region bordering the Caspian Sea. It's said that the dangerous activity – apparently always practised without a safety net – began as a means of crossing the mountain gorges... Then I came across the following quote from funambulist, Andrea Loreni, which suggests to me that it might equally have originated as an art form that was taught in the context of the rites of passage to adulthood.

> *Today what I teach is not a technique to stand on the tightrope. I teach my way to face fear, a new situation, an obstacle, all of these aspects that are well represented by the tightrope. A balance practice like this goes beyond the acquired technique in order to involve the body-mind whole in a self-transformation process which could be considered a denudation, an analysis, a rooting, or exceeding of our own limits in order to become tightrope-empty.*[37]

And why two bulls, four horns, as shown in those petroglyphs? They seem to confirm that there was always a couple side by side. The same can be said of the Egyptian Narmer palette which shows two bull heads presiding over the complex scenes there; and the same again on an artefact from the Jiroft culture of ancient Persia. Mr and Mrs Bull appear together in more than one circumstance, a cosmic and sometimes a comical pair.

GUD appears in the lexical entries as GU-UD, the cord of the sun, a ray perhaps or a means of measurement:

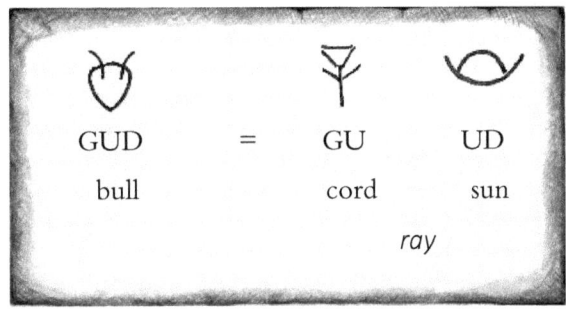

GU is given as 'cord' 54 times at 3000-2500 BC. It's also given as 'net', perhaps the strong cord used to make nets for hunting and fishing. The obvious interpretation here of 'cord of the sun' as 'ray' leads back to the symbol RA discussed in the context of Harran and its stargazing Sabians:

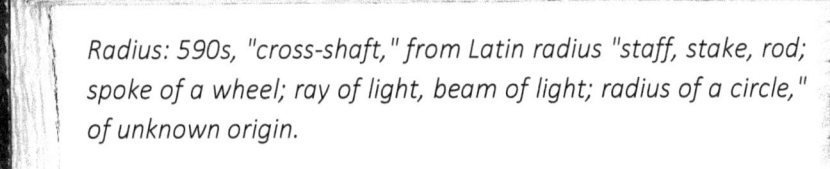

Radius: 590s, "cross-shaft," from Latin radius "staff, stake, rod; spoke of a wheel; ray of light, beam of light; radius of a circle," of unknown origin.

Egyptian Hathor, pictured on page 57, must not be overlooked in this connection. She gazes out from all four sides of her pillars at Dendera and Karnak, the celestial cow, nurturer and Matriarch of the skies. Thanks to the lexical entries for GUD, the threads of the common symbolic language begin to untangle themselves. The bull, the cow, the cord and the eternal stone. Where will they lead?

7
The Umbilical Cord and the Flow of Water

UM

rope

The UM of 'umbilical' and of Portuguese 'umbigo' has a Sumerian origin. UM is given as 'reed rope' twice at an early period. As already mentioned, Turkish 'gobek' and Portuguese 'umbigo' are both equivalent to the English word 'navel' and can be understood to refer to the maternal cord.

An attempt is made in etymological dictionaries to link the word 'umbilicus' to the root 'navel' despite the absence of any similarity in their pronunciation.

> *Umbilicus: 'navel,' 1610s, from Latin umbilicus 'the navel,' also 'the center' of anything, from PIE root.*
>
> *Omphalos: also omphalus, "sacred stone," 1850, from Greek omphalos, literally "navel," later also "hub" (as the central point), from PIE *ombh-alo-, from root *nobh-/*ombh- "navel" (see navel).*

It's as if an effort had been made at some point in time to muddy the waters between the tummy button and the umbilical cord. It seems more logical to look for a separate etymology for the umbilical cord through Latin umbilicus and link that, through UM, to the Greek word 'omphalos'. This is the sacred stone, notably at Delphi, considered to be the navel of Earth and, like most of the words here, from an unspecified PIE root.

The roots of the omphalos stone are unknown. That is because they are profound and Sumerian. The artefact resembles a mound, perhaps best described as the shape of a beehive, and it is wound around with rope or, in some instances, with snakes. I would contend that the rope or snakes are the portion of the artefact that give the stone its name, a direct reference to the matriarchal umbilical cord – not the navel! The core element, the stone, derives from NA, source of 'navel'.

> *Navel: Old English nafela, nabula, from Proto-Germanic *nabalan (source also of Old Norse nafli, Danish and Swedish navle, Old Frisian navla, Middle Dutch and Dutch navel, Old High German nabalo, German Nabel), from PIE root.*

Although this is a slight deviation from the main subject of the umbilical, there's the possibility that the etymology of navel, with its Greek connotation of sacred stone, is linked to Sumerian NAB. Lexical entries show this to correspond to NA-AB:

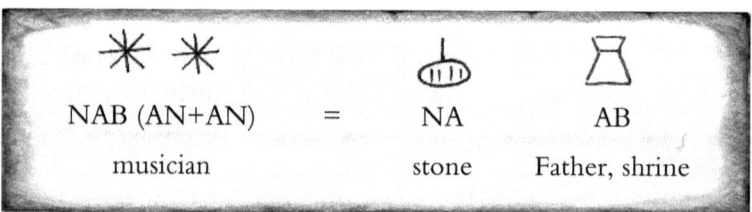

| NAB (AN+AN) | = | NA | AB |
| musician | | stone | Father, shrine |

NAB, composed of two 'sky' symbols, is given as 'musician' 5 times at the earliest period. NA-AB might translate to 'stone of the shrine', 'stone of the Father', 'stone of the ocean' and, particularly in the context of 'kanab' on line 56 of *The Story of Sukurru*, was taken to mean 'sands', the sands of time. There is another reference to NA as origin of 'navel' on page 217.

In conclusion, the long forgotten English words, 'umbe' and 'umbego' are surely descended from the same UM source as the Greek word 'omphalos' and offer an intriguing angle on the ways in which a combination of the phonetic forms of symbols UM, BE and GU existed together and were understood until relatively recently:

> *Umbego (English): To go around, to go about, encompass, encircle, surround. From Middle English umbegon, from Old English ymbgān ('to go around, go about, surround'), from Proto-Germanic *umbi ('around'), *gānan ('to go'), equivalent to umbe- + go. To go around, To go about; encompass; encircle; surround.*

Another connection between Turkish Gobek, the navel/umbilical, Sumerian GU-BE or BE-GU, and the site of Gobekli Tepe is found in a unique carving there. This piece of stone was found at the site and is now displayed in the Sanliurfa Museum:

Visually more graffiti than carving, the image is unlike any other found so far at Gobekli Tepe. We might well wonder if the perpetrator ever got into trouble for it. Apart from the obvious strangeness of the head, not unusual in ancient images of the cosmic Matriarch, there is the bizarre portrayal of the vulva. It may be that this was done as deliberate provocation, a desecration of the sacred matriarchal image. But, given the unnatural shape of the head, it's most likely a serious (or not…) depiction of one aspect of the cosmic figure.

It introduces the possibility of an origin to the concept of the double cord seen on the UM symbol and inferred by the GU-BI, 'binary cord', combination. Only the birth of twins could result in two umbilical cords. But there is another way to visualise the dual cords; one as the earthly attachment at birth, the other as the less visible 'silvery' cord that is said to attach to the spirit, described by people in deep meditative states or close to death.

Given that 'umbe' meant 'around' and 'umbego' meant 'to go around', there is the possibility that the Sumerian phonetic value GU gave us the verb 'to go'; a second candidate for that word. I have already considered GA as a source of it. These meanings all recall the Greek omphalos stone with its encircling threads. An example of UM with BI is shown below.

On line 158, a choice is offered to the hero:

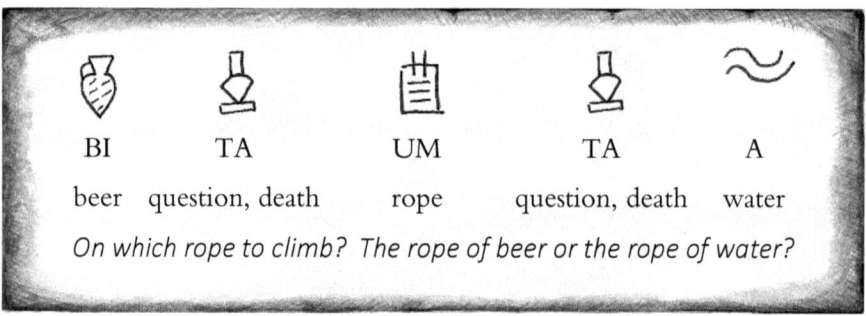

Here is another example of a Sumerian line to be read from the centre out. The centre is UM, the rope, with its intriguing double cord. It should be remembered that the full meaning of a text like this can only be gleaned when the earliest symbols are shown. The text of *The Story of Sukurru* did not come down to us in its original form. I re-created it as closely as possible by searching out the earliest symbols and matching them with the simplest of their phonetic values. What you see here is no longer in existence on any of the known tablets. Phrases like this appear only in abstract and visually unyielding cuneiform of a later time, mostly with different phonetic values applied, a linguistic quagmire. Perhaps one day someone will find a stash of the earliest editions. But, in the meantime, this is the best that can be done to rediscover the world of the first Sumerians. Here I exaggerate the gaps on either side of the two-corded central UM but perhaps the originals were separated into different squares. The cleverness and meaning of the phrase are completely bypassed and lost in The Instructions of Shuruppak, the academic version of *The Story of Sukurru*. It could not have been otherwise.

On each side of the cord is TA, given as 'what?' and translated by me to 'question' and to 'death'. It's the earliest known written reference to the philosophical principal of Tao which is said to have its origin in China. See page 177. A fundamental understanding was doubtless an essential element of the Sumerian culture and, as the language was worldwide, I make no guesses as to the place of origin. Perhaps it was the land that is now China.

The Story of Sukurru is a humorous one. Will it be death by water or death by beer? Sumerian TA was also used to signal that the word preceding it was a noun, a physical object. Another reading of it might give 'Will it be bios (life) by hanging on to the cord or death in the water?' On a more superficial level, perhaps a lifestyle choice, to get drunk or not. Most of all, it appears to be another reference to the passage to manhood, choosing between the maternal cord of milk or the cord of beer, in the course of a ritual enacted at a dedicated site.

Two cords of choice might be imagined in more than one way, not least as a reference to a team of acrobats playing out the various scenes of rising and falling, of throwing cords around the two horns of the stone bull man. Ups and downs are at the heart of the musical performance that is *The Story of Sukurru* - as above so below.

But the two cords of UM signal another metaphor, this one concerning the headwaters and carved-out channels of the Tigris and Euphrates rivers. The left-hand river as seen from the sky is the mildly flowing Euphrates. The right-hand cord is water, that of the fiery Tigris. Perhaps they would fit better the other way around. Anyway, they have a mutual source. Two by two, the twins were born with separate but parallel umbilical cords. And they have a common task. They are life-giving.

In *The Water Kingdom – A Secret History of China*[38] Philip Ball discusses the importance of water in terms of the myths and spiritual teachings of China. That is far from the only subject of his excellent book but was, for obvious reasons, the part that interested me the most. It resonates with the Sumerian translations undertaken so far. Water is life. His book reminded me that this must never be forgotten in the process of seeking out forgotten and profoundly significant meanings. The symbol for water expresses the flow not only of rivers, streams, and mountain gullies, but also the breaking waters of childbirth, both Earthly and Cosmic, the revitalizing flow of energies, fluids throughout our planet, including our own bodies; two small parallel wavy lines for symbol A carrying all that weight.

8
Springs, Fountains and Waterspouts

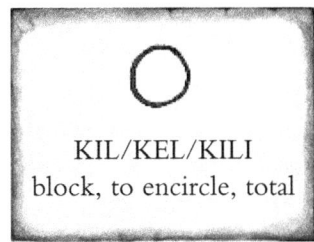

KIL/KEL/KILI
block, to encircle, total

Symbol KIL is straightforward, a circle or square shape. Represented by a large number of phonetic forms, some shown above but others completely different (LAGAB, ELLAG, RIM...), it's given with quite a few meanings between 3000 and 2500 BC:

- 'ball' 37 times preceded by the symbol for wood or tree,
- 'to be thick', 'to be big' 9 times,
- 'block', 'stump' (of tree) 10 times,
- 'to be short', 'tight' 56 times,
- 'to enclose, to confine, to encircle' twice,
  (Other given meanings have been left out here),
- 'important' given once.
- 'To break' appears only once at 2000 BC but is attested in context at an earlier period on line 50 of *The Story of Sukurru*.

Suppression of pagan knowledge, detrimental to religious dogma, began with the destruction of the language of the Matriarch. It continued with the destruction and usurpation of Her sites. In places where the knowledge was too deeply entrenched in natural surroundings, temples to newly founded religions were built on top of the ancient stones.

> *No one shall go to trees, or wells, or stones or enclosures, or anywhere else except to God's church, and there make vows or release himself from them.*
> The Penitentials of Theodoris. 7th century AD.
>
> *No Christian place lights at the temples or at the stones, or at fountains and springs, or at trees, or at places where three ways meet...* St. Eligius, 7th century AD.[39]

Despite the attack on all fronts, age-old pagan ceremonies at water sources were still in existence across Europe in the 7th century AD, by which time both oppressed and oppressors were perhaps less aware of the reason behind the original choice of such sites; testimony to the enduring subliminal nature of pagan wisdom. Water sources are natural gateways to other worlds. There are many, so many that it is difficult to know where to begin. But Sumerian KILI or KL sounds take us straight to the source of ancient knowledge. Let's begin with just one example.

Here's what Clive Essery, a dowser and investigator of ancient sites, wrote when I asked him about the church at Kilpeck:

> *We didn't look for water when we dowsed there unfortunately, but we did find 13 pagan altars around the site, and two Saxon Christian altars that are outside the present church to the North. Two of the group also believed that they had found a small stone circle under the naval of the church, either 5 or 6 stones. I think that an earlier survey than I attended (I have done 3 surveys there now) showed at least two water courses running on a North-South alignment under the current altar. I vaguely remember somebody saying that they had found one entering from a North direction that didn't pass through the building - possibly a blind spring under the altar?*

Kilpeck is the name of the village of the Church of St Mary and St David in Hereford, England. The church dates to around 1140 CE and is famed for its extraordinary façade sculptures which include a carving known as a 'Sheela-na-gig', a grotesque female figure holding open her vulva. I interpret that well-attested figure as representing the cosmic Matriarch at the time of her breaking waters, when childbirth is imminent and, in this case, a celestial stone is set to come forth. Did the flood come before the stone from the sky? There is a section in *The Story of Sukurru* between lines 249 and 252 which refers to this. It is my opinion that the Sheela-na-gig once served as a reminder of a great natural catastrophe and that it is still reflected in her name; Sumerian NA is 'stone', while GIG has the given meaning of 'troublesome'.

KIL is the most important and ubiquitous of generic place names left to us from extreme antiquity, and still in existence across a wide swathe of languages. Through Middle Dutch, we find kill as water channel. In the ancient Norse language, kell is a spring. The Celts take their name from this symbol and it is particularly widespread in Irish place names. These from Etymonline:

> *kill (n.2) 'stream, creek,' 1630s, American English, from Dutch kil 'a channel,' from Middle Dutch kille 'riverbed, inlet.' The word is preserved in place names in the Mid-Atlantic American states (such as Schuylkill, Catskill, Fresh Kills, etc.). A common Germanic word, the Old Norse form, kill, meant 'bay, gulf' and gave its name to Kiel Fjord on the Baltic coast and thence to Kiel, the German port city founded there in 1240.*
>
> *kil- first element in many Celtic place names, meaning 'cell (of a hermit); church; burial place,' from Gaelic and Irish -cil, from cill, gradational variant of ceall 'cell, church, burial place,' from Latin cella.*

I don't paint with a broader brush than the analysts who created PIE (Proto-Indo-European) when I look for words generated from the original Sumerian KIL/KILI/KEL sounds. The PIE statistics consider 'kel' to be the origin of words containing 'col' or 'cal' in them. That is not the case here. Words that don't retain the same vowel sounds as those given for the Sumerian symbols are not mentioned, whatever the truth of the matter. Accusations of cherry-picking to fit the overall subject might still be levelled, but I stick to my guideline of considering only the words or syllables that closely correspond to the Sumerian phonetics. That's why KEL would also be acceptable as the kil-origin of Latin cella, 'chamber' or 'cellar', celare, 'concealed' and 'kept secret', and, interestingly, cellere, 'to raise'.

A Sumerian watercourse is given as phonetic ID_2, combining three symbols:

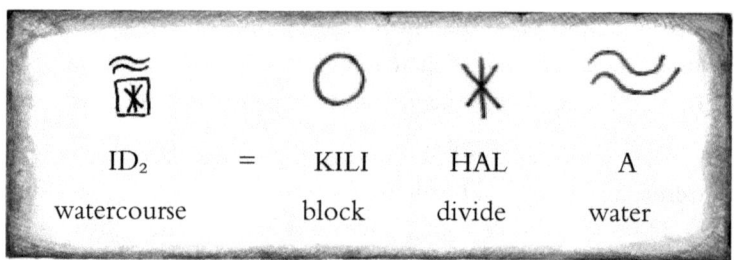

ID₂ appears a couple of times in *The Story of Sukurru*, once on line 94 (see page 60) where the oldest and strangest mention of Noah's ark is found and again on line 190 shown here below. This is the line that follows on from the mention of GU_2-BE. See page 64:

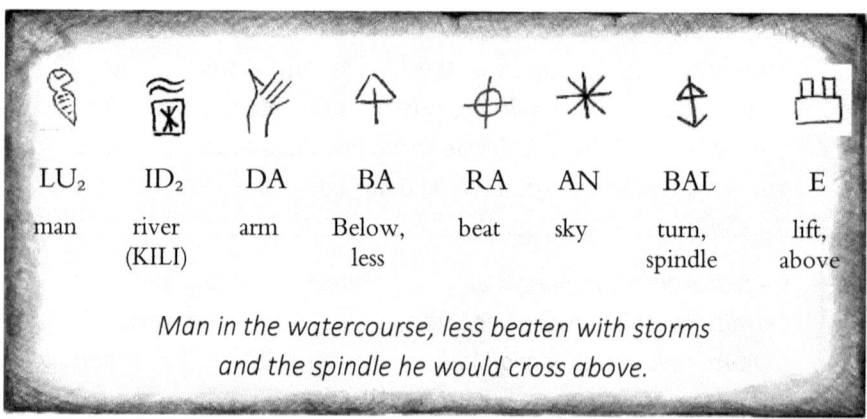

Man in the watercourse, less beaten with storms
and the spindle he would cross above.

DA, the arm, is given as 'side' and 'vicinity' 102 times at the early period. ID_2 with DA might signify the river bank, but, in the context where DA can also be understood as the arm that holds the spindle waiting to strike if he surfaces, it is likely that 'man' is lying inside the canal or under the water. It would have been the safest option.

GU₂-BI on the preceding line with KILI here are at the origin of the name of Gobekli. That said, it can be argued that the place doesn't have any apparent water source nearby. The two great Mesopotamian rivers don't flow close even if they can be said to pass by on either side. Did they ever? Does the geology of the region show the existence past or present of an aquafer and perhaps a spring? I don't know. However, it is known that the fields around are fertile, that people gathered there, and a lot of meat was eaten. Presumably, they would have chosen the place because it had good access to water nearby for growing crops, allowing them to make good use of the many millstones found there and presumably brewing beer. That is the only logical explanation. The line of text infers the presence of a natural watercourse, but it also suggests a hefty manmade flow of beer.

KIL/KEL

KIL or KEL are given in the lexical entries with two possible combinations, KI with EL or KI with IL:

a)

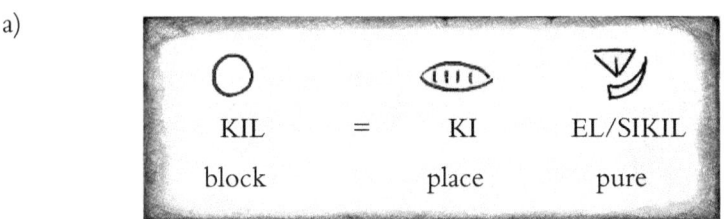

KI-EL, 'place of the fine horn', 'pure place', 'place of purification', where phonetic EL, also given as SIKIL, is a symbol of purity, given 5 times at 3000-2500 BC. There is a long Sumerian proverb where PI with EL have the meaning of 'pure pitch', understood as a musical note of absolute perfection. This is also attested in context in Line 35 of *The Story of Sukurru*, where the hero is seduced, not by the beauty of a companion, but by a song about clay tablets and writing. PI alone might signify 'perfection' but with EL, it goes one step beyond, perhaps to ecstasy.

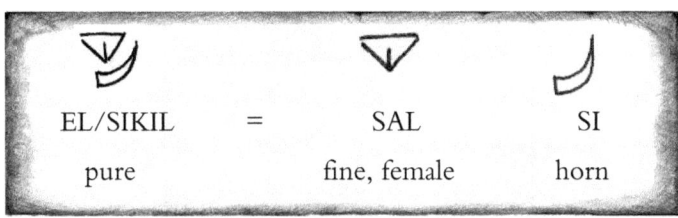

EL is formed from two symbols: SAL, 'fine', 'feminine', symbol of the vulva, also evoking a chamber, and from SI, 'horn' and 'to remember'. SI is given as 'horn' 9 times at 3000-2500 BC, and as 'to place' 61 times. The possibility of phallic inference can't be ignored.

> *Salon: from French salon 'reception room' (17c.), from Italian salone 'large hall,' from sala 'hall,' from a Germanic source (compare Old English sele, Old Norse salr 'hall,' Old High German sal 'hall, house,' German Saal), from Proto-Germanic *salaz, from PIE root.*

The horn and chamber pictured to represent this symbol of purity, can translate to an enclosed place, a chamber or cell, where a sound of great purity is heard, very likely that of a 'fine horn'.

A lexical entry for SIKIL gives SI with KIL and one other shows SI-KI-IL, reinforcing the horn element but associating it directly with KIL, the block, perhaps as a verb, the encircling. Add SAL as 'chamber' and the combination becomes increasingly intriguing:

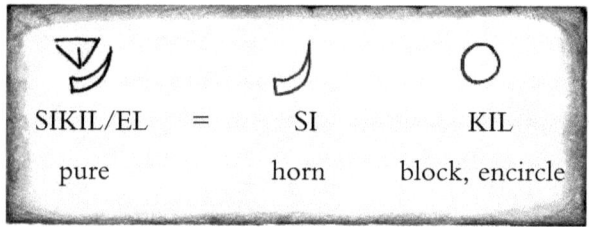

SIKIL/EL   =   SI   KIL
pure   horn   block, encircle

SI can also be understood as a waterspout and, of course, the horn as drinking vessel. SI-A, horn of water, is the oasis, the waterspout, and origin of the name of Siwa, a large oasis in the Sahara Desert. To raise the horn implies to drink. Gobekli can still be associated with beer drinking through the KLI element of its name.

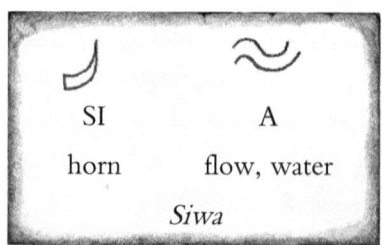

SI   A
horn   flow, water
       Siwa

Thanks to SI, the horn, there is an element of music or at least of sound, and also of flowing liquid, of abundance, incorporated into the KIL/KEL symbol, perhaps a place of stone where water bubbling from a spring can be heard. I found a place like that in a coastal village of the French Basque country; a small covered structure made up of stone slabs, hidden behind the pretty village centre, between the cottage gardens. A narrow public footpath leads up to it from the carpark. The water still trickles down from a hidden source and the atmosphere is quite magical. Of course, it has been associated with a Catholic saint, but the place is much older than any religion can claim.

b)
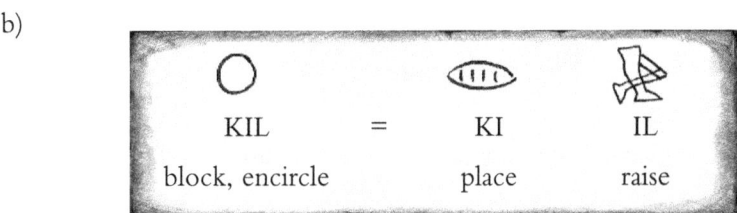

There are a couple of lexical entries which demonstrate that EL and IL are easily understood as synonyms. The second lexical combination for KIL/KEL is KI-IL. IL, also phonetic EL_2, is easily recognisable as a human, sometimes truncated, figure with one leg raised and possibly crossed over the other. They might be climbing, stepping up, or rising in some way, leading back to the earlier association of Gobekli with ladders, acrobats and bull-leaping ceremonies. $KI-IL_2$ translated to 'the raised place' in line 33 of *The Story of Sukurru* (see page 243). But the symbol might equally refer to a spiritual rising, 'the place of rising'. The two together have no single meaning in the dictionaries whereas SI, the horn, with IL have the given meaning 'to split apart'.

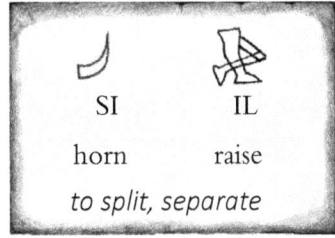

Although the horn doesn't appear in KI-IL, its mention in KI-EL indicates that it is to be factored into a global understanding of the symbol KIL.

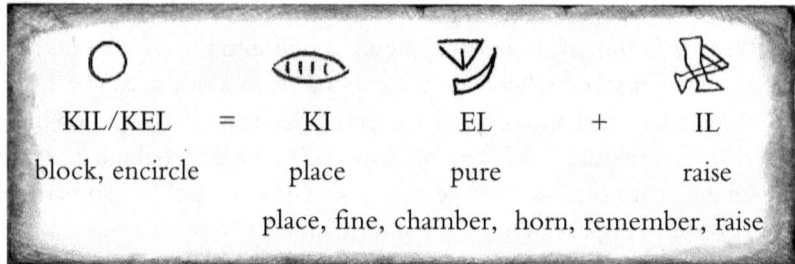

To summarize, KIL/KEL incorporate KI-EL (KI-SAL-SI) or KI-IL which lead to the following possible interpretations:

- The pure (EL), raised (IL) place (KI) where the fine (SAL) horn (SI) is raised (IL), place (KI) of remembrance (SI), of purification (EL), of separation (SI-IL) and rising (IL).

That is just the beginning. So far, only two phonetic forms of the KILI 'block' have been investigated. There are quite a few. The subject is vast.

> *Kel (Hungarian): to rise, with Hungarian kelt, to revive, resuscitate.*

ME-KI

There is an important lexical entry that tends to confirm the concept of KIL as a place of burial rituals and enlightenment. Two entries giving almost identical versions of the phrase are found. The difference lies in the use of IL or EL. They read as follows:

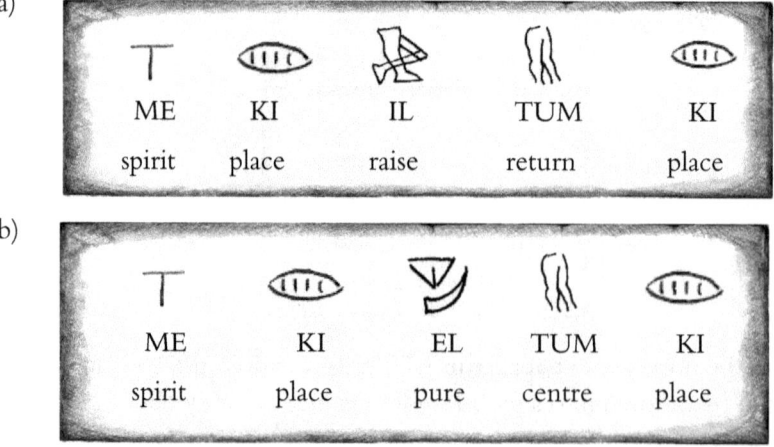

90

The two central pictograms of (a) show human figures side by side, truncated with a raised or crossed leg or standing straight, shown just from the waist down. The given meanings of TUM include 'back' as in 'to return' and 'middle'. I take this symbol to be the origin of 'tomb' and 'tumulus'. In this phrase, IL and TUM are surrounded by the place KI. The tomb or tumulus is in the middle of the place. IL might indicate that the centre, the navel, is raised but also refer to the rising of the spirit. ME-KI can be understood as the place of the spirit. ME has other important given meanings, of which 'magic', which will be discussed in great detail in later chapters.

> *Tomb: c. 1200, tumbe, early 14c. tomb, from Anglo-French tumbe and directly from Old French tombe 'tomb, monument, tombstone' (12c.), from Late Latin tumba (also source of Italian tomba, Spanish tumba), from Greek tymbos 'mound, burial mound,' generally 'grave, tomb.'*
>
> *Tumulus: ancient burial mound, 1680s, from Latin tumulus 'hillock, heap of earth, mound' (see tomb).*

To Kill

It's not possible to complete the analysis without mentioning this. It would be pleasant to prove that no sacrificial killings were carried out in those most ancient of times but that isn't possible either. Is our verb 'to kill' just a coincidence, entirely unrelated to the place names and to other topics that incorporate the sounds KIL or KEL or KILI or KLI?

> *Kill: c. 1200, 'to strike, hit, beat, knock;' c. 1300, 'to deprive of life, put to death;' perhaps from an unrecorded variant of Old English cwellan 'to kill, murder, execute,' from Proto-Germanic (...) from PIE root.*

I went looking for another explanation. Finally, it was the Great Hermes who gave me hope. I might be wrong about this, of course, but I choose to hope that the mindset that created places like Gobekli Tepe and even the Giza pyramids was that of people who felt no need to shed blood for anything other than their daily food. I want to believe that they had a higher moral compass than later cultures. Of course, killing for food, which certainly happened, requires some means of expressing that concept but at least it isn't a vengeful action and also not the only meaning of 'to kill'.

I began to look into the complexities of alchemy and hermeticism after detecting the presence of Hermes in the Sumerian texts. It is beyond my remit to explain more fully what it all entails, and I can only encourage others to do as I did, first listening with fascination to the hypnotic voice of Terence McKenna in the recording of his Lectures on Alchemy and then reading the books that he recommended. The Forge and the Crucible by Mircae Eliade[40] goes some way to explaining the incorporation of the notion of death by 'killing' into ancient rituals without the need to turn to the more obvious theme of physical human or animal sacrifice. It explains that the term encompasses the processes involved in the reduction and transmutation of metals in Western alchemy while also covering the notion of personal cleansing and awakening of 'divine substances' in Indian alchemical wisdom.

Use of the verb 'to kill' in those contexts suggests the existence of something far more subtle than a dedicated block of stone at the top of a pyramid where throats were cut and blood was shed for murky reasons. The alchemical activities would have taken place at sites where certain qualities, energies, natural forces were particularly propitious. The mention of it here can only begin to shed a small ray of light on age-old alchemical processes paralleled by some form of equally ancient initiation rites. And it does nothing to dispel the fact that, if the source of many words is found in the Sumerian symbols, then 'killing' as we know it in its most cruel form is sourced here too in Sumerian KIL.

KILI

KILI is another phonetic value of the same symbol. This time the lexical entries give KI with LI.

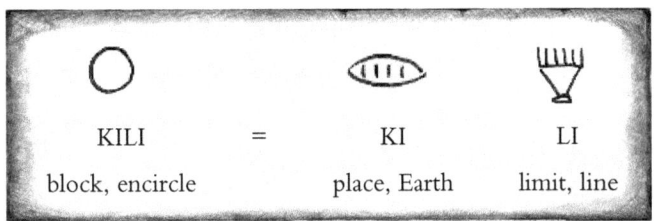

KI is given 282 times with main meanings of 'place', 'ground', 'earth'. It's also used as suffix after a place name, for example, Sukurru-KI, Sukurru which is a city. KI is discussed in the context of Enki on page 35.

> *Key: mid-14c., 'fasten with a wedge or key' (implied in keyed), from key. From 1630s as 'regulate the pitch of a musical instrument by means of a key,' also in the figurative sense 'give a tone or intensity to.'*

KI with LI give 'the limit of Earth', 'ley line markers', 'a delimited place', definition of a boundary stone. Taken as the key, I would suggest it indicates that this is where important points of Earth's energy paths can be found and used. Taking the original compound meaning of KIL into account, it becomes possible to enlarge on the overall meaning:

- A source of water (KIL in ID_2) and encircling blocks (KILI) where cosmic energy (ley lines KI-LI) meets Earth (KI), where a fine horn (SIKIL) is raised in a chamber (KI-EL/KI-IL), where the key to spiritual rising is found (KI-IL), where the souls of the dead (kill?) are purified and rise (SIKIL).

LI

LI is not mentioned as relating to stone in any way. Neither is it given as 'line', 'limit', or 'ley', but it is given as 'branch' or 'twig' 47 times at 2500 BC. I'm tempted to suggest that this would be the branch or twig of the water diviner but have no other evidence for that.

LI can be compared to another symbol, ŠA, discussed in chapter 15.

> *Litho-: before vowels, lith-, word-forming element meaning 'stone, rock;' from Greek lithos 'stone, a precious stone, marble; a piece on a game board,' a word of unknown origin.*
>
> *lee (n.) Middle English le, leoh, from Old English hleo 'shelter, cover, defence, protection,' from Proto-Germanic *khlewaz (source also of Old Norse hle, Danish læ, Old Saxon hleo, Dutch lij 'lee, shelter'). The original sense is uncertain.*
>
> *Latin linea 'linen thread, string, plumb-line,' also 'a mark, bound, limit, goal; line of descent,' from linum 'linen'.*
>
> *Limit c. 1400, 'boundary, frontier,' from Old French limite 'a boundary,' from Latin limitem (nominative limes) 'a boundary, limit, border, embankment between fields,' perhaps related to limen 'threshold.'*

9
Cursing Stones of Gods and Bull

GUD is the symbol of the bull, taking the form of a simplified image of the animal's head and horns. But the bull can also be found in one of the combinations of KLI shown below:

BUL

rock, shift

'To rock' or 'to shift' is given 6 times at the 2000 BC period for KILI, the block, with EŠ, three, at its centre. There is no trace of an earlier example of it. Presumably, this is the symbol that gave their name to the Mesopotamian bulla, hollow balls of clay containing small counters. This is also the origin of both 'bull' and 'boulder'.

> Bull: 'male of a bovine animal,' c. 1200, bule, from Old Norse boli 'bull, male of the domestic bovine,' perhaps also from an Old English *bula, both from Proto-Germanic *bullon- (source also of Middle Dutch bulle, Dutch bul, German Bulle), perhaps from a Germanic verbal stem meaning 'to roar,' which survives in some German dialects and perhaps in the first element of boulder. The other possibility [Watkins] is that the Germanic word is from PIE root.

> *Boulder: 1610s, 'water-worn rounded stone of medium or large size,' variant of Middle English bulder ston 'stone worn round, cobblestone' (c. 1300), from a Scandinavian source akin to Swedish dialectal bullersten 'noisy stone' (large stone in a stream, causing water to roar around it), from bullra 'to roar' + sten 'stone.' Or the first element might be from *buller- 'round object,' from Proto-Germanic *bul-, from PIE root.*

BUL represents the roaring bull as metaphor for the combination of rushing waters and the boulders that once traced and carved out mountain gorges. In that process, great rocks were worn down into 'boules', French for 'ball', of stone. The founding symbol KILI is also given as 'ball' under its phonetic value ELLAG/ILLAG.

> *Bull 'papal edict, highest authoritative document issued by or in the name of a pope,' c. 1300, from Medieval Latin bulla 'sealed document' (source of Old French bulle, Italian bulla), originally the word for the seal itself, from Latin bulla 'round swelling, knob,' said ultimately to be from Gaulish, from PIE root.*
>
> *Bull (modern term: Bullshit): There seems to have been an identical Middle English word meaning 'false talk, fraud,' apparently from Old French bole 'deception, trick, scheming, intrigue,' and perhaps related to modern Icelandic bull 'nonsense.'*
>
> *Sais christ to ypocrites ... yee ar ... al ful wit wickednes, tresun, and bull.*[41]

We discover that the modern use of 'bullshit' as a violent way of denouncing nonsense is of ancient origin. Who would have guessed? It may well be that the papal bull is inherited from BUL in its most placid meaning of boulder, the rounded stone, leading to Latin bulla as stated above, and that it is nothing more than a reference to the form of the round wax seal of those all-important papal documents. Who knows?

As mentioned earlier, a particularly large number of Irish place names begin with or include KIL/KEL/KILI. For example, there is an Irish village called Kell on an island called Achill. A keel is a manmade stone formation having a wedge-shape or ridge and found at ancient pagan sites. Kil means 'wedge' in Scandinavian languages too. The following reference to an Irish keel provides the missing link between Sumerian KIL and BUL, between the block and the bull, by adding another word of importance to this study; the bullaun.

> *Bullaun: Irish: bullán; from a word cognate with 'bowl' and French bol.*
>
> *Keel and bullaun: ...at Ballyvourney, Co. Cork, at a keel or low cairn, composed of stones and earth, evidently an ancient pagan cemetery. On the summit of the mound lay a bullaun, with a circular cavity or basin, overshadowed with low-growing bushes on which hung rags of various colours, votive offerings of pilgrims who were accustomed to encircle the mound upon their knees in the course of the sun. Persons afflicted with bodily ailments resorted hither esteeming earth from the mound and rainwater from the bullaun, to be specifics for their complaints...* [42]/[43]

FIG. 10.
St. Bridget's Stone, Killinagh, near Blacklion. Reproduced from the *Journal* of the present Society of Antiquaries of Ireland.

The bullaun is a natural concave formation in rock where rainwater gathers. Rounded pebbles or larger stones have been found sitting alongside or on top of some. There are different stories about the uses of these top stones. In the above quote, healing appears to be the only motive for visiting bullauns, and that story makes no mention of the movable pebbles. It was the pilgrims themselves who turned. The pebbles were known as cursing stones or stones of God. From the following two quotes, it seems that they had a different use according to the direction in which they were turned:

> *In the island of Iniskea, adjoining that of Achill, there used to be, and probably there still is, a cursing stone at the mouth of a holy well. Anybody who wanted the immediate gratification of vengeance must "go to the stone, turn it round three times and pray that his enemies might not prosper or get length of life'. (...) In fact, it is a stone that will put an end to bad people in a short time."*[44]

Some cursing stones have particularly well-executed and ornate crosses and circles on them. That decoration is necessarily significant in some way. It's reminiscent of the circle and cross that combine to form LU, the light. These are not all artefacts that bring 'primitive' immediately to mind[45]:

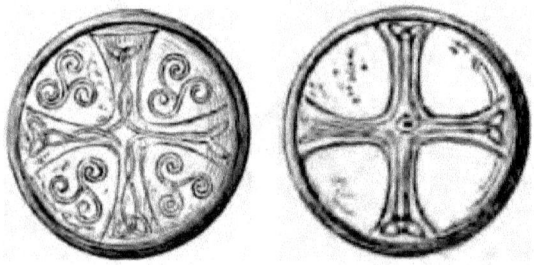

A hollowed-out stone with another round stone that fits over or into it seems like a good description of a grinding stone.[46] And grinding is a more practical use than wishing or cursing, but one does not negate the other. Such top stones have been found in numerous countries. If they can be conflated with grinding stones and linked with the hollowed-out cuplike forms of bullauns, then it can be said that they are found all over the world and at the earliest times. There are examples of hollowed-out cup-shaped stones at Gobekli Tepe. Round grinding stones and round cursing stones fit neatly with the meanings of millstone and cursing given for HAR/HUR. See the chapter on Harran.

There is also a link to be made with Greek Hermes. Stone-throwing customs in Eastern Europe were group rituals serving to root out and to curse the culprits of crimes. You wouldn't want to be cursing the innocent for fear the curse be turned back against you. Another stone-throwing ritual of uncertain origin is carried out at Mina in Saudi Arabia. It's a complicated ritual known as the stoning of the devil. This takes place in close proximity to the Kaaba where people gather to circulate in anticlockwise direction around a mysterious black stone encased in a wall. It may or may not be coincidence that Sumerian MI and NA have the meanings of 'black' and 'stone'. They are found together in numerous lexical entries.

> *There was a four-cornered statue of Hermes [a Herma] by the side of the road, with a heap of stones piled at its base..*[47]

Hermes is intimately connected with - and even integrated into - a pile of stones. Another interesting fact told in the Greek account of Hermes is that he was born on Mount Kyllene, another KIL. The keel, the cairn, the bullaun, the rotating cursing/wishing stones and now Hermes himself. These are some hitherto unconnected threads that begin to weave together. But that is not the end of the story.

The Keel

KL is the sound that never stops giving. The symbol itself is of the utmost simplicity, either a circle or a square, and found at the earliest known period. It appears to do little justice to the complexity of its uses but the same might be said of any square or circle until it fits into the context of geometry. The following is its final offering here, and the result of the obvious link between keel, cairn and bullaun shown above:

> *Keel: lowest timber of a ship or boat from bow to stern, from Middle Dutch kiel, (cognate with Old English ceol "ship's prow," Old High German kiel, German Kiel "ship"), of unknown origin.*

I refer the reader to the lexical entries mentioned on page 89 where KI, the place, is combined with IL, to rise, giving the possible translation of 'from the place to rise' or 'from Earth to rise'. My contention is that places with names that include the KIL/KLI form are associated not only with a life-giving flow but also with the ships that sail on both earthly and cosmic waters. The ancient stone circles represented, if not the ships' keel, then the blocks on which the keel rested until those waters carried it upwards. It should be remembered that KIL, the block, is the main symbol of ID_2, the watercourse.

The celestial ship, called the 'basket' in *The Story of Sukurru*, was that of Noah but it appears to also have served in the passing of souls from Earth to sky and back again, with the suggestion of duality and choices seen in line 158 (presented on page 80), based on the complex philosophy known to us as Tao. The keel is naturally associated with the story of a very real and great flood.

Was Noah's Ark round like a circle of stones, round like the circling planets, like the weave from the loom of the celestial Matriarch, like the cursing mouths of the cosmic millstones? According to Dr Irving Finkel in his book, *The Ark Before Noah*[48], that is what the fragment of a clay tablet dated to the Old Babylonian period of ca. 1900-1700 BC is telling us in the Akkadian cuneiform style of writing. He makes the link with boats known as 'coracles', as did I in the process of translating *The Story of Sukurru*. My translation of that word, used for the round reed-plaited boats that once plied the twin rivers of Mesopotamia, came from the context in which KUR and RA were found together, particularly in line 178 shown below.

> *Coracle: "round boat of wicker, coated with skins," used by fishermen on the coast of Wales and parts of Ireland, 1540s (the thing is described, but not named, in the Anglo-Saxon Chronicle from 9c.), from Welsh corwgl, from corwg, cognate with Gaelic curachan, Middle Irish curach "boat," which probably is the source of Middle English currock "coracle" (mid-15c.). From an unknown source.*

Of course, citing the Mesopotamian coracle in a section devoted to the ship's keel might seem a little strange, given that a coracle's main feature is its roundness and lack of timber frame or integrated steering device. But nevertheless, all forms have their place in Noah's story. It is in keeping with other 'nonsense' aspects – such as the dodo's flight – used for humour. It's also possible that the very earliest meaning of the keel was more general and covered all types of ships' undersides on the condition that they rise with the water. Perhaps the most important was that the vessel did not keel over.

Line 178 is part of the cursing scene carried out by the Sumerian equivalent of biblical Ezekiel who, sitting on a rooftop, finds himself confronted by the figure in a 'hanging basket' and consequently becomes very annoyed about the situation. One epithet of this Ezekiel is KA-ZU, knower of words, the word specialist! KA can be understood as the word of a cosmic figure, while ZU takes the form of a pyramid.

Measure the height of the man in the fiery coracle, that his straw go up in smoke!

The theory of an important link between stone cairns and ships' keels is supported by the ancient burial customs that have come to light in various parts of the world; stones aligned to take the shape of ships found in Scandinavia, Germany and other places, some of them encircling burial sites, and also the Egyptian practice of burying funerary boats, notably the magnificent example found and restored at the site of the Great Pyramid of Giza. See page 213.

KUR-RA is mentioned again on page 156 in the context of a mythological wisdom school. The churning mountains, the round coracle as woven container, a type of basket, and cosmic ship, the three mounds; should any notion of a preserved written link between them be dismissed out of hand?

Then again, it would take a daring person to reach even further back in time and suggest that the round stone circles at Gobekli Tepe, filled with all sorts of animals and birds, some of them compartmentalized according to species, a prehistoric zoo dominated by two huge and apparently human figures, a place where beer and bull were quite obviously at the heart of the matter…it would take a daring person to suggest all that has anything to do with an original version of Noah's Ark, a version that would be at least 11,000 years old. Or to suggest that *The Story of Sukurru* was written to perpetuate that memory. Nevertheless, a round zoo was to be found floating in the sky with a great specialist on board on line 167. I admit to going slightly overboard with his qualifications, using A, ZU and SAG twice over for the following, but it might well have been what the scribe intended to convey:

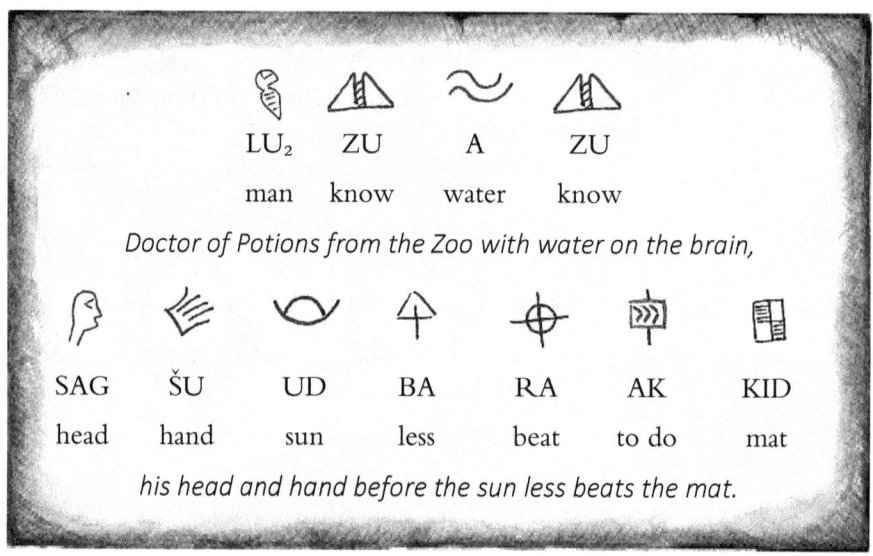

The placing of the first four symbols implies that the man had intimate knowledge of water because that's all there was to know from his boat at the time of the great flood. On another deeper level, note that there are two pyramids representing knowledge shown here with some kind of flow between them. I chose the path of humour because it fits with the overall tone of the work, but the following symbol SAG is origin of sagacity which, with ZU placed before it, indicates knowledge belonging to a sage. Or perhaps that someone had lost their head…?

The zoo- of zoology stems from Greek zoion with the meaning 'living being', 'animal' and is from the usual PIE root. See page 168.

10

Signs of the Magician

A few years back while trawling the CDLI website for photos of the most ancient pictograms, I came across an image from the pre-writing era, i.e. before 3500 BC. The provenience of the tablet was given as Susa, modern-day Shush in Iran. Having the recently discovered stone circles of Gobekli Tepe fresh in my mind, the association was quasi-immediate. There are two T-shaped forms side by side, linked by a circle, that have been stamped onto several different areas of the tablet. The most notable circles at Gobekli Tepe have two very tall T-shaped standing stones at their centres.[49]

Looking closer, I also noticed that the image below the T-shaped forms has the quite distinct appearance of a rodent venturing out of its hole. That is not unlike one of the carvings on a central pillar where an animal of some kind seems to appear from under a (possibly) human arm:

 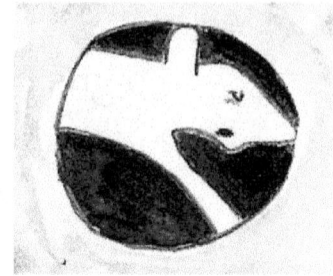

Suggesting an association between an unidentified image on a clay tablet dated to around 3500 BC from an area in Southern Mesopotamia and structures at a newly uncovered prehistoric site further north, a site that has lain underground since around 9600 BC, is not for the faint-hearted. But once it is understood that Sumerian T is synonymous of 'magic' and the 'magician', many things become worthy of consideration. Meet ME:

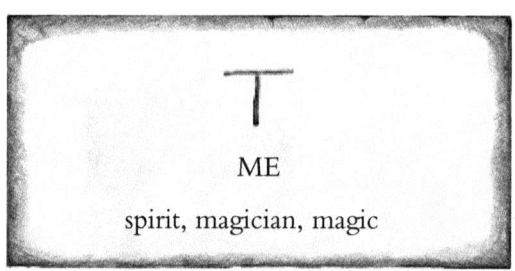

ME

spirit, magician, magic

The meanings given here are not the result of an overworked imagination. They are all ME as offered by Sumerian dictionaries and notably the ePSD. ME is given as 'being' and 'divine properties enabling cosmic activity' once at the 3000-2500 BC period and 4 times at 2500 BC. It isn't a great stretch to amalgamate those vague meanings into 'spirit'. It's given as the verb 'to be' 1,448 times at the earliest period. Then, hidden behind the phonetic value IŠIB, ME is also given as 'sorcerer, magician' and 'spell' 7 times, which, in my opinion, takes the spirit to a whole new level. ME/IŠIB is discussed in chapter 18.

The pictogram of ME is a simple one that looks for all the world like a capital T. See it here on a clay tablet from the Uruk IV period[50], next to symbol EN meaning 'master, noble' and 'end'. Read here from right to left, ME-EN is found again on page 250:

104

But is ME me?

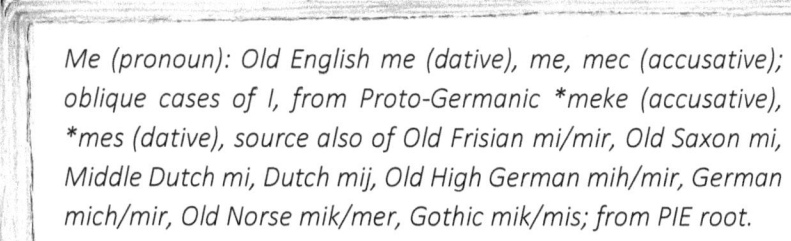

Me (pronoun): Old English me (dative), me, mec (accusative); oblique cases of I, from Proto-Germanic *meke (accusative), *mes (dative), source also of Old Frisian mi/mir, Old Saxon mi, Middle Dutch mi, Dutch mij, Old High German mih/mir, German mich/mir, Old Norse mik/mer, Gothic mik/mis; from PIE root.

There is one way to find out if the T-shaped symbol is at the origin of a very personal pronoun, the one we use to talk about self; That is to look closely at its positioning in the context of a Sumerian literary text. On lines 55, 57 and again on line 59 of *The Story of Sukurru*, in the section following mention of fire and cannabis, ME is shown between two symbols of the eye:

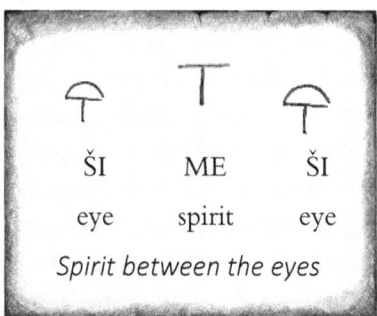

Although my rendering of this quite extraordinary and threefold-reiterated combination of symbols is probably far removed from the way they would once have been drawn, the result is nevertheless relatively plain. These are

105

not only words in a text. They form a picture, the image of a nose and brows shown between (and probably above) two upturned ocular globes.

> *Medium: 1580s, "a middle ground, quality, or degree; that which holds a middle place or position," from Latin medium "the middle, midst, center; interval," noun use of neuter of adjective medius "in the middle, between; from the middle" from PIE root.*

Given the context of the section of text where ŠI-ME-ŠI appears, with shamanistic activity, the smoke of a mind-altering substance and the source word for 'cannabis' spelled out in line 56, there can be no doubt of the character of ME. It's the indication of the pineal gland, more commonly known as the third eye, source of magic and place of the spirit.

The above combination in *The Story of Sukurru* has implications beyond that of shedding light on the alchemical nature of these pre-cuneiform symbols. It demonstrates that this literary text is far older than the clay tablet on which it was found. Put simply, in 2600 BC, the Mesopotamian writing system was already in the process of becoming abstract. It would not have been possible to fully appreciate the original subtleties of the language once these symbols had been transformed into cuneiform. The phrase must necessarily date back to a time when the original pictograms were the preferred writing system, at least back beyond 3000 BC. ŠI-ME-ŠI is evidence that the 2600 BC edition of *The Story of Sukurru* is a copy of something far older. It can be likened to a modern-day edition of any ancient writings. Although it is unthinkable that our medium of paper survive a period of five thousand years in the way that fired clay tablets might, the philologist born in the year 8000 who finds nothing but the 2020 copy of Shakespeare, devoid of an explanatory biography, might be forgiven for concluding that Hamlet was a story of and written in our time.

Clearly, the full-blown beauty of the original language was destroyed by its conversion into cuneiform. And it's the magical ME that brings us the proof. After the cuneiform tragedy, the further transformation into alphabetical form destroyed all hope of understanding the profound meanings of the symbols, particularly true and noteworthy in this case. But, as I am attempting to demonstrate here, all is not lost.

The many ancient carvings of faces and figures where a prominent brow and nose appear but other features are either left out or grossly unrealistic, tending towards but not meant to entirely convey normal human faces, leave us stumped as to their meaning. The distinguishing and uniting feature of most of them is the prominent T-shape, sometimes with a flat horizontal line for the brows, sometimes more curved and life-like. The effect can be strange, alien. The Easter Island Moai statues offer a good example. And a number of stone faces of that type were found placed next to the T-shaped pillars at Gobekli Tepe. The description of these discoveries and the accompanying photos of the 'masks' are commented on the archaeologists' website.

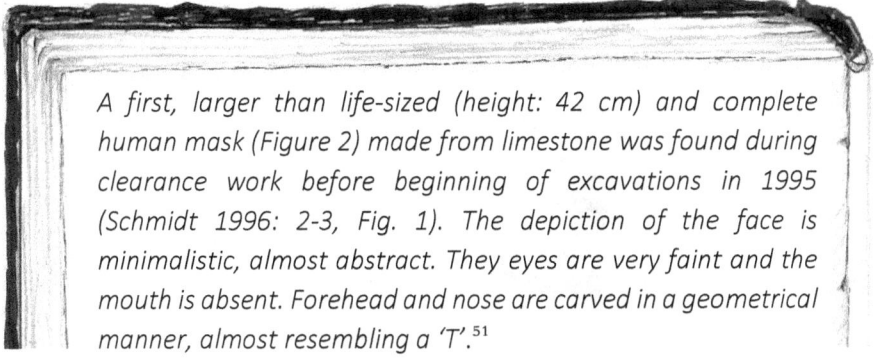

A first, larger than life-sized (height: 42 cm) and complete human mask (Figure 2) made from limestone was found during clearance work before beginning of excavations in 1995 (Schmidt 1996: 2-3, Fig. 1). The depiction of the face is minimalistic, almost abstract. They eyes are very faint and the mouth is absent. Forehead and nose are carved in a geometrical manner, almost resembling a 'T'.[51]

I had the good fortune to visit the museum at Sanliurfa where artefacts found at the sites of Gobekli Tepe and Nevali Cori are housed. Below are three of those stone faces. Two are stand-alone but the third is that of a figure with what appear to be folded wings:

Returning to the subject of the twin T-shaped pillars on a tablet from the Uruk V period (page 103), my suggestion of a possible link to the far more ancient Gobekli Tepe was made public by British author, Graham Hancock, who found it to be of interest. This heresy provoked an archaeologist working at Gobekli Tepe to demonstrate that the T-shaped object was nothing more than an element of a weaving machine. To show that I (or more importantly Graham Hancock) was wrong, he put forward the evidence of another clay tablet from the same series found at Susa in modern-day Iran, this time a weaving scene where very similar but not identical forms appear. The archaeologist's theory is that the T shapes cannot be depictions of Gobekli pillars because they are part of a weaving scene. See the T-shaped pillars laid out flat or from an awkward aerial perspective, on the right side[52]:

In between times, I found another version of the T-shaped pictogram stamped onto a bulla, this one not from the same series, and dated to pre-Uruk V, anywhere between 8500 BC and 3500 BC. Bullas, mentioned on page 95, are hollow balls of clay containing small counters and given as pre-writing. They are thought to have been used for trading. From the general dating of these artefacts, it can be assumed that academia does not rule out the possibility of such a scene at an extremely ancient epoch.

The bulla shows the same two pillars with a human figure holding up an arm towards one of them. But, in this image, there is the addition of an animal in profile with its paws firmly planted just above the Ts and close enough to identify it as part of the same stamp. Taking into account the peeping rodent on the first tablet, it appears that animals have as much right to be associated with this stamp as weavers. See the detail below[53]:

My full response to the accusation of cherry-picking can be found in the section of Graham Hancock's website which he generously makes available for articles written by others on a broad range of subjects[54]. To cut a long story short, the archaeologist's suggestion had the effect of stimulating my curiosity as to a possible link between the T-shaped stone pillars and the thread of the weaver. This is perhaps straying a little far from the subject of Sumerian symbol ME but it all ties in together eventually.

I then found several intriguing Hittite scenes which go some way to confirming the existence of wool or flax being wound around large T-shaped stones. Hittites occupied a broad area of northern Mesopotamia, which includes the region of Harran and Gobekli Tepe, during the second millennium BC. Vases found at Hüseyindede Tepe[55], situated in a mountainous region of Turkey south of the Black Sea, show several examples of bound T-shaped pillars in ceremonial scenes. Another has a depiction of bull-leaping but no pillars. The dating somewhere in the second millennium BC doesn't help to fill the blanks between Gobekli Tepe and 3500 BC but it goes a long way to proving that T-shaped images were widely known in the region, that they are associated with winding materials but not necessarily directly connected with weaving scenes. If the drinking scene also found on a Hittite artefact had been the only example, such festooned pillars would perhaps have been forever associated with beer - and only with beer.

There are others; this detail below from a long bas-relief carving on an outer wall of the Hittite city of Alaca Höyük, situated to the east of Sanliurfa and Gobekli Tepe. This time no weavers or drinkers, but a figure holding a hand up to the bound T-shaped stone. And there is another character, as ubiquitous as any Mesopotamian god but not yet mentioned in this section; the sacred bull perched on its pedestal, witness to a ceremony, perhaps even the main attraction of it[56]:

The undeniably T-shaped pillar is bound in some kind of material and this time almost the same height as the figure. Notice the similarity of the hand gesture with that of the figures in clay. Again, this image is not proof of a connection through dating. The carved wall was created at a much later date than the pillars of the Gobekli Tepe site. But it's reasonable to assume the images were based on scenes in places known at the time of the clay bulla, pre-3500 BC. Perhaps there existed materials other than clay for recording such things, unknown to us because long gone. In other words, it is not necessary to have seen the pillars of Gobekli Tepe to know about T-shaped pillars. Gobekli Tepe was not the only place to have them. As mentioned on page 55, they are recorded elsewhere. The stones of Karan Tepe haven't yet been excavated. They are perhaps also to be dated to the 9th millennium, but their very abundance evident at ground level should suggest that the knowledge of them was likely to be perpetuated.

The tablet and bulla images of the double T-shaped stones are given as pre-writing and have no phonetic value attached to them. However, the T-shape is that of Sumerian ME, a symbol meaning 'spirit', 'magician', 'sorcerer' and 'spell'. When we look at ME - and for the pleasure of stating the obvious - the letter T of the modern alphabet comes to mind. That is not fortuitous. We are looking at the origin of all things T. To complete the picture, another symbol must be considered. ME, the spirit, and TE, the tether, are inseparable.

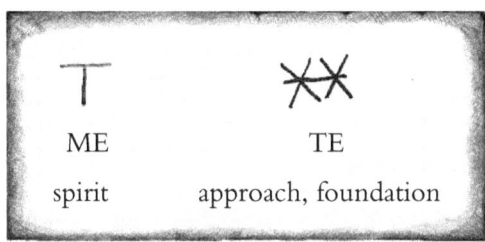

ME	TE
spirit	approach, foundation

Symbol TE is formed of two crosses with a single central line between them, the most obvious explanation being that TE refers to a distance between and a joining of two points. Here below a neat version appears on a tablet from the Uruk IV period[57]:

TE is given as 'to be near to' and 'to approach' just once at the earliest period on ePSD. It's the founding syllable for words that involve bringing together. TE has some extremely interesting and useful phonetic alternatives, discussed in detail in chapter 19.

> *Tether: late 14c., 'rope for fastening an animal,' not found in Old English, probably from a Scandinavian source akin to Old Norse tjoðr 'tether,' from Proto-Germanic *teudran (source also of Danish tøir, Old Swedish tiuther, Swedish tjuder, Old Frisian tiader, Middle Dutch tuder, Dutch tuier 'line, rope,' Old High German zeotar 'pole of a cart'), from PIE root.*

> *Tend*: 'to incline, to move in a certain direction,' early 14c., from Old French *tendre* 'stretch out, hold forth, hand over, offer' (11c.), from Latin *tendere* 'to stretch, extend, make tense; aim, direct; direct oneself, hold a course,' from PIE root. **ten-* 'to stretch.'

ME with TE, which might translate to 'the tethered spirit', are very much concerned with measuring. This is the lost origin of a word of the utmost importance to all those seekers of knowledge in matters of ancient measurements:

> *Me-* : Proto-Indo-European root meaning 'to measure.'
>
> *Metre*: 'poetic measure,' Old English *meter* 'meter, versification,' from Latin *metrum*, from Greek *metron* 'meter, a verse; that by which anything is measured; measure, length, size, limit, proportion,' from PIE root.
>
> *Mete*: 'boundary,' now only in phrase *metes and bounds*, late 15c., from Old French *mete* 'limit, bounds, frontier,' from Latin *meta* 'goal, boundary, post, pillar.'
>
> *Mete*: 'to allot,' Old English *metan* 'to measure, mete out; compare, estimate' (...), from Proto-Germanic **metan* (source also of Old Saxon *metan*, Old Frisian, Old Norse *meta*, Dutch *meten*, Old High German *mezzan*, German *messen*, Gothic *mitan* 'to measure'), from PIE root.

The combination of ME-TE is given as 'one's own' once on ePSD and is understood as 'self' in later Akkadian. It's also given as 'appropriate thing' and even as 'image' although without dating. I offer the added meaning of 'nose', an entirely earthly attribute in our modern understanding but no doubt of greater significance in antiquity. TE indicates the cord that stretches between two points marked by a cross, and it is probable that the length of it was measured by winding it around the T.

From ME-TE to Tau

Letter T of the Greek alphabet, tau, is said to derive from the Phoenician letter taw which took the form of a cross. If we look at them as their symbolic forms, that is not immediately obvious. The fact is that a T is not an X. But, of course, now we're considering an alphabet, a completely different ball game where sounds first took precedence over form. It has been suggested that the Phoenician X derives from an Egyptian hieroglyph that has the meaning of 'mark'. None of the mainstream suggestions bring the old Sumerian language into the equation. Why would they? In truth, Greek tau derives directly from Sumerian ME with or without TE, possibly by way of a more obscure writing system known as Old Canaanite.

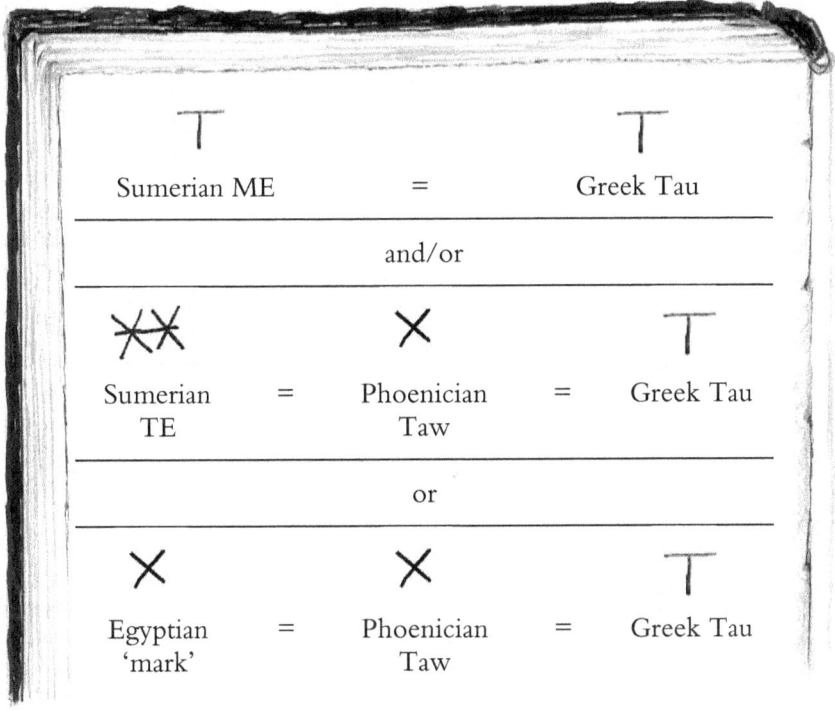

Why is the truth about the source of Greek tau important? A letter in a modern alphabet is rarely anything more than a sound without inherent meaning in isolation, unless for a grammatical purpose. However, there is information to be gleaned from Greek tau; that it represents the number 300, for example, according to the alphanumeric code known as gematria, and easily found within the list of Greek numerals. If my theory of Sumerian ME, combined with TE, as the source of Greek tau is acceptable, then it can be considered that ME and/or ME-TE also had a value of 300. Considering that ME-TE is the very origin of 'metre' and that it might well have been related to that number at its Sumerian origin, such a corresponding numerical value might open some rusty doors onto ancient mathematical knowledge.

Saint Anthony of Egypt
Saint Anthony of Egypt was a hermetic monk who lived during the 4th century AD. He was the inspiration behind the Order of Saint Anthony, also called the Hospital Brothers of Saint Anthony, which was founded in 1095 in southern France. The purpose of the French Order was to care for victims of the deadly disease of ergotism, known as St. Anthony's Fire and the symbol that represented them was the Tau, also known as St. Anthony's Cross. An example of it is still visible on the lintel of a building in the village of Biot where a chapel dedicated to Saint Anthony first stood[58], later replaced by a hospital run by the monks. It sits to the left of two symbols, one looking for all the world like Sumerian ŠI, the eye, (which would give ME-ŠI), and the other appearing to be a Templar cross. Biot is a picturesque village in the Alpes-Maritimes region of France, gifted to the Knights Templar in 1209 by the Count of Provence. It's not proven that the Tau symbol was that of St. Anthony, or whether the Order knew it to be his. But, since they took his name, that seems likely. A cross reference between the well-known stories of his trials in the wilderness and the symbol of Tau implies that it represents resistance to demons. Its presence on a lintel signifies that it was a protective sign. That it appears there in the company of a Templar cross lends credence to the suggestion that the 'Hospitaliers' were intimately connected to the Knights Templar at some point in time. Were the Knights Templar aware of the Sumerian origin of the Tau? See pages 220, 236 and 238 for other mentions of Saint Anthony of Egypt.

ME-DA versus MA-DA

Lines 119 to 122 of *The Story of Sukurru* shown here below (page 116) present a particularly useful and amusing illustration of the use of ME within the text. The context for this scene was easily found thanks to the first four symbols indicating that this was our hero, the basket expert, through MAL, the basket, and ZU, to know but also because KUŠ-LU-EŠ$_2$, the native fleece, had already made its appearance on lines 106 and 107.

> *Now the men of Thebes and those who after their example abstain from sheep, say that this custom was established among them for the cause which follows:--Heracles (they say) had an earnest desire to see Zeus, and Zeus did not desire to be seen of him; and at last when Heracles was urgent in entreaty Zeus contrived this device, that is to say, he flayed a ram and held in front of him the head of the ram which he had cut off, and he put on over him the fleece and then showed himself to him.*[59]

The twice-repeated combinations of ŠI-ME-DA and ŠI-MA-DA are being opposed here. There is the 'spiritual side' and there is the 'land side'. I took the latter to mean that the baser concern of the leader, his earthbound sentiment of personal pride, was being tested by his situation.

Mada, found in Hindu scriptures, confirms that conclusion. It's the term used to mean 'pride', 'intoxication' and 'arrogance', the fifth of six passions to overcome. Herodotus writing about Egyptian rituals mentions a curiously similar myth concerning Thebes, modern-day Luxor, shown here above.

ŠI-ME, the 'eye of the magician' or 'the spirit eye', is transcribed in line 119 as 'forehead', indicating the place of the pineal gland, and then as 'the spirited leader' in line 122. Between the two occurrences, we find ŠI-MA on line 120, the 'leader of the land', but also 'the eye of Ma'. All four incidences are followed by DA, symbol of the arm which indicates the location. All four follow on from KUŠ-LU-EŠ$_2$ which translated to 'skin-sheep-native', the 'native fleece'. KUŠ is another phonetic form of SU, given as 'skin' numerous times at the early period. They both correspond to the pyramidal symbol that is a close relative of ZU, knowledge.

119 – 122

THE NATIVE MAN, BASKET EXPERT, THE NATIVE SHEEP SKIN'S FOREHEAD HOLDS LESS HIGH.

THE NATIVE SHEEP SKIN, THE LEADER'S PRIDE TO SWALLOW ON HIGH.

THE NATIVE FLEECE, THE LEADER AND THEIR SPIRIT TO GROW OLD ON HIGH.

IN THE HANGING BASKET, THE SPIRITED LEADER HIS PADDLE TURNS.

MEHIDA and MU

My conclusion that ME originates with the abstract form of human nose and brows (with the inference of signalling the pineal gland) holds true, but that isn't the only way to look at it. There are likely a few different ways to consider the T shaped symbol without detracting from its ultimate sense of measurement and magic. ME combined with symbol HI leads to an age-old riddle:

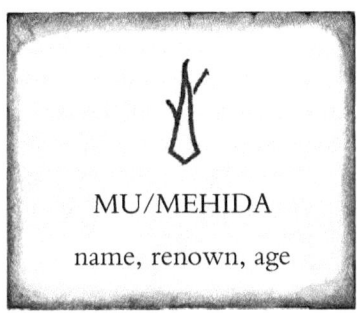

MU/MEHIDA

name, renown, age

MU is given as 'name, line of text, son' 81 times and as 'year' 298 times at the early period. It was translated in the opening lines of *The Story of Sukurru* to 'age', the bygone age of the great flood. I used it again as 'renown' because it is the symbol that combines the fame of an individual or place with the age in which they existed. Frequently collocated with UN and according to context, MU-UN was translated to 'homeland', and, in the same vein, NU-MU-UN was understood as foreign because 'not the homeland'.

Symbol MU is mentioned here because it has the phonetic value MEHIDA. Found just once opposite ME-HI-DA in the lexical entries, this leads to more intriguing places and associations:

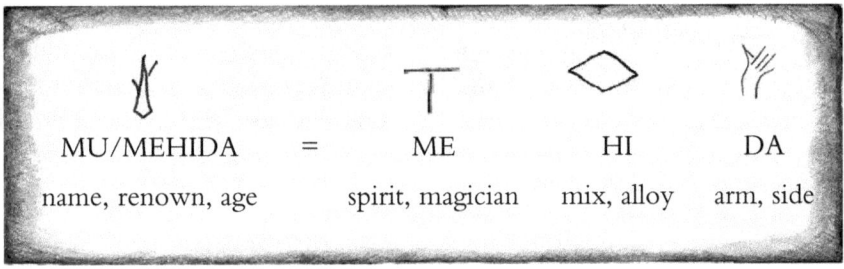

MU/MEHIDA   =   ME   HI   DA

name, renown, age   spirit, magician   mix, alloy   arm, side

ME combined with HI, passage of the spirit, forms a shape closely resembling the Egyptian ankh symbol. See them side by side here above and compare to the hieroglyph in the centre of the photograph on page 119. Together, they give the origin of Greek Hymen, god of marriage and the virginal membrane.

> Hymen: 1610s, from French hymen (16c.), from medical Latin, ultimately from Greek hymen "membrane (especially 'virginal membrane,' as the membrane par excellence); thin skin," from PIE root.

DA, symbol of the arm, can also be translated as 'by the side of', 'next to', and 'vicinity'. The possible translations of ME-HI-DA include 'by the arm of Mehi', 'next to Mehi', 'where the spirit entrance is'. But who then is Mehi? The plot thickens when we discover that, according to Hitchcock's Bible Names Dictionary published in 1869, the word Mehida translates to 'a riddle' and 'sharpness of wit'.

> The something-in-the-body, the that-which-moves the thing inanimate, this surely's not a body, for that it moves the two of them—both body of the lifter and the lifted? So that a thing that's lifeless will not move a lifeless thing. That which doth move [another thing] is animate, in that it is the mover.
>
> Thou seest, then, how heavy laden is the soul, for it alone doth lift two bodies. That things, moreover, moved are moved in something as well as moved by something is clear.
> Corpus Hermeticum[60]

Symbol MU is linked to the movement of time through its given meaning of 'year' and its extensive use in the Sumerian King List placed next to the numbers given there. Is MU, period of time, the first syllable of the sounds we employ to indicate motion, movement, or mutation? And, of course, the moon.

Motion: late 14c., 'suggestion; process of moving,' from Old French mocion 'movement, motion; change, alteration' (13c.), from Latin motionem (nominative motio) 'a moving, a motion; an emotion,' from past participle stem of movere 'to move' from PIE root.

Mutate: 'to change state or condition,' 1818, back-formation from <u>mutation</u>. In genetic sense, 1913, from Latin mutatus, past participle of mutare 'to change' from PIE root.

Moon: Old English mona, from Proto-Germanic *menon- (source also of Old Saxon and Old High German mano, Old Frisian mona, Old Norse mani, Danish maane, Dutch maan, German Mond, Gothic mena "moon"), from PIE root.

Sumerian MU is collocated with BI, the beer, the bee, binary and bios-, numerous times on the Sumerian King List, always placed next to the numbers. My thought in that regard is that MU-BI indicates a method of counting time, a binary movement, perhaps a lunisolar calendar. There is more to MU than meets the eye; It resembles the sedge symbol found in Egyptian hieroglyphs and the two have a further connection. The Egyptian sedge hieroglyph is commonly associated with the bee. Here below is a detail from an inscription on a pillar at the Temple of Karnak in Luxor where the bee and sedge hieroglyphs surround the ankh:

It came to mind, seeing the Egyptian hieroglyphs, that they sometimes look as if they could be read from the middle out…

In the meantime, and for those who are reading all of this in an orderly fashion from left to right, bear in mind the **ME-TE** combination. It haunts the heart of more than one Greek hero and leads further into an understanding of the Sumerian origin of everything.

11

Prometheus

> *Prometheus: The name is Greek, and anciently was interpreted as literally 'forethinker, foreseer,' from promethes 'thinking before,' from pro 'before' (Both Latin and Greek pro- are from PIE) + methos from PIE root.*
>
> *Prometheus, himself a Titan, forewarned by his oracular mother Earth or Themis (for she bore either name) that the victory should be won by craft, whereas his brethren placed their sole reliance on brute force, rallied with her to the side of Zeus and secured his success.[61]*

Prometheus, a central character in Greek mythology, is said to have stolen the secret of fire from the gods and given it to mankind, along with a myriad of other teachings. His attribute as bringer of wisdom is reminiscent of Hermes Trismegistus and Egyptian Thoth. He was a thief and a trickster, perhaps to be assimilated to a fox, capable of confounding Zeus, the most powerful of gods. Conflating wisdom with trickery and theft leads to a strange place. The bull plays its part in this story, its body to be divided up for a meal, part of it for the gods and the rest for humanity. Prometheus decided to trick the gods into leaving the greater portion of the meat to mankind. The Greek story makes it crystal clear that the bull is nothing more than the food of gods; it serves no other purpose. There are no comparisons to be made between god and bull in this myth. Prometheus was caught and punished mercilessly, tied to a rock, his liver constantly eaten and regenerated and eaten again by an eagle, an endless cycle. Nothing in his actions shows wisdom. Rather it shows that this was a compassionate figure dedicated, above all other considerations, to the well-being of humanity, a benefactor, sacrificing his own integrity for that cause.

Prometheus combines ME with TE in his name, and he combines the stone, the binding and the bull in his story. The binding is a prominent feature of the tale. Prometheus Bound, the ancient Greek tragedy written by Aeschylus during the 6th century BC. has ensured the hero's immortality:

> *Prometheus himself sacrifices two bulls. When he had first placed their entrails on the altar, he put the remaining flesh of the two bulls in one heap, covering it with an oxhide. Whatever bones there were he covered with the other skin and put it down between them, offering Jove [Zeus] the choice of either part for himself.* [62]

The two middle syllables of the name, ME-TE, are also found at the heart of his equally unfortunate brother, Epimetheus. While intrigued by their names, I have two concerns with their stories. The first is the existence of a bunch of selfish spiteful gods, and the second is the obvious misogyny involved in the portrayal of Pandora, wily man-eater who seduces Epimetheus, putting her nose into matters that don't concern her, causing untold damage by opening that box. I flare the same attitude as that of the hand that composed the Adam and Eve account. This is the character assassination played out on biblical Eve and again on Mary Magdalen. The Instructions of Shuruppak, original translation of *The Story of Sukurru*, is included in my 'suspicious' list. References to women are contemptuous and disapproving, divisive - gods versus man, man versus woman, woman as the temptress and cause of evil. The narrative is unwise, ill-intentioned. These are surely re-writes or mistranslations. There must be deeper, older levels to explore. There is wisdom in there somewhere. There is hope.

A major key to everything, the measure of it all, is ME-TE and an opportunity to turn that key comes when we find proto-Prometheus in his original role, in context in *The Story of Sukurru*. References to Prometheus are identifiable in the section from lines 68 to 70. It begins on line 67 with the banishment of NAR, the fox, to Tartarus, (or, as originally transcribed here, *sent to cut the tar*). TAR, given as 'cut', was shown twice, which points to it being the origin of the Greek place name. This corresponds to the Titans banished by Zeus to Tartarus at the same point within the Greek myth. The wily fox who is known for cheating when using scales is mirrored in the conflict caused by Prometheus with Zeus over the apportioning of the bull:

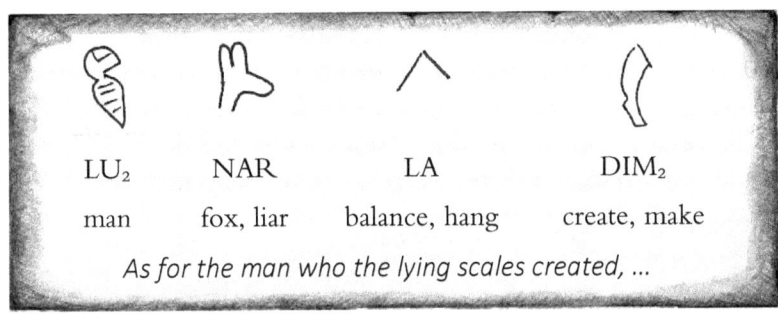

It's not possible to entirely match the characters and the events in *The Story of Sukurru* with the myths of their much later counterparts. They appear to overlap quite wildly. See page 278 and line 36 for another reference to the fox. But the evidence for a proto-Prometheus goes beyond just one or two coincidences. Already shown to be a swindler who was not going to get away with his little games much longer, line 68 goes a considerable step further by integrating the symbols that were to become the essence of his Greek name:

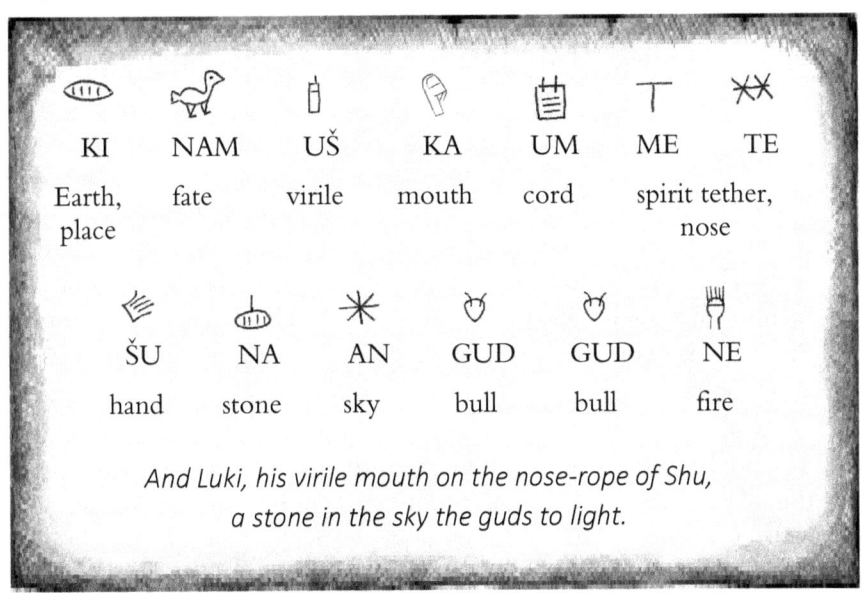

It's intriguing to note that this section, which is definitely part and parcel of the warnings given about an impending flood, appears to conflate Prometheus with Loki. The translation of these thirteen symbols was aided by the fact that Luki, aka Loki of Nordic mythology, had already appeared in the text. He was true to form, a disrupter of tranquil lifestyles, and he had to be dealt with. The less-than-delightful qualities of man as noisy and argumentative, leading to their downfall, is mentioned more than once in ancient texts. This is surely the earliest of them all. But, unlike the story of Loki and despite being situated in the sky, the deciders are not gods as we might imagine them.

- The full title of Loki is 'Man of Earth' where LU_2 precedes KI. Without trace of LU_2 here, it is translatable as 'On Earth' or 'In the place'. However, line 61 not only gives his name in full but LU_2-KI is followed there by the same two symbols NAM and UŠ as in line 68 above. I decided that it was inferred in line 68 and repeated it in order to keep the text, already murky in other places, as understandable as possible. That said, proto-Loki can be read as a more general reference to the failings and the fate of mankind on Earth.

- ME with TE, source of 'metre' with the addition of UM, the rope, in first place become the 'measuring cord'. ME-TE also translates to 'nose', giving the nose-rope. Is this the origin of Prometheus' name, a nose-rope and a measuring cord magically used to establish the dimensions of everything in the cosmos?

- ŠU-MU, the renowned hand (or wing) of the vulture, had already made her appearance on line 49. ŠU is the bird's 'hand' or rather its claw that hold the end of the spirit's nose-rope, leading the strange stone up to the skies. The hand is also a reference to measurement. The Narmer image is mentioned again in this context on page 128. This is the bird that tortures Prometheus in the later myth. It would more likely be a vulture that tears at his flesh.

- The double symbol of GUD offers a further link between this portion of the text and the scene portrayed on the Egyptian Narmer palette. 'God' really was once a bull, or rather a pair of bulls. The unusual choice of translation was my way of pointing that out. Otherwise, it might have read 'Mr and Mrs Bull to light', but certainly not 'the gods to light'. Remembering that GUD can be broken down into GU-UD, 'cord of the sun' or 'brilliant cord', there is an underlying reference to celestial measurements. This double GUD also sits well with the story of Greek Prometheus and the division of a bull into two portions. But it mustn't be forgotten that the Sumerian version is the earliest of them.

- NE is used here as 'light' but it can be understood as 'fire' and thus as a relevant verb in final position: 'to burn'.

- Symbols UŠ and KA, the virile voice, give the source of our word 'chaos', further indicating that Loki and Prometheus, both found lurking in line 68, have a common Sumerian origin.

The three symbols, UM-ME-TE, central to the name, appear together only once during the 280 lines of *The Story of Sukurru*. The addition of PIR as prefix and UŠ as suffix would result in an interesting translation. UŠ is not missing but appears earlier in the line. UD/PIR appears soon after on line 70. Perhaps there is a clay tablet somewhere with all five in that order. They would have looked something like this:

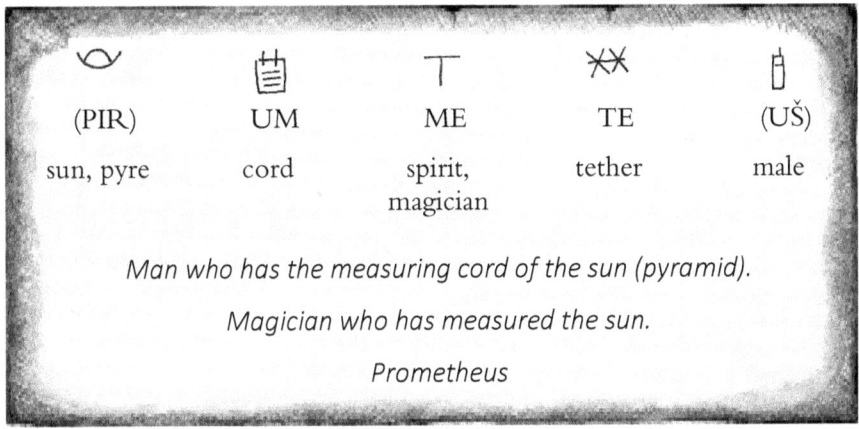

(PIR)	UM	ME	TE	(UŠ)
sun, pyre	cord	spirit, magician	tether	male

Man who has the measuring cord of the sun (pyramid).

Magician who has measured the sun.

Prometheus

The following lines 69 and 70 hide a further reference to the story of Prometheus with their four iterations of the symbol DIL also given as phonetic AŠ, pronounced 'ash'. The two lines are identical apart from the first two symbols which indicate the cosmic characters who have made the terrible decision. They are (line 69) UR-SAG, Dog-Head, presumably Sirius, and (line 70) AN-UD, the sun which, as shown above, can be given as PIR. UR can also be read as 'lion' while AN before UD might indicate the only 'godly' emphasis of the entire text and is translated to 'exalted'.

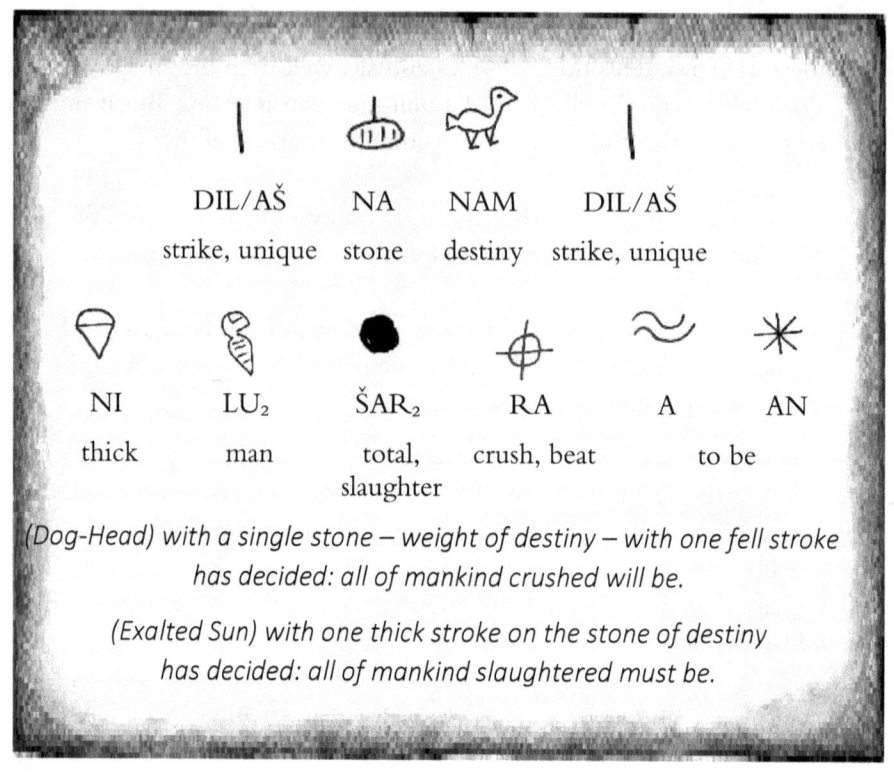

Above is the reiterated line (69-70) with four strikes in all, where Sirius and the Sun decide the fate of mankind, a fine example of the different ways the same set of symbols can be understood, always taking context into account.

DIL/AŠ surrounds the stone. It's given as 'one' 10 times at the 3000-2500 BC period and as 'sole', 'unique' twice. It's also given without dating as the 'stroke of a stylus'. It's possible to make a connection between phonetic AŠ and the ashes of fire.

> *Ash: "powdery remains of fire," Old English æsce "ash," from Proto-Germanic *askon (source also of Old Norse and Swedish aska, Old High German asca, German asche, Middle Dutch asche, Gothic azgo "ashes"), from PIE root.*

but also to establish the link between DIL and Prometheus thanks to the Greek author, Pliny the Elder:

> *The storing of fire in a fennel stalk (was invented) by Prometheus.*[64]

Fennel and dill are very similar aromatic plants with hollow stems, both members of the plant family known as umbellifers.

> *Dill: 'umbelliferous plant with yellow flowers, extensively cultivated for its aroma and oils,' Middle English dille, from Old English dile 'dill, anise,' a Germanic word of unknown origin.*
>
> *Umbel: 1590s in botany, from Latin umbella 'parasol, sunshade,'*

The above quote allows another connection to Gobekli and to UM-BE-GO through the UM-BI of umbellifer. See the etymology of 'umbego' on page 79. The cluster of flowers exploding from the hollow stalk of an umbellifer is a fitting metaphor for a burst of light spreading from the point of a tube or rod. The UM in Prometheus' name is the umbilical cord through which a life-giving substance flows. Which will it be? Fire or water?

The repetition of DIL/AŠ in these two lines is significant, perhaps a veiled reference to measurements, but, if the text is to be believed, intimately connected to a terrible fate. If Greek Prometheus' story contains even a small element of something real and is seen through the prism of this section of *The Story of Sukurru*, there would appear to be a terrible blow accompanied by fire. There is more to be gleaned from *The Story of Sukurru* than its superficial narrative; a real warning about the fate of mankind and a numerical code hidden in its symbols. There are two vertical lines here, two blows…or four?

Sirius and the Sun

> *Twas the season when the vault of heaven bends its most scorching heat upon the earth, and Sirius the Dog-star smitten by Hyperion's [the Sun's] full might pitilessly burns the panting fields.* [63]

Bearing in mind that *The Story of Sukurru* is thousands of years older than the Greek texts mentioning the deadly duo in the sky, there is further confirmation of the importance given to Sirius in another line where the origin of the star's Greek name Seirios is found. Line 186 has ŠE-IR followed by TA:

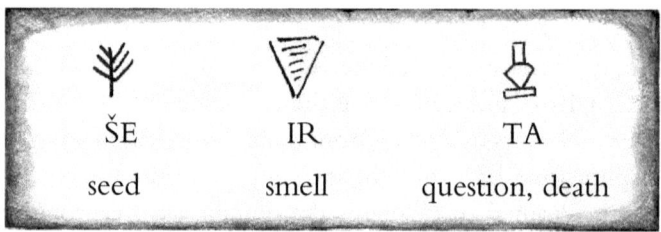

If all goes well, the seed will become a plant in flower and the smell will be that of its scent. But, if the heat of the sun is overwhelming, the smell will be that of death. TA after ŠE-IR poses the question. Which will it be?

The original Prometheus, punished for stealing the fire of the gods, can't be claimed by the Greeks. He was already shown on the Narmer Palette, an artefact discovered in Egypt and dated to around 3100 BC, a time that corresponds to the existence of the early Sumerian writing. The character appears there in a bizarre and so-far unexplained form and position, on the nose-rope of a bird just below the heads of Mr. and Mrs. Bull, the GUDs. The bird, possessing both claw and hand, holds the nose-rope with ŠU, the hand:

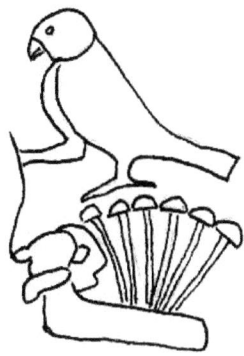

Consider the similarity between this strange figure, encased in a stone and dragged off by his nose, and the much later Greek Herma, also rectangular blocks of stone with a head projecting from one end, understood to have been used as markers of boundaries. The character on the Narmer palette, shown above, has six sticks implanted in his back with round knobs that suggest a light or flame. There exists another ancient figure encased in rock with just its head emerging above ground level. It might well have been the inspiration for both the Prometheus of the Narmer palette and the Greek Herma stones. I'm referring to the guardian of the perimeter of the pyramids, the Great Sphinx of Giza.

I am ambivalent about the nature of the magical gift that Prometheus stole for mankind and suspect that it might be something more sophisticated than the wherewithal for hunter-gatherers to light a fire. Whatever it was, some terrible catastrophe from the sky destroyed it. ME-TE, source of Greek mete and meteor (see page 180), followed by the four strokes or blows of AŠ strike me as particularly ominous.

Theseus

Theseus is another intriguing Greek character who combines the bull with the unravelling of a cord in his story:

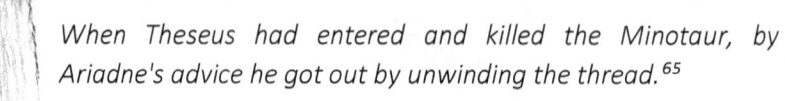

When Theseus had entered and killed the Minotaur, by Ariadne's advice he got out by unwinding the thread. [65]

The journey of Theseus to kill the dangerous Cretan bull necessitated a guiding thread to enter and to leave the Minoan labyrinth. The ambience of this story is not mirrored in the benign images of the bound T-shaped pillar on the Hittite wall where an apparently benevolent bull stands watching from its pillar. Nevertheless, we find the T in one form or another, the winding thread, the standing stones, whether as pedestal or walls of a labyrinth, and the bull at the end of them. This combination of elements is not coincidental.

Prometheus, Epimetheus, and Theseus are much older than ancient Greece whose legacy of myths is part of a wider game of hide and seek. These characters have a foot in more than one camp at a time and their adventures cross into other layers of history barely hidden below the surface. Someone is laughing in the background, a hearty roaring sound. We mustn't forget to hang on to Ariadne's thread as we try to unravel it all. The terrain is unlevel and slippery but not impossible to retrace. One end of the cord has been offered. Where will it lead us next?

12

The Ancient Clews

> *Clew - A roughly spherical mass or body. 'ball of thread or yarn,' northern English and Scottish relic of Old English cliewen 'sphere, ball, skein, ball of thread or yarn,' probably from West Germanic *kleuwin (source also of Old Saxon cleuwin, Dutch kluwen), from Proto-Germanic *kliwjo-, perhaps from a PIE root*

The Hittite bas-relief shown on page 110 combines T-shaped stone pillar, thread, and bull while the Greek myth of Ariadne and Theseus entails a stone labyrinth, thread, and bull; the three clues to a common origin grounded in KIL. The clew gives the link between KIL, the place of stone, and the thread. Ariadne gives Theseus a clew of thread which will serve to guide him in the labyrinth as he hunts for the Great Bull.

> *clue (n.) 'anything that guides or directs in an intricate case,' 1590s, a special use of a revised spelling of clew 'a ball of thread or yarn' (q.v.). The word, which is native Germanic, in Middle English was clewe, also cleue;*
>
> *Cluse (French) a narrow mountain pass or gorge, from Latin clusa, past participle of cludere, variation on claudere (see above) from PIE root.*

The ball (KIL under the phonetic value ELLAG) of thread (GU the 'cord') is used to lead Theseus (TE, symbol of the bringing together, the tethering) through the labyrinth in search of the bull (GUD).

Cluse, a French term for a mountain gully or gorge, is another link between KIL/KL and GU_2, the Sumerian symbol with the meaning of gully, and between two syllables of GU₂-BE-KLI. An écluse is the French term for a lock, a mechanism on a waterway, canal or river that allows boats to navigate safely. A valve.

Another Clue
Why the connection between a T-shaped pillar and weaving? Why a Hittite ceremony involving the same form of pillar, the thread and the bull? The images show us that there was once a tradition of tying yarn or pieces of cloth around T-shaped pillars, whether of wood or stone. There are similar rituals around the world today; rows of colourful Tibetan prayer flags tied along string to rocks and poles in the mountains, a tradition of uncertain origin, and the so-called Celtic 'rag trees' in Ireland, where small pieces of cloth are tied to the branches of specific trees, said to bring good luck. See the chapter on cursing stones for mention of this tradition in the context of keels, cairns and bullauns in Ireland.

a) Namkha
Another Tibetan ritual called Namkha caught my attention. The name is of Sumerian origin and the following is an intriguing glimpse at one explanation of a tradition linked to woven threads. The origin of the namkha is lost in time, pre-Buddhist, unknown. The object itself has been perpetuated and is relatively simple to make. It's comprised of winding threads of different colours around two sticks placed together in the form of a cross:

> *Ngak'chang Rinpoche comments: 'These threads symbolise the 'thread' that is the literal meaning of the word 'tantra' and describe the manner in which each point in time and space is the warp and weft of the loom of experiential / existential emptiness.', Sky-weaving with threads the colours of the five elements: blue, green, red, white, and yellow – space, air, fire, water, and earth respectively. The threads are woven around a matrix of wooden dowels in a form which displays the basic kyil'khor (mandala) of the elements.*[66]

I looked for a collocation of NAM, the bird of destiny, with KA, the word, in the lexical entries and found what I had hoped to find. If there is doubt about a Sumerian equivalence for the Namkha tradition, this combination is the most reasonable proof possible. Associated with HER which has the meaning 'to bind' and is discussed in detail in Chapter 18, the lexical entry shows:

NAM	KA	HER
for	word	bind

For the purpose of binding words.

Although lacking in context, it indicates that something or someone serves to bind words, perhaps that a verbal contract is established or that a law is proclaimed. There is another ancient custom entailing the winding and binding of a thread that has come down to us through the ages and is of unknown origin. This one is Celtic. It's known as hand-fasting, a form of engagement or marriage where vows are made while the hands of the couple are tied together.

Thanks to that all-important Hittite scene (page 110), we can see for ourselves that the bull or sacred cow on its pedestal presides over a ceremony. From the description of the Celtic hand-fasting tradition here above it can be deduced that this involved a verbal pact. The image of the bull is carved into at least one of the stones at Gobekli Tepe. Perhaps marriage vows were made there too. The place must surely have had more than one use for the community; from rites of passage to adulthood, then marriage and its contractual form, and finally the burial rites. Perhaps all the stages of life, all the binding contracts were established in that way, in the sight of the Great Bull.

Is it the word of the Great Bull that binds or its eye on the words of others? To bind implies the establishment of boundaries. Is this the most reasonable explanation for our current understanding of the word 'god' with its connotation of a sacred practice, a place under the eye of the Bull where words were made good? A fitting place. There is much more to say on the subject of HER and it will be said in Chapter 18.

b) Eye of the Bull, Eye of God

'God's Eye' is the name given to a similar piece of weaving done on two crossed sticks in a Mexican tradition. Beginning at the middle and working outwards, threads of different colours come together to create an attractive square. As I understand it, an 'Eye of God' is almost identical in form and meaning to the Namkha, the weaving of a thread round and round a central pair of crossed wooden sticks for the purpose of making a wish. Once completed, they are both sacred objects. There is another interesting name associated with the Eye of God; Namma. In Sumerian, this gives NAM-MA, 'for the land' or a task done for/in the name of Ma, the Matriarch, in which case it would also be in the name of truth. Ma and the feather of truth cannot be disassociated. They are synonymous. The combination corresponds well with a binding agreement. NAM and MA appear together on several lexical entries.

> *Bull's eye, also bullseye: 1833 as 'center of a target,' from bull + eye. So called for size and color. Meaning 'shot that hits the mark' is from 1857. Bulls-eye also was used from 1680s of various sorts of circular holes or objects with them.*

The Eye of God and the Namkha can be cross-referenced with the cursing stone of the bullaun which has a cross carved on it and is also 'wound' in one direction or another for the purpose of cursing or wishing.

I wonder if the direction of the cursing stone and the weaving of the thread one way or another might be significant in navigational terms; going from east to west with the sun or from west to east. How to get home? That was a problem for Homer's Odysseus and also for Greek Theseus. The most obvious cosmic equivalent to the bull's eye is Aldebaran, eye of the Taurus bull, one of the four Persian Guardians of the Heavens. Aldebaran is associated with the star cluster known as the Pleiades, the seven sisters, who it appears to follow.

Once we begin to unravel the ball, the clew of thread, it's difficult to know where to stop and how to avoid becoming entangled. Here is another tug at the net of the Great Weaver. It takes us back to Tibet and to the citation in which the namkha is discussed in the context of a mandala. The Tibetan name for mandala is Kyil Khor, another thread leading back to Sumerian KIL and forward to KUR, discussed page 155.

The Tibetan word for mandala is kyil-khor, meaning centre [kyil] and surrounding [khor], reminding us that the term encompasses the entire host of mandala deities, including the principal deity in the centre and his/her surrounding retinue.[67]

13

The Idigna Bird of the Taurus Mountains

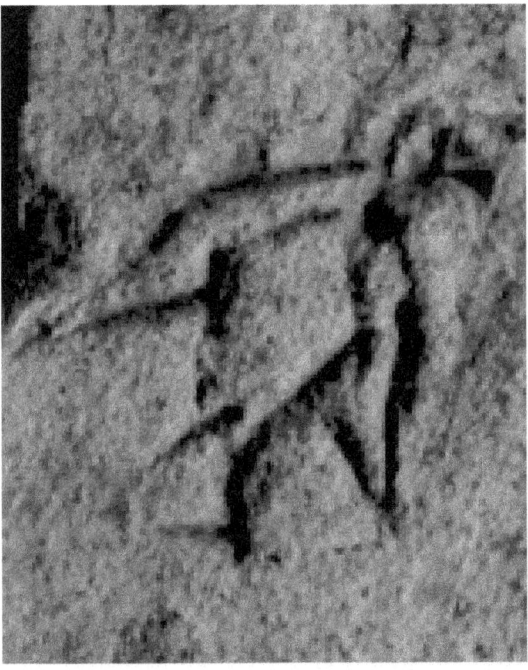

IDIGNA (a)[68]

The Idigna bird is a rare species that appears in person, so to speak, on just three of the earliest tablets shown on CDLI. I came across it by chance when looking at the symbols that were said to represent the Mesopotamian river Tigris. Typing IDIGNA into the CDLI search page at the Uruk periods, I expected to find three symbols but instead an unknown bird appeared. The pictures here above and below on clay tablets date from the earliest Uruk IV period, ca 3350 to 3200 BC:

IDIGNA (b)[69]

IDIGNA (c)[70]

IDIGNA, also known as DALLA, is given as 'bright, impetuous, fierce' twice at 3000-2500 BC and as 'ring, crown' once. It seems certain that Idigna was once the name of the river known today as the Tigris. But when was it given either of those names? The Tigris and Euphrates rivers spread out on either side of the lands today known as southern Turkey and down through the whole of Iraq, parts of ancient Mesopotamia. Taking their source in the Taurus mountains, they serve to fertilise the valley before emptying into the Persian Gulf. At a place between and below their headwaters lie Harran, Edessa (modern Sanliurfa), and the ancient site of Gobekli Tepe in modern-day Turkey. I would suggest that the reclusive Idigna bird once dwelt there too, somewhere between the headwaters of the Tigris and Euphrates rivers, perhaps at the very site of Gobekli Tepe. There are already quite a few birds carved on pillars there and, as I write this in 2019, up to fifty stone circles still to excavate, so who knows what carved treasures have yet to be found?

The three tablets containing the Idigna bird on CDLI were all inscribed at a time before abstract cuneiform symbols took over from pictographic forms. All show a full frontal of a bird with wings on each side, slightly spread, and the triangular shape of the tail feathers below. On the second tablet (b), it appears to point its beak upwards, and is accompanied by what seems to be a version of the round symbol, LU, (see page 11) above its right wing. The third (c) is already more abstract and thus probably from around the end of the Uruk IV period, later than the other two. It sits beside the image of a basket, MAL, and AN, the sky. With the sky inside the basket, MAL with AN becomes AMA, the mother, origin of Latin amare, love.

I first came across IDIGNA in the context of a translation. This is what I found:

As already demonstrated, the earliest Sumerian literary texts made use of placement of the symbols to indicate meaning. I take an unorthodox view of this line of text where the following three symbols, not shown here, are ordinarily understood to mean 'Euphrates', leaving IDIGNA to indicate 'Tigris'. It's said that the second symbol ID_2 refers to and is the prefix to a second river, and that the translation gives 'the river Tigris and the river Euphrates'. My interpretation of the phrase is based on previous experience with this type of setup. The two ID_2 surround IDIGNA. Two waterways, or one that is split into two, surround a bird. We are told that this bird is synonymous of the Tigris. For me, the above indicates that it should be placed either in the middle of a river or at the headwaters, the source, where one river becomes two. My contention is that this is a bird not of one river but between two rivers at their source, or more precisely the point at which they diverge, where they are weaned.

Symbol ID_2, shown on either side of IDIGNA and discussed on page 86, remains somewhat elusive. Composed of three symbols, KILI, the block or encirclement, with HAL the division (or hall) inside, and accompanied by A, the water, is given as 'river', 'watercourse', and 'canal' 112 times. Since a river and a canal are both watercourses but quite different in origin, the symbol remains open to some serious thought about its use in context. Are we looking at natural flows or manmade? Do these combined symbols encompass different types of flows on the condition that they all split rock? Should HAL be understood as the division of the rock or as a chamber, a hall, carved out of it? A mountain gorge is carved by water flow, a natural cave also, while a canal is made by man.

Phonetic IDIGNA is also represented in the later cuneiform texts by a combination of three symbols: MAŠ, GU_2 and GAR_3 which is why I was

139

surprised to discover the bird on the oldest tablets. This is how it looks in the lexical entries:

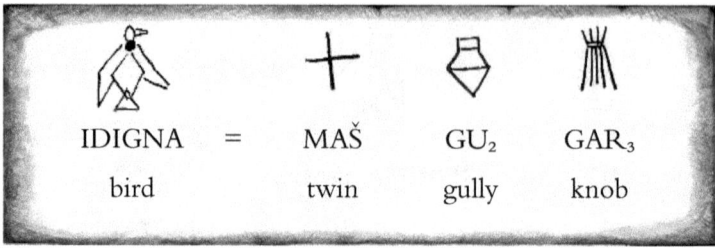

MAŠ

MAŠ is most often translated as 'goat' in Sumerian dictionaries. However, it also has the meaning of 'twin' and can be found in the name of the constellation of Gemini, the twins (MUL MAŠ TAB BA). Phonetic MAS as goat is relevant in other contexts, not least that of the pagan flute player, Pan. See line 93 of *The Story of Sukurru*, possibly the origin of the 'scapegoat'.

In the lexical entries showing the combinations of symbols related to the Idigna bird, there is one case where the symbol MAŠ is replaced by PAP. Either they were synonyms or whoever wrote those lexical lists could not be sure of the correct reading of the original symbol. PAP and MAŠ can both be transcribed as forms of the cross, one upright and the other skewed. Perhaps the scribe considered them to be identical in meaning only in certain contexts:

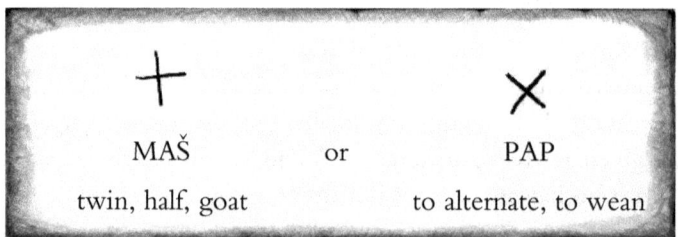

PAP/BAB was discussed in the first chapter in the context of water management. One meaning of PAP is to alternate, but it can also mean to estrange or to wean.

MAŠ as 'twin' fits the notion of the two rivers, Tigris and Euphrates, having the same place of birth in the Taurus mountains. Between PAP, to estrange, and MAŠ, the twins, this is the parting of the ways after birth, weaned from the mother and separated one from the other. We are still firmly in the realm of the headwaters in the Taurus mountains, birthplace of two rivers. We are also looking at the one and only situation that involves two umbilical cords at the same time. UM-BI indeed!

PAP is mentioned twice on the lexical page of IDIGNA alongside NA_2, the bird's nest.

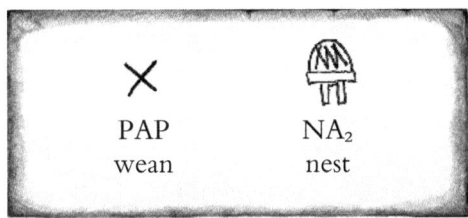

Is there a metaphor to be found between the birthplace of twin rivers and the weaning from the nest of a great bird? This is reminiscent of lines 124 and 125 in *The Story of Sukurru* where the two youngsters, a boy and a girl, brother and sister, are carried away by ZU, symbol of knowledge but apparently also a bird, to her beautiful nest of straw. I took this to be the straw of the Milky Way. If we return to the notion of the Milky Way as original womb, then there is the suggestion that the rivers Tigris and Euphrates are twins born from the cosmic womb.

GU_2/TIG

Once again, GU_2 is present in this study, this time surrounded by two symbols new to the discussion, and this time GU_2, the throat or gullet, is intimately linked to the image of a bird that is in turn acknowledged as related to the Tigris and, by extension, to the headwaters of the Mesopotamian river system. At least one end of it!

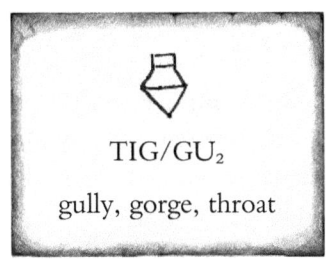

In Sumerian dictionaries TIK/TIG corresponds to one of the phonetic values of GU_2, already cited as one of the founding symbols of the name Gobekli. Working backwards from Tigris, the current name, is not ideal. There is no way of confirming the connection here but it's worth a note. The name of the river is, of course, generally associated with 'tiger'.

> *Tiger: Old English tigras (plural), also in part from Old French tigre "tiger" (mid-12c.), both from Latin tigris "tiger," from Greek tigris, possibly from an Iranian source (...)*

Notwithstanding the possibility of symbol GU_2/TIG as an origin for 'tiger', its meaning and the form of it correspond surprisingly well, in my opinion, with the markings on the throat of the central bird carved on pillar 43 at Gobekli Tepe:

It can be argued that they are not exactly the same but consider the possibility that the gullet of the bird carved around 9600 BC gave rise to a symbol found in a language from the same part of the world around the 3350-3200 BC mark, that symbol having the given meaning of gullet or neck or throat...

GAR_3

The third symbol, GAR_3 (far right) is given as 'knob, pommel', or' unit of measurement' 3 times. Unfortunately, this symbol remains enigmatic. It might be said that it resembles some kind of haystack or indicates that something has been tied at its topmost point.

The Light

IDIGNA-b shown on page 138 has a curious round black blob at the point of its left wing (righthand side of the image). It looks like a ball held at the same position as the one in the detail of pillar 43. It may be damage due to the age of the tablet or even a quirk from the angle of the photograph, but still. The weave of the cloth in which the moist clay had been stored is quite apparent all around it, undamaged. It looks like the Idigna bird was, at some distant time, shown holding a ball balanced on the end of its left wing. May the reader consider my arguments and draw their own conclusion.

This is a study of symbols as elements of a writing system. The Idigna bird is all the more fascinating for being both a bird and a word. Thus, we have two related words appearing together on tablet (b):

LU was discussed in the section on Babel in the context of I-LU, the illumination, multiplying of light. A translation of the above two symbols together might give 'fierce light' or 'crowning light' with inferred reference to the moon. The juxtaposition of the images shown on tablet (b) recall the same positioning of symbol LU with a lion – certainly a feline – carved onto a stone at Gubedra in Ethiopia.[71]

I-DI-IG-NA

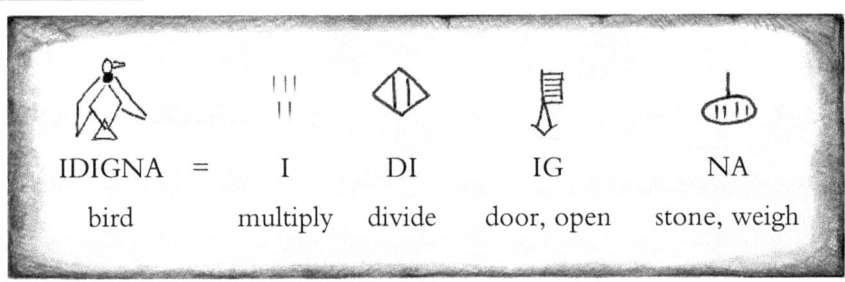

According to the Sumerian lexical entries for phonetic IDIGNA, this comes from a combination of the above four symbols:

- I with DI indicate a mathematical element, multiplying or spreading and dividing. I was discussed as the source of the Fibonacci sequencing, an organic spreading or multiplying. (See page 10). DI, symbol of division, is given as 'to equal, compare, compete and rival' 79 times. It's also the symbol of judgement, putting an end to disputes by equitable division. But it might also refer to the division of water if applied to the two waterways that surround the Idigna bird. It might well constitute the symbol that is both complementary and opposed to I, the multiplying and the dividing.

- I-DI appear in front of IG, the sign of the door, of opening or guarding. I-DI-IG could thus be the choice between a large flow or none at all according to a door closed or opened, some kind of bottleneck. The idea of a river dam or weir comes to mind as with the section on BA-A-BU in chapter 1 and harks back to the importance given to water in ancient texts. That said, the all-important symbol A doesn't appear in the name of the Idigna bird.

- IG with NA give a 'stone door', unless NA is used here as the verb, to 'give weight' or 'to weigh'. The most obvious translation would be 'multiplying and dividing at the stone door', which, in the absence of A, implies more than a mechanical device concerning irrigation. It could apply to astronomical calculations made at a place where stones provide a reference or an entrance to the skies. Without more context, there is no absolute conclusion to be drawn. Wishful thinking is not an option.

There is just one page of lexical entries dedicated to IDIGNA on ePSD. We find the river connection with ID_2. We also find the three symbols mentioned at the start of this section and generally given as the Sumerian name of the Tigris river. When the Sumerian pictograms were finally replaced by the abstract wedge-shaped cuneiform symbols, the Idigna bird disappeared from view and these three symbols were chosen to replace it within the later writing system of Assyria. There must have been a good reason for that.

ZUBI

ZUBI is another interesting collocation found with MAŠ, the twin, in the lexical entries for IDIGNA and given as 'watercourse' once at 3000-2500 BC. It reinforces IDIGNA as being more indicative of the headwaters of both rivers than of the Tigris alone.

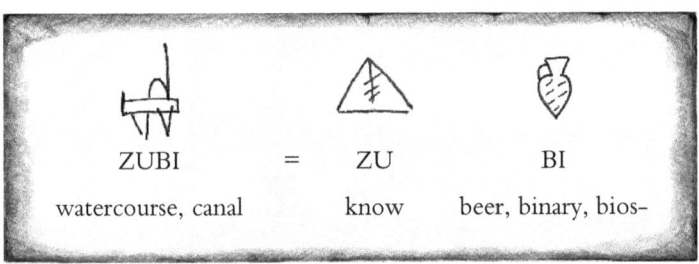

| ZUBI | = | ZU | BI |
| watercourse, canal | | know | beer, binary, bios- |

ZUBI is broken down on the lexical entries to ZU, to know, with BI, beer, binary or bios, the life-giving fermentation process. It could read 'knowledge of the beer' or 'life to know'. It must be a great Sumerian play on words if, as I suspect, it applies equally to the headwaters of the Tigris and Euphrates, to the Sabian 'Beer-Heart', to Gobekli Tepe and to the beer making and celebrations that took place there; ZU-BI, 'knowledge of both', or even SU-BI, 'sinking of the beer'.

ZU-BI is also linked in the lexical texts to PAP-NA$_2$, linking 'knowledge of beer' with 'weaned from the nest', booted out of the nest of ZU, one brutal alcoholic way of entering adulthood. That fits extremely well into the cursing section of *The Story of Sukurru* ending with line 247:

> Fired with beer, that the noble young son in the straw reflect on his birth in the land!

Another tablet from the slightly later Uruk III period (here below - d^{72}) shows an increasingly stylized IDIGNA. The head, not very well defined on the earlier pictograms, is now absent altogether and replaced by a square block at neck level which has two short parallel lines above and two diverging lines from its centre below that form the chest of the bird. On other increasingly abstract Uruk III tablets, the wings, straightened and considerably slimmed down, become the predominant features of the symbol and Idigna becomes unrecognisable as the bird that it once was.

IDIGNA (d)[72]

The neck with its two protruding vertical lines now resembles the UM sign mentioned in the section on UMBI page 77.

It's likely that the Idigna bird became the symbol of just one river, the Tigris, sometime after the 4th millennium. Perhaps the bird's head and neck were always a reference to the two rivers, gradually morphing into the abstract UM and the binary umbilical cord. Looking again at image (d), that might well be a big square block of stone in its throat. KIL perhaps?

14

Bird of Prophecy

The image of the Idigna bird is very different from the four types shown here below. We see its underbelly, a bird in flight, and it doesn't show up with the regularity of these symbols. Meet the other birds:

The Birds

HU, also phonetic MUŠEN, is given simply as 'bird' once at the early period and is taken as the generic term, used as prefix for different types of bird. It's also given once as 'wild goose'.

DAR, which has a distinctive duck-like form, is given as 'to be speckled' 6 times and 'to be hatched' which, notwithstanding the egg, refers to writing and to the cross-hatching when it appears on Sumerian symbols. DAR is the flock of birds that form a single line in the sky on line 139 of *The Story of Sukurru*. See them flying in formation to fully understand the use of this symbol. Another reference to this scene appears on line 161, where they accomplish their task. The same birds are given there as A-HU, the water birds, which demonstrates that these phonetic forms and symbols are somewhat interchangeable.

RI, also phonetic DAL/TAL, has an intriguing meaning of 'dividing line' 9 times at 2500 BC. This is the bird of 'collecting', 'gathering' of water and of words. Used with A, it becomes RI-A, origin of Greek Rhea, and of the flood, the collecting of water. Used with NA, it becomes NA-RI, the words collected in stone, the permanence of a text, but also the flying stone. The phonetic forms TAL and DAL are immensely important too. See the chapter concerning Greek Talon. Also consider the similarity with DALLA, another phonetic form of the Idigna bird.

The dodo, like the Idigna, is a bird that doesn't conform to the norm, only symbolized by its prominent features, two big feet and sometimes the addition of its stone, giving DU-DU or DU-DU-NA, the heavy dodo. It was probably easily identifiable in this way because the dodo's awkward stance, inability to fly and its bizarre habit of swallowing stones were once well-known.

> 𒁺 𒁺
> DU + DU
> foot + foot
> go, bring, sailor

The double symbol DU.DU is given as 'to go' 6 times at the early period, 'to bring' 10 times and as 'sailor' 90 times accompanied by MA_2, symbol of the ship. The etymology of the dodo's name is given as unknown, but it's believed that the bird became extinct because it was too easily caught and used as a food source by sailors. The following quote was added to the notes accompanying line 66 in my translation:

> *'The keeper called it a Dodo, and in the ende of a chymney in the chamber there lay a heape of large pebble stones, wherof hee gave it many in our sight, some as big as nutmegs, and the keeper told us that she eats them (conducing to digestion)..'*[73]

Line 66 of *The Story of Sukurru* is part of the oldest known account of the secret warning of an impending flood given to Noah; It involves prophecy, a bird, and stones:

> *'For the leader in water a lofty destiny shared with the lofty dodo, flight of the noble.' Tears from the heart of the reed façade, 'And both from their homeland stones estranged.'*

Nonsense and negation are comedic devices used more than once in *The Story of Sukurru*. There will be no chance of escaping a flood on the back of a flying dodo because the dodo doesn't fly. And it will carry its heavy homeland stone in its gullet, making the impossibility of flight even more evident. The dodo was a natural comic character:

Admittedly the bird in the above detail from a Sumerian seal[74] has sufficiently large wings to keep afloat - or flying - and we don't get to see its feet, only those of its rider or sailor, but it is surely one depiction of the scene described in line 66, a hero riding to the sky on the back of a bird, one version of an age-old joke. The oldest version of it can be seen on Pillar 43 of Gobekli Tepe where the human figure astride the bird has completely lost their head.

The head is a symbol of sagacity pronounced SAG or SAN in Sumerian. There is more to this story line than an easy joke.[75]

Sage: "wise," c. 1300 (late 12c. as a surname), from Old French sage "wise, knowledgeable, learned; shrewd, skillful" (11c.), (...) from PIE root.

Sane: 1721, back-formation from sanity or else from Latin sanus "sound, healthy," in figurative or transferred use, "of sound mind, rational, sane," also, of style, "correct;" of uncertain origin. Used earlier, of the body, with the sense of "healthy"

NAM, the Bird of Destiny

NAM

for/in order to/purpose

NAM, also phonetic SIM, is given as 'determined order, will, fate, destiny' but also as 'locust' 12 times. This last, combined with the fundamental meaning of fate, calls to mind the biblical tale of the Egyptian pharaoh and the plague of locusts mentioned in Exodus.

The meaning of NAM has varied very little over a few thousand years between a testament and the utterance of a prophecy, both dealing with a future situation. Globally, this bird has always been involved with fates and destinies, a fact confirmed by its use in context in the translation of *The Story of Sukurru*.

Naam: (English) from Old English nám, from Old Norse nám, (uncountable) obsolete legal - The act or process of taking property for the purpose of compensation.

Latin nam: (Conjunction) for, thus, because.

Hebrew naam: to utter a prophecy, speak as a prophet, (to declare) (source Bible Hub)

Hebrew naam with its meaning of 'prophecy' links directly to 'destiny' and 'fate' given for NAM but adds the element of foresight. Sumerian 'fate' leads fairly smoothly into the obsolete English legal term 'naam' where property is to be attributed as compensation.

It must be said that NAM appears with perfect timing and quite regularly throughout *The Story of Sukurru* to take events forward in a timely fashion. In fact, it's the rare exception of a Sumerian symbol used mainly as a function word for grammatical purposes in that text, rather than predominantly as a word with inherent meaning. When it wasn't directly coupled with a neighbouring symbol, I used it as 'for' or 'to'. NAM helped tremendously in the translation process, marking the separation of clauses, facilitating comprehension of the text, and moving it all along; cause and effect. I am always happier to be dealing with a line that includes NAM. But notwithstanding the value of NAM as a conjunction, all the symbols in these earliest Sumerian texts have inherent meaning as monosyllabic words.

A wonderful illustration of the usefulness of NAM is found in lines 27 to 28 of *The Story of Sukurru* where the reasons for wanting to reach the sky are explained in several stages:

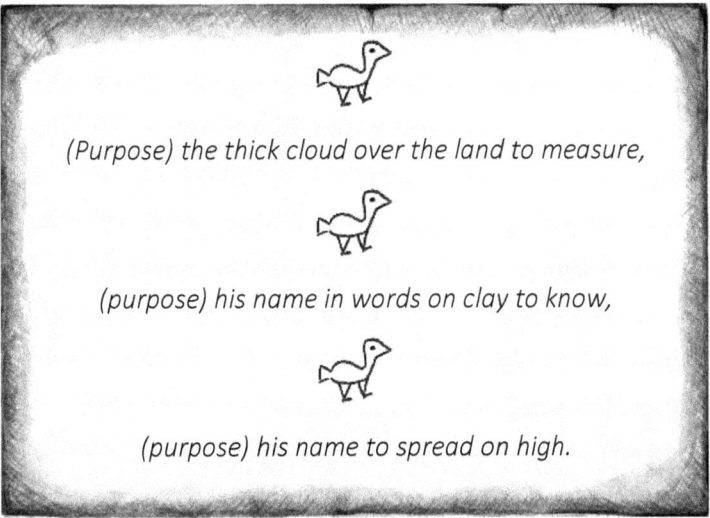

This section mirrors the way in which the temple was to be constructed, built upwards, a thought process, a succession of steps mirrored by reiteration of NAM…NAM…NAM, a three-tiered building, one way of designing a ziggurat, perhaps the ground plans for the Tower of Babel…? This is, after all, the script of a kind of musical comedy, a medley of well-known stories. Becoming increasingly conscious of the style of the original work which certainly involved rhythm, I added images to compensate just a little for all the nuances that have no doubt been lost. And that's why this page was illustrated with three NAM birds between the lines; there was a sense of paying homage to the author's intentions and out of gratitude for the clues that the knowledgeable little bird had gathered and fed to me.

NAM is found in lexical entries alongside NA-AM, stone and wild bull, possibly translating to 'weight of the wild bull' or 'stone of the wild bull'. At first glance, there appears to be nothing connecting the meanings of these two symbols to the fragile figure of the NAM/SIM bird.

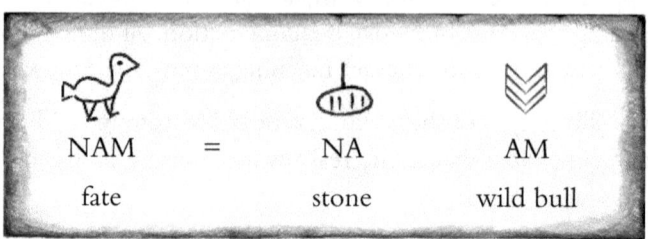

NA

NA as 'stone' and 'weight', is given 9 times at 3000-2500 BC. Depending on context, NA is a reference to the stone on which writing is gathered, where prophecy could be written, testament made. NA is the inversion of AN, the sky or lightness of the air, giving AN-NA or NA-AN, stone of/from/to the sky, a stone roof, and as opposing adjectives; heavy and light.

In *The Story of Sukurru*, the stone is used as counterweight to the Feather of Truth on line 40. In ancient Egyptian death rituals, it was said to be the dead person's heart that was weighed against the feather. As this story is a humorous one, we find another comedic device. The dice were more heavily loaded against the poor soul. But perhaps he really did have a heart of stone:

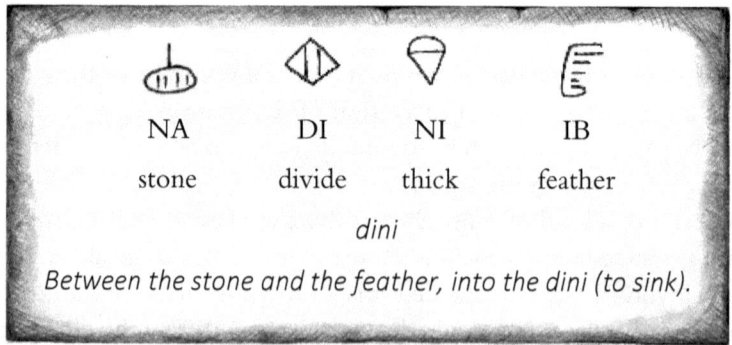

'Dini' was one name given to karstic waterways (underground fresh-water streams, caverns and sinkholes) in ancient Greece while 'din' is the term for a faith or type of religion in several languages. Note that symbols NA and IB indicate the two opposing sides of the scales.

It's possible to make a linguistic connection between DU-DU-NA, the heavy dodo or the dodo and stone, and the notion of prophecy via the Greek island of Dodona. The following quotes contribute to a better understanding of the reason for an image of the Sumerian hero sitting astride his bird (see page 149) rather than in a more conventional cosmic ship. They take us into the domain of Homer and Odysseus. Through the observations of Herodotus, they also take us to ancient Egypt, to Thebes, home of the majestic temples of Luxor and Karnak.

> *and Argus, by Athena's advice, built a ship of fifty oars named Argo after its builder; and at the prow Athena fitted in a speaking timber from the oak of Dodona.* **Apollodorus**[76],
>
> *That, then, I heard from the Theban priests; and what follows, the prophetesses of Dodona say: that two black doves had come flying from Thebes in Egypt, one to Libya and one to Dodona; the latter settled on an oak tree, and there uttered human speech, declaring that a place of divination from Zeus must be made there; the people of Dodona understood that the message was divine, and therefore established the oracular shrine.* Herodotus[77]

AM

AM is given as 'wild bull' 47 times. This symbol presents a couple of dilemmas. The bull would have been a mighty animal. AM is given several times in collocation with AL, presumed to be the hoe, in Sumerian proverbs. The marriage of wild bull and hoe is unlikely. AM, a wild animal, won't be used for ploughing earthly fields, and it would surely have had horns. The symbol doesn't reflect that at all. On page 164, I put forward the argument for AL being understood as 'bellows'. From the bellows to the bellowing, a wild bull bellowing is a more plausible scenario than a wild bull ploughing.

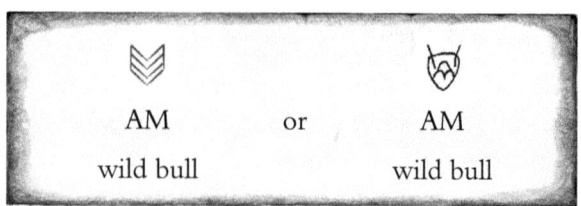

AM seen here on the left is found on tablets from the Uruk III period, ca. 3200 to 3000 BC. AM appears to be a cross-hatched version of AMAR, the calf. Given the most animal-like version of AMAR where ears are shown, it's possible that AM should be understood as a calf rather than a mature bull. The horned bull is commonly represented by GUD, discussed at length in the sections on Gobekli.

While CDLI has photos of tablets showing the symbol here on the left, both the ePSD and L'Ecriture Cunéiforme give the symbol of AM as a combination of GUD with KUR, the mountains, at its centre, seen here above on the right, and indicate that it appears only from the Ed III period, with nothing recorded for the earlier Uruk periods.

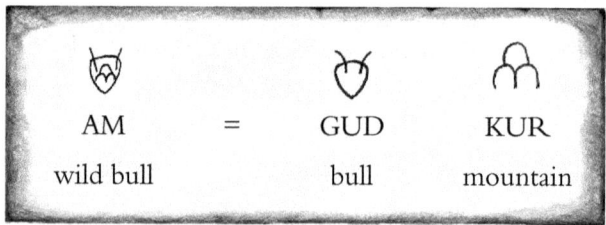

Whatever the form of the symbol, they both have the given meaning of wild bull, a central character to the ancient world in the context of prophecy, stones, and mountains, the world of NAM and NA-AM. From that conclusion to the suggestion of a prophetic wild bull is not an impossible leap.

> *Egyptians celebrated the Festival of the Apis Bull, which lasted for seven days. (...) It was thought that any child who smelled the breath of the Apis had the ability to predict the future. In fact, the Apis itself was often consulted as an oracle. Egyptians asked the bull a question and then offered it food: if the bull ate the food it was a good omen, but a rejection of the food was a bad omen.*[78]

KUR

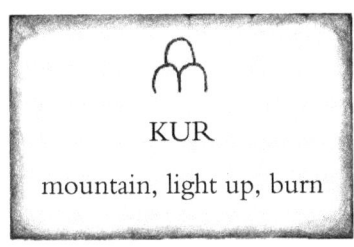

KUR

mountain, light up, burn

KUR is given as 'to burn', 'to light up', 5 times at 3000-2500 BC and as 'mountain' 46 times at 2500-2000 BC. It's also given as 'underworld' 59 times. Situated inside GUD, it changes the meaning from 'bull' to 'wild bull', the undomesticated animal of a mountainous region. The most evident meaning from the pictographic form of KUR is 'mountain', but there are quite a few meanings and phonetic forms associated with the symbol.

In fact, KUR is a hard nut to crack despite the distinctive form, three mounds closely linked, or perhaps a pile of stones. There are too many possibilities rather than too few:

> *Core: early 14c., 'heart or inmost part of anything' (especially an apple, pear, etc.), of uncertain origin, (...) from Latin cor 'heart,' from PIE root.*
>
> *Cure: c. 1300, 'care, heed,' from Latin cura 'care, concern, trouble,' (...) 'means of healing, successful remedial treatment of a disease' (late 14c.), from Old Latin coira-, a noun of unknown origin.*
>
> *Curia: c. 1600, one of the ten divisions of each of the three ancient Roman tribes; also 'the Senate-house of Rome,' from Latin curia 'court,' from PIE root.*
>
> *Curious: mid-14c., 'subtle, sophisticated;' late 14c., 'eager to know, inquisitive, (...), also 'wrought with or requiring care and art;' from Old French curios 'solicitous, anxious, inquisitive; odd, strange' (...) directly from Latin curiosus 'careful, diligent; inquiring eagerly, meddlesome,' akin to cura 'care' (see cure (n.))*

There are seven pages of lexical entries on ePSD where KUR is collocated with RA, an unusually high number. I came across the Maori word for 'wisdom school' thanks to the work of Laird Scranton in his book dedicated to their ancient culture[79]: Wharekura, a temple of wisdom teaching where 'kura' has the meaning of 'school'. One line of *The Story of Sukurru* where the two symbols KUR-RA are found together comes in an enigmatic and intriguing section, lines 266 to 268, in the company of ME-EŠ, translated there as 'the spirit of the three'. It suggests that three choices are being given, presumably to mankind; the volcano, the mouse-hole, or the KUR-RA. See page 101 for another interpretation of KUR-RA as celestial coracle. See page 219 for a another more recently discovered possibility for ME-EŠ.

Lines 266 to 268, along with two lexical entries showing KUR-IA, lead me to wonder if the three mounds represent the mythical original wisdom school:

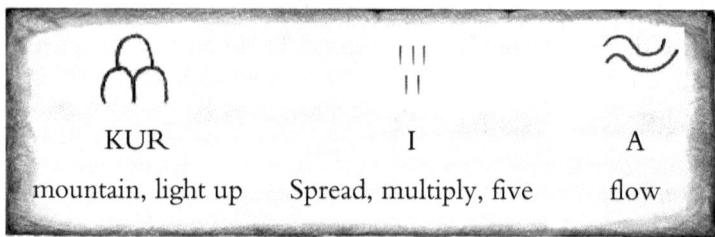

There is also the enigmatic term 'khora' discussed by Plato in Timaeus 48e:

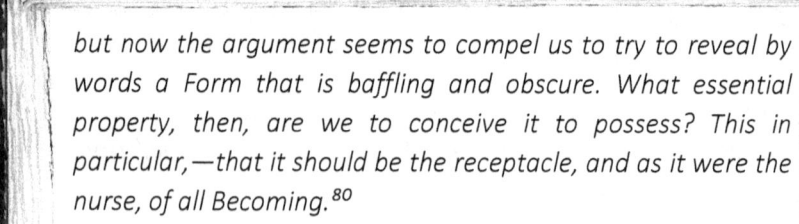

but now the argument seems to compel us to try to reveal by words a Form that is baffling and obscure. What essential property, then, are we to conceive it to possess? This in particular,—that it should be the receptacle, and as it were the nurse, of all Becoming.[80]

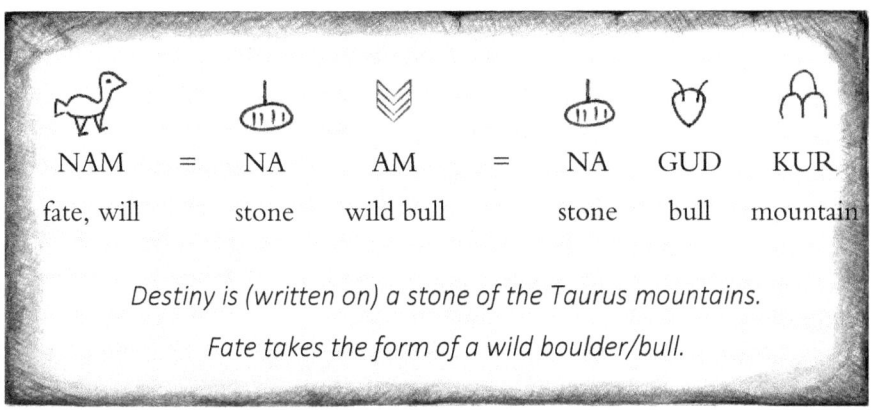

The above interpretations stem from the NAM symbol and its lexical equivalents. But it also reflects the translator's cultural input. It would be less likely to have emerged if I hadn't read about our vulnerability to meteorites, particularly those of the Taurid showers, hadn't known the story of Moses on the mountain, or seen the stones of Gobekli Tepe, and hadn't taken on board the suggestion that our ancestors might have wanted us to be aware of a cyclical catastrophic event, encoding that knowledge in symbols and perhaps architecture. The interpretation is given without literary context and therefore, unlike *The Story of Sukurru*, I don't vouch for it. But still…

The bible story of Moses on the mountain insists heavily on the impossibility of co-existence between God-given stone tablets and the golden calf worshipped below by an unruly, pagan crowd. If the prophetic writings and the calf were once two closely associated pagan symbols - possibly even integrating a message about a boulder - the necessity to oppose them violently one against the other, to separate them for all time would be understandable.

Lines 49 to 51 (see page 312) describe a scene of broken tablets, symbolised by two KILI blocks side by side, in the usual humoristic manner. KIL is given as 'to break off' once at 2000 BC. The bird, who goes unmentioned in the biblical version of Moses with his tablets, is given there as 'the renowned wing'. ŠU-MU, origin of Sumul, a Canaanite deity and mother vulture. The vulture is the rapacious bird that eats the flesh of corpses, an act that is part of a natural cleansing and life-sustaining cycle:

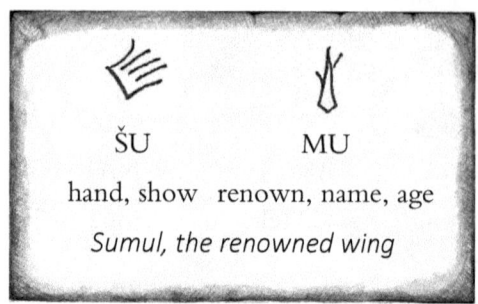

ŠU — MU
hand, show — renown, name, age
Sumul, the renowned wing

In the notes to *The Story of Sukurru*, I suggested a link to Egyptian Muu dancers who were said to use hand gestures to usher funerary processions into the necropolis. MU, also given as 'month', is linked to the movement of time. That would lead easily to the gesturing hand (or wing) of death, indicating that the time had come.

The tablets are dropped by the hero of the tale and broken out of panic when Sumul calls out his name, understood as the signal of imminent death. Symbol AM, a strange abstract form, might even be said to resemble two conjoined tablets. NA-NAM, weight of destiny!

NA-NAM

The combination of NA with NAM is given as 'consent' and 'to assent' 3 times. They appear together seven times in *The Story of Sukurru* and their collocation in the text reinforces the importance of the stone/bird relationship.

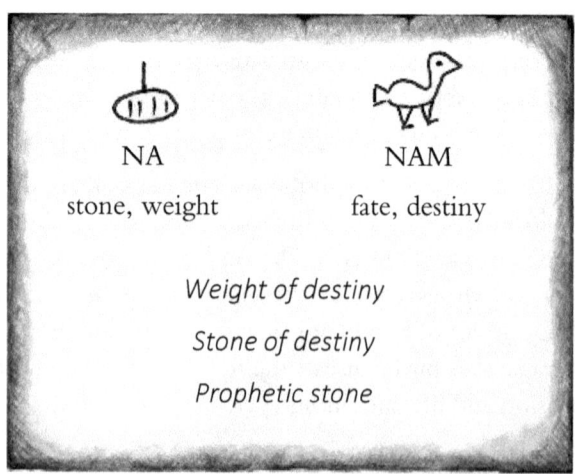

NA — NAM
stone, weight — fate, destiny

Weight of destiny
Stone of destiny
Prophetic stone

NAM, the bird with well-defined legs, is now associated with a second, this time external, stone. Taking the lexical NA-AM into account, the above might read NA-NA-AM, the two stones of the wild bull or a more general indication that this is a plural. The understanding of this phrase as 'consent' complies with the idea of a fate too weighty to be withstood. But it also fits with the consent that comes with a binding verbal agreement made at the T-shaped stone and in the sight of the bull. See page 133.

This powerful combination of stone and bird brings to mind the ubiquitous winged stone images found in Mesopotamian, Egyptian and other cultures. See here the imposing symbol that meets the eye when you stand under one of the gigantic doorways in the outer walls of the Karnak temple complex at Luxor in Egypt and look up:

Feel the weight of destiny in every stone of that impressive place… the overwhelming atmosphere of grandeur and gravitas that reigns there.

NA-NAM…

15

Shaman and Alchemist

> *Shamans from the Amazon are now mounting a kind of reverse activity. When I've asked Shamans about the sickness of the West, they say it's quite simple: You guys have severed your connection with spirit. Unless you reconnect with spirit and do so soon, you're going to bring the whole house of cards down around your heads and ours.*
> Graham Hancock[81]

There is a fine line, so to speak, between two Sumerian symbols that are both linked to syllable SHA of 'shaman'. One is LI, the boundary line, discussed in the context of KILI on pages 93-94. The other is shown below. The two symbols are almost identical, so much so that I have not come to an absolute conclusion about their differences. Perhaps the direction of the smoke?

ŠA/ARA

heart, altar

ŠA is given as 'heart', 'inner body' and 'an official' once at the 3000-2500 BC period and 64 times again as 'heart' after that. Ara is the name of the constellation known by the Greeks as the altar of the gods. The pictogram of ŠA/ARA, copied from a tablet of the Uruk IV period, is the earliest rendering of it that we possess. The picture is that of a container balanced on a small stand with smoke rising from it, evocative of the smoke of a shaman's brew rising to the sky. The constellation of Ara as shown on ancient sky maps matches this symbol although in a more elaborate style.

But Greek Ara also takes us back into the realms of cursing and to the Arai who were female spirits of the underworld invoked for purposes of revenge. ARA breaks down in the lexical entries to A-RA, the churning waters. A shaman as we understand the positive, benevolent figure in modern times cannot be matched to the popular cursing theme of *The Story of Sukurru* or other dark tales. My thought is that they have only the stirring of a brew in common. Whatever is at the heart of the Arai is another story. Perhaps it relates to the dousing of RA discussed on page 47.

Alchemy is a word that, in the minds of many, conjures up images of old bearded men melting metals and stirring pots in the hope of finding the recipe for gold. For others, it evokes the soulmate, the sublime alchemy between two people that is difficult to express through more common words – but still a notion of mixing and harmony exists.

ŠIM

alchemist, brewer

ŠIM is given as 'brewer' 7 times. With LU$_2$, man, it's given with that meaning 223 times at the 2500-2000 BC period. The symbol has conveniently retained its laboratory-equipment image, that of apparatus for some type of alchemical process, a large neck allowing to pour liquid in and a smaller exit tube below. ŠIM is, of course, the alchemist. That said, our modern versions of the alchemist or chemist pronounce the word either as a hard K or as the softer SH of Š, found in French 'chimie', and the word has been linked to the ancient name Kemet meaning Egypt. Kemet is discussed in Chapter 18:

> *Alchemy: 'medieval chemistry; the supposed science of transmutation of base metals into silver or gold' (involving also the quest for the universal solvent, quintessence, etc.), mid-14c., from Old French alchimie (14c.), alquemie (13c.), from Medieval Latin alkimia, from Arabic al-kimiya, from Greek khemeioa (found c.300 C.E. in a decree of Diocletian against 'the old writings of the Egyptians'), all meaning 'alchemy,' and of uncertain origin.*

ŠIM is found in lexical entries with ŠI and IM, the eye and the clay:

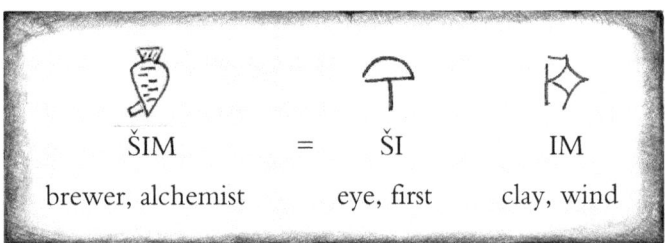

ŠI is given as 'eye' 8 times and as 'first, earlier, front, face' 134 times. I have added 'leader', a meaning synonymous with 'first' derived from context. It goes – almost – without saying that this is the origin of our verb 'to see' and is interesting to consider as a candidate for the noun, the 'see' that is the throne of the highest-ranking member of a community (also from a PIE root). The drawing of ŠI shown here was copied from the only example that I have come across so far[82]. ŠI has a variety of other phonetic values but none of them appear in a search of the tablets referenced for the Uruk periods on CDLI. EPSD favours the phonetic value IGI as the earliest known for this symbol. However, ŠI was equally, if not more, important. For the most part, I haven't wandered from the academic choices as to the most ancient sounds. This is an exception. MAL instead of GA_2, for 'basket' was another.

IM is given as 'clay, mud' 21 times at the early period, and as 'wind' twice. It can also be read as EM and understood as the mirror sound of ME. They appear side by side on numerous lexical entries and might translate to 'clay of the Magician' or 'the spirit wind'. Their collocation and mirrored sounds signal a close link between them although it isn't an obvious one:

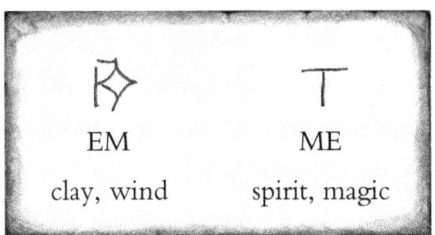

An inverted combination of ŠI-EM/IM appears in *The Story of Sukurru* on line 10 where it provides a very solemn, formal ending to the introduction. ŠIM, the brewer, is also the 'Clay Eye' in the sky, the eye recording all on clay, witness to and perhaps author of the Tablets of Destiny. The witnessing

163

on a clay tablet appears early on, at the end of the re-telling of the flood that swept over Sukurru, leaving the people of that land clinging desperately to life:

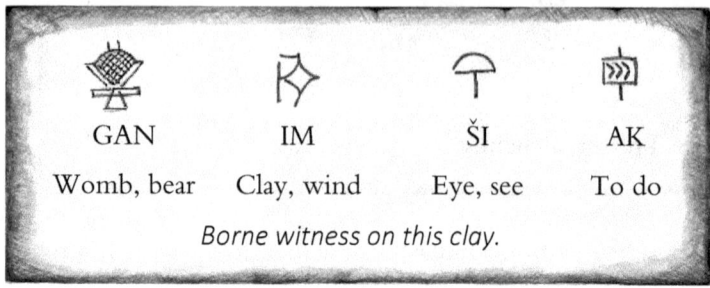

ŠI with IM translated to 'eye' and 'wind' leading to other more humorous associations. We find 'wind in his eye', the same combination of those two symbols used in a different context in line 13.

GAN, the womb, is given as 'child-bearing' and the curious combination 'be it' which might be taken as a form of 'So be it'. It is also true that GAN is a major alchemical reference, symbol of the crucible. See it on page 165. The translation of line 10 is justified in the following manner:

- GAN with IM, that which is born/borne on clay,
- ŠI, the eye, as witness,
- ŠI as 'see', reinforced by AK, 'to do', becomes the act of witnessing.

The clay tablet is born and the act of witnessing too. They are both carried out or borne. Etymological dictionaries inform us that the distinction between born and borne is recent. That is not to say that IM and ŠI don't also have the meaning of 'clay eye' in this phrase; to use either/or logic on Sumerian symbols is to miss the point of them. The Clay Eye and the Eye on the Clay are one and the same. The close proximity of GAN, the crucible, with the two symbols that form ŠIM, the brewer, conveys an underlying current of meaning. It might signify the action of the alchemist, and the wind of the bellows under the crucible.

AL

But what of the al- in alchemy? We are fortunate to be able to contemplate one of the very few carefully executed versions of the early Sumerian symbols. AL is on the right, next to an equally well-formed symbol GAN that served as the basis for my copy[83]:

GAN　　　　AL

AL is given as 'hoe' 3 times at 3000-2500 BC and 733 times after that. I have looked for images of agricultural tools and shapes that might possibly have been the originators of this symbol as a hoe, but nothing corresponds. What I do see in the above is a fire-provoking instrument, the bellows, its long funnel hanging down, sat next to a vessel that is shown to be full. AL will serve to blow wind on the fire at the base of the crucible.

One of the books recommended by Terence McKenna on the subject of alchemy (see page 92) and the ancient rituals involved in that enigmatic practice is The Forge and the Crucible.[84] The bellows is mentioned there in the context of its use by various African tribes and the sacred nature with which it is understood to be endowed. The author notes that the Ogowe, not possessing such an instrument themselves, were in awe of the bellows owned by the smiths of other tribes.

See page 177 for AL as the source of 'all'.

The Clay Eye

The symbolic eye figures on the hull of the ship of Odysseus. It appears on the Greek Siren vase in the British Museum[85] and served to illustrate the Clay Eye of line 130 of *The Story of Sukurru*:

RI, symbol of the bird, is used here in context to indicate flight, but it has much broader implications. RI which has the phonetic values TAL and DAL is discussed in relation to Greek Talon and to Hermes. It is a most important bird. RI/RE has a phonetic mirror image, IR/ER, to err and to perceive.

The Egyptian eye-shaped amulets made of clay and known as the 'Eye of Horus' take their source in the Sumerian clay eye. There was a time when Egyptian and Sumerian cultures were one. I don't pretend to put a date on it or give any other theories in archaeological and historical terms. My only resource is the evidence of the symbols and the translations that result from them. I have made no effort to force a contentious theory into being. *The Story of Sukurru* has more than one obvious reference and the Egyptian amulet, said to represent Horus, symbolises the all-seeing eye in the sky. When? I have no way of knowing but it must have been well before the oldest known Egyptian dynasty appeared - at a time before division of any sort. See page 215 for more on the eye and the ship.

Cannabis

Line 56 gives an insight into another combination linked to the notion of alchemy and spiritual flight. From the preceding line 55 and the following lines 57 to 59, it's not difficult to identify the scene as that of a hallucinogenic substance sending smoke to the sky. The obvious interpretation of symbols KA-NA-AB was to combine them into a single word, cannabis:

> Cannabis: 1798, "common hemp," from Cannabis, Modern Latin plant genus named (1728), from Greek kannabis "hemp," a Scythian or Thracian word. Also source of Armenian kanap', Albanian kanep, Russian konoplja, Persian kanab, Lithuanian kanapės "hemp," and English canvas.

The Greek form, kannabis, might stem from a more direct link between KAN_4 and NA, the stone gate, as this collocation can be found in several lexical entries. Nevertheless, KA is also a celestial mouth and thus another gateway.

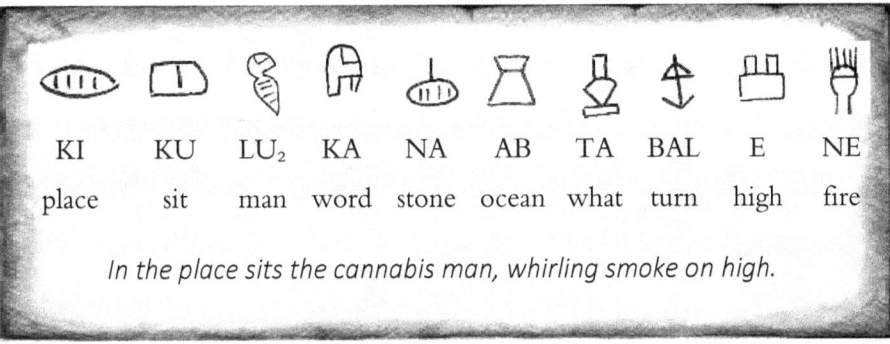

KI	KU	LU$_2$	KA	NA	AB	TA	BAL	E	NE
place	sit	man	word	stone	ocean	what	turn	high	fire

In the place sits the cannabis man, whirling smoke on high.

There are various possibilities from the three symbols together and bearing in mind the overall meaning of cannabis; the heavy word of the Father, the word of the Father to weigh, the stone mouth of the shrine... but not one that stands out more than another. NA with AB, stone of the ocean, equates to sand. However, NAB, comprising two signs of AN, the sky, is found in lexical entries opposite NA-AB and has been suggested as the origin of 'navel' on page 78.

Fermentation

Continuing with the more obvious symbols linked to alchemical activities, BI, the symbol for beer, is also that of 'binary' and origin of Greek bios, the fermentation and the bringing to life of the brew – a process necessitating the intervention of ŠIM, the brewer.

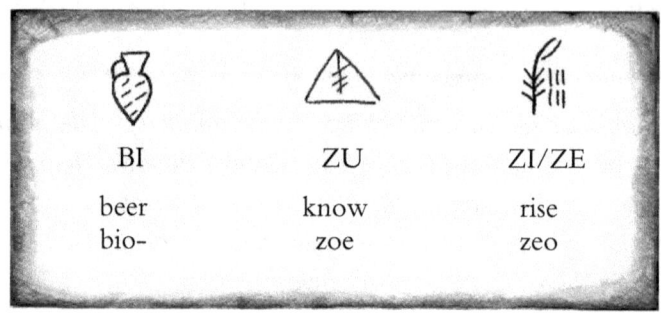

Other symbols that take their roots in alchemy are ZU, symbol of knowledge in the form of a pyramid with ladder and origin of Greek zoe, and ZI, given as 'life', a symbol resembling an ear of corn with enigmatic vertical strikes, usually six, accompanying it. ZI/ZE, origin of 'zeal', was personified as Greek Zeus and is discussed on page 233. The three symbols are the sources of Greek words for 'life' and 'living'.

> Bio-: word-forming element, especially in scientific compounds, meaning 'life, life and,' or 'biology, biology and,' or 'biological, of or pertaining to living organisms or their constituents,' from Greek bios 'one's life, course or way of living, lifetime' (as opposed to zoe 'animal life, organic life'), from PIE root.
>
> Zoe: Greek, 'life,' from PIE root.
>
> Zeo: Greek, 'to boil', 'bubble' from PIE root

It appears from their given meanings that the concept of fermentation is at the heart of alchemical language, fitting well into the preparation of beer and the world of the Great Brewer. Another phonetic value of ŠIM is ŠIMBIZI which, according to the lexical entries, can be dissected into ŠI-IM-BI-ZI leading to more than one possible translation. Also see ZUBI on page 145.

SHIM or SIM? / SHIN or SIN? / SHIM or SIN? / SHIN or SIM?

According to the etymology dictionaries, Greek syn and sym come from the same unspecified root:

> *Syn-: word-forming element meaning 'together with, jointly; alike; at the same time,' also sometimes completive or intensive, from Greek syn (prep.) 'with, together with, along with, in the company of,' from PIE root*
>
> *Sym-: assimilated form of syn-, from Greek form of syn- in compounds with words beginning in -b-, -m-, -p-, -ph-, -ps-.*

If the same logic is applied to the Sumerian phonetic values, ŠIM, the brewer, becomes a close relative if not a synonym of NAM/SIM, the bird of destiny. ŠI-IM, the clay eye in the sky, might then be understood as synonymous of or closely related to NA-AM, the winged stone, discussed in the previous chapter. Linking all of the symbols gives the following result:

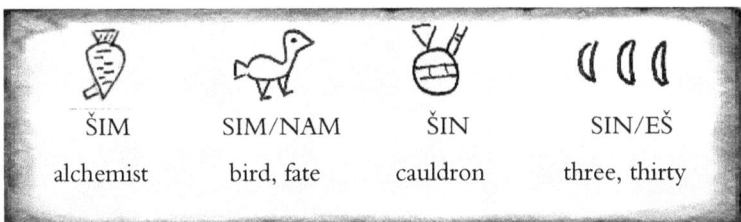

ŠIN is given 6 times as 'cauldron' at the 3000-2500 BC period while the image of SIM/NAM appears on clay tablets at the earliest Uruk IV period, ca 3350 to 3200 BC. Already discussed in the previous chapter, its unassuming air hides another important character in the order of things; NAM/SIM, the bird of destiny, is the mythological creature that will make its name in the history books as the Simurgh, a great leader of birds.

> *Simorgh: The creature represented the union between the Earth and the sky, serving as mediator and messenger between the two.*[86]

This interpretation of its name is not supported by evidence from the Persian etymology which appears to derive Simurgh from Sen or Sina. However, the amount of confusion generally existing between the sounds of sym and syn inspires me to insist. The Sumerian bird, whose name is SIM and whose function it is to take us from one stage to another, will have his day in court.

Written in the 11th century AD by Persian author Farid ud-Din Attar, The Conference of the Birds is a long poem about the journey of a flock of different species of birds, a journey undertaken to find the king of all the birds, the Simorgh. Interspersed with moralising parables, it has since been translated at different times in different styles, some preferring to be faithful to the original meter, others adapting the text to better please a foreign audience. It's a difficult balance to strike. Each version has its merits. The following lines come from that of Edward Fitzgerald translating in 1889.

> *It was in China, late one moonless night,*
> *The Simorgh first appeared to mortal sight –*
> *He let a feather float down through the air,*
> *And rumours of its fame spread everywhere...*[87]

The core of the Conference of the Birds is true 'wisdom' literature, a label that was erroneously awarded to the original translation of the Sumerian text known as *The Instructions of Shuruppak*. There can be no comparison. At the risk of displeasing some but with no disrespect intended, I do believe that Attar based his poem on a far older text and that his Simorgh was a profoundly Sumerian bird; that is to say, an elder, a sage.

The number of birds, SIN, three or thirty, is of importance in The Conference of the Birds. After a long and difficult journey during which the attributes and weaknesses of each species are highlighted, just thirty birds make it to the end of the road:

> *But Thirty—thirty desperate draggled Things,*
> *Half-dead, with scarce a Feather on their Wings,*
> *Stunn'd, blinded, deafen'd with the Crash and Craze*
> *Of Rock and Sea collapsing in a Blaze*
> *That struck the Sun to Cinder—fell upon*
> *The Threshold of the Everlasting One,*[88]

There they discover that the Simorgh is the reflection of self:

> *If there the Simorgh's form does not appear;*
> *No one can bear His beauty face to face,*
> *And for this reason, of His perfect grace,*
> *He makes a mirror in our hearts - look there*
> *To see Him, search your hearts with anxious care.*[89]

Synonymity, similarity and the Simorgh.

> *Similar: 'having characteristics in common,' 1610s (earlier similary, 1560s), from French similaire, from a Medieval Latin extended form of Latin similis 'like, resembling, of the same kind,' from Old Latin semol 'together,' from PIE root*

The Sumerian language takes us back to the source of the story, before the Simurgh of the Persian story, before the Eye of Horus of Egyptian lore, and long before the medieval themes of bearded wizards stirring their pots. It takes us back to a philosophy, an alchemical understanding that has been rendered increasingly obscure over millennia. It will take a Great Magician to unravel the nauseating concoction, to melt the elements in His great crucible, and to stir them all together once again to form a more comprehensible whole.

16

Talon, the Metal Robot

This is a Greek coin depicting Talon, the metal robot of Homeric fame, a faithful and extremely precious reproduction of a much older portrayal[90]. The proof of that lies in the message spelled out on it:

Talon is preparing to throw rocks. He holds one in his right hand and is ready to follow up with a second in the left. His massive wings are unfurled, his great strength on display. He means business. Note the impressive six-pack and the upturned T form of the genitals. Although this is a well-worn coin, the round staring eyes, the prominent T-shape of nose connected to brow and the bull's horns above his head are all still visible.

> *Talon: c. 1400, talounz 'claws of a bird or beast,' probably originally from Old French talon 'heel or hinder part of the foot of a beast, or of a man, or of a shoe; foot-step' (12c.), from Medieval Latin talonem 'heel,' from Latin talus 'ankle'*

Talaria was the Latin name for the winged sandals of Greek Hermes who was also Mercury, messenger of the gods, while Talon's name is quite naturally associated with his well-known weakness at his heel or talon. In the section below, it's proposed that Talon/Talos might be a bull.

> *Putting to sea from there, they were hindered from touching at Crete by Talos. Some say that he was a man of the Brazen Race, others that he was given to Minos by Hephaestus; he was a brazen man, but some say that he was a bull. He had a single vein extending from his neck to his ankles, and a bronze nail was rammed home at the end of the vein. This Talos kept guard, running round the island thrice every day.[91]*

The importance of the myth of Talon associated with the image on that ancient Greek coin can't be overstated. It lies partly in TAL/RI, the Sumerian bird, with its link to the etymology of talon, and the general emphasis that is put on claws, ankles and heels with this symbol. It relates to 'clew' where Ariadne's life-giving gift of a ball of thread or clew to Theseus is analogous to the single vein of life that runs through the body of Talon from ankle to head, also linking to French 'clou', the nail that holds his life-blood in place. There are numerous phonetic and visual clues here. The word 'clue' itself must come from the Sumerian riddles that gave us all these words.

Talon as a bull, shown on this coin with horns, and the single thread running through him, contributes a further link to the bull-yarn connection that is made in several different places here; the Hittite wall carving with yarn-laden T-shaped pillar and sacred bull, the story of Theseus in the labyrinth, the woven Eye of God…

On this precious coin, Talon's feet divide the letters of his name between three spaces; a stand-alone capital T, followed by AL in the middle, and completed with ON to the right; T-AL-ON, his given name in Greek, all three placed next to the talons of the winged creature. If the coin stamper had had free choice over the arranging of the five characters involved in the name – whichever way it's spelled – they might have divided it up with two on the left, one in the middle, and two on the right, TA-L-ON, for the purpose of symmetry. But this wasn't random. It was a faithful copy of a much earlier image. The following demonstrates the first and most obvious way in which the symbols between the feet of this mythical figure were meant to be read:

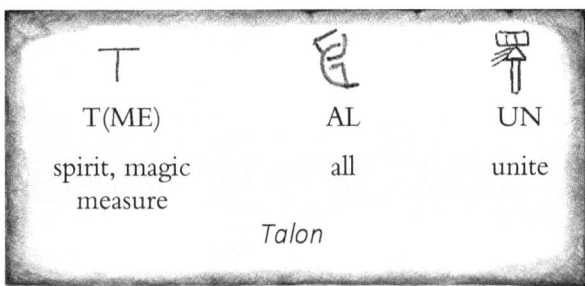

T(ME)	AL	UN
spirit, magic measure	all	unite

Talon

Evidence that the image of winged Talon/Talos comes to us from a more ancient source than this Grecian copy lies first in the T at the side of his right foot:

- ME-(TE), the measurement, tether of the spirit, and TE (ME), perhaps the temerity of anyone who approaches his island.

- T with AL give 'the spirit of all', leading to 'the measurement of everything'. See page 164 for AL, symbol of the alchemist's bellows and here with ME-TE, the magic performed by their use.

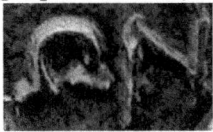

- UN is given as the Land (of Sumer) 17 times at the 3000-2500 BC period and as 'people' 280 times at a later period. I have translated it to 'unity' from contextual use, a word that doesn't detract from given meanings.

With the addition of UN, Talon's name gives 'the measurement or the magic of everything united in one', an essentially alchemical reference. Greek Talon is a messenger. Continuing with the analysis, a further reference can be found:

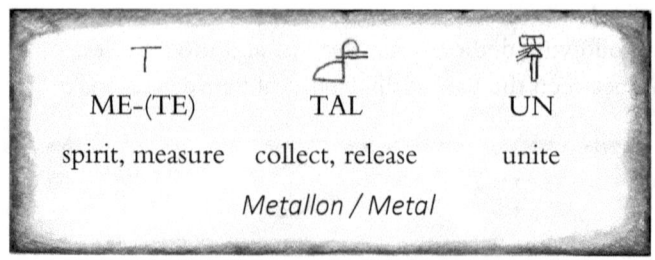

With the name of the bird, TAL, derived from the first two segments, T-AL, we find ME-TAL, hidden reference to the material of Talon's body.

> *Metal: mid-13c., from Old French metal 'metal; material, substance, stuff' (12c.), from Latin metallum 'metal; mine, quarry, mineral, what is got by mining,' from Greek metallon 'metal, ore' (senses only in post-classical texts; originally 'mine, quarry, pit'), probably from metalleuein 'to mine, to quarry,' of unknown origin,*
>
> *His body and his limbs were brazen and invulnerable, except at one point: under a sinew by his ankle there was a blood-red vein protected only by a thin skin which to him meant life or death.*[92]

The phrase 'with its issues of life and death' shows the vein of Talon to be the link to mortality; that is if the story is to be understood as one of a physical bronze giant. There is more information hidden in this image of the great metal robot:

RI, also known as DAL/TAL, collector bird, and one of a flock, a gathering together of birds and words, is a close relative of the Idigna bird through phonetic DAL. The following are derived from lexical entries showing TAL and DAL:

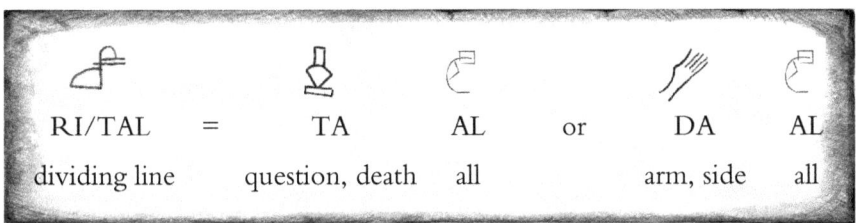

RI/TAL	=	TA	AL	or	DA	AL
dividing line		question, death	all		arm, side	all

One of the given meanings of RI/TAL is 'dividing line' which has a connection to the notion of mortality discussed above. TA is given as 'what' 85 times but only at the late 2000 BC period. TA has been translated by me to 'question', an easy variation on 'what' but also as 'death'. This is the founding symbol of Tao, the most ancient of philosophies grounded in the quest for knowledge of life and death, a symbol of duality and choices. The sound gave the opening symbol of Greek Thanatos, god of death, but TA should be understood as a division between life and death, the questioning of it, rather than a one-sided symbol with the meaning 'death'. Greek Talon is a demonstration of this concept, the most imposing of figures who, while capable of killing others with his rock, nevertheless carries within him the ultimate fragility, the vein that divides between life and death.

AL is discussed in the context of alchemy on page 165.

> *All: Old English eall 'every, entire, the whole quantity of' (adj.), 'fully, wholly, entirely' (adv.), from Proto-Germanic *alnaz (source also of Old Frisian, Old High German al; German all, alle; Old Norse allr; Gothic alls), with no certain connection outside Germanic. As a noun, in Old English, 'all that is, everything.'*

DA is given as 'side' and 'vicinity' 102 times. The translation to 'arm' is not difficult thanks to the pictogram itself. It's tempting to look for it in Latin damnare, to damn or to doom, and in Greek Damocles, the character who found himself with a sword hanging by just one hair over his head; DA-AM, 'arm of the wild bull' perhaps? This combination does appear with DAM in the lexical entries. Suffice to say here that DA, the arm of Talos, with the rocks he is holding in both hands, does not bode well for sailors. Dao is another spelling of Tao.

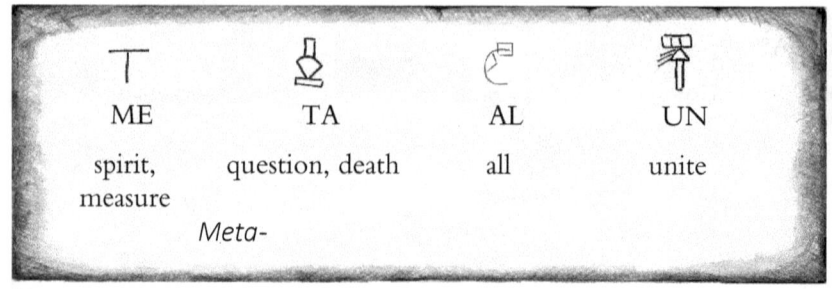

All of this leads to ME-TA, the spirit and question of death, while remaining within the domain of the alchemist and magician who is mixing, mixing...

> *Meta- word-forming element meaning 1. 'after, behind,' 2. 'changed, altered,' 3. 'higher, beyond;' from Greek meta (prep.) 'in the midst of; in common with; by means of; between; in pursuit or quest of; after, next after, behind,' in compounds most often meaning 'change' of place, condition, etc. from PIE root.*

The Greek coin has AL between the legs of the figure, while both versions of the bird, TAL and DAL, but also the Idigna bird, DALLA, incorporate this symbol. AL was identified as the alchemist's bellows in the previous chapter and, as such, fits neatly into the Sumerian combination that gave us metal: ME-TA-AL, between the spirit and the force of the bellows, there is change (see meaning of 'meta' above) into (the three symbols 'all' together) METAL. Contained in a word that we know so well without ever dismantling its parts, melting them down, is the full description of an alchemical process . I wonder who that was...

> *If that, indeed, the 'many' be the 'good,' and not the 'one,' in which are 'all.' Indeed the difference between the two is found in their agreement; 'All' is of 'One' or 'One' is 'All.' So closely bound is each to other, that neither can be parted from its mate.*[93]

It might also be that this giant is responsible for our word 'tall':

> Tall: 'high in stature,' 1520s, probably from Middle English tal 'handsome, good-looking; valiant; lively in speech; large, big; humble, meek,' from Old English getæl 'prompt, active,' from Germanic *(ge)-tala- (source also of Old High German gi-zal 'quick,' Gothic un-tals 'indocile').

UN

The UN of Gothic un-tals (see 'tall' above) is an interesting part of this etymology leading to 'indocile' as is the surprising 'humble' and 'meek' suggested for the later English 'tall'. I u̲nderstand that 'un-' is a negative here corresponding to the 'in' of 'indocile' – it undoes something. It's the prefix used to show reversal, deprivation and removal according to etymological dictionaries. Gothic un-tals would be 'not-tall' which equates to 'not docile'. So small is fiercer…? Tall as synonymous of docile corresponds with the later Middle English 'humble, meek' applied to someone who is otherwise particularly noted for their imposing and rather lovely appearance. A humble giant! Quite unexpected and not at all suited to our impression of Talon/Talos. Note that this version of un-, the undoing, is opposed to the Sumerian UN of unity; the land and the people, being one… or not? But understanding UN-TAL as the Gothic version of Sumero-Greek TAL-UN, the reason for the given meaning of 'indocile' becomes more evident. Quite a puzzle!

There is a curious reference to prefix un- in the Etymonline version:

> Un- : The most prolific of English prefixes, freely and widely used in Old English, where it forms more than 1,000 compounds. <u>It underwent a mass extinction in early Middle English</u> but emerged with renewed vigor in the 16c. to form compounds with native and imported words.

Early Middle English would be around 1100-1450 AD. Why was that? And what's it to be? Unique as in 'alone in a crowd', united as in 'all together as one' or un- as in the 'undoing of it all'? They're all given as stemming from the same PIE root.

Incorporating TAL into ME on one hand and TAL with UN on the other yields an enigmatic result:

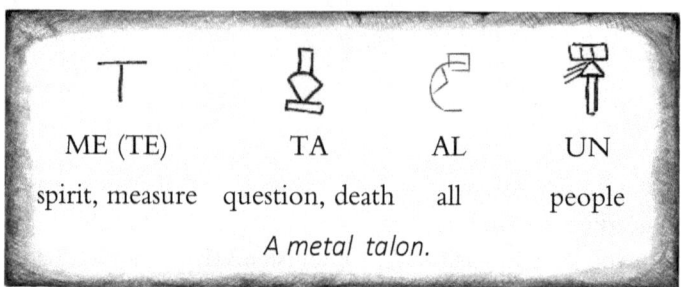

ME (TE)	TA	AL	UN
spirit, measure	question, death	all	people

A metal talon.

There are other levels to this combination of Sumerian symbols, the story of Talon, and the image on the Greek coin. If he is a bull, as the horns on his head and some Greek texts suggest, he can be linked to the constellation of Taurus, another name beginning with the TA 'question of death' syllable, and his stones become boulders (see etymology of boulder pn page 96) or perhaps meteorites. Is there a connection to be made between Talon, the metal man with horns, and the meteor shower known as the Taurids?

> *Meteor: late 15c., 'any atmospheric phenomenon,' from Middle French meteore (13c.) and directly from Medieval Latin meteorum (nominative meteora), from Greek ta meteora 'the celestial phenomena, things in heaven above,' (...) (see meta-) + -aoros 'lifted, hovering in air,' related to aeirein 'to raise' from PIE root.*

Crete

On another related subject, Talos throws his rocks from the shores of the island that we know today as Crete. He circles the shores of the island three times every day for the purpose of protecting it from invaders. The origin of the place name, Crete, is unknown but thought to be that of Kres, father of Talon.

> *The inhabitants of Crete claim that the oldest people of the island were those who are known as Eteocretans, who were sprung from the soil itself, and that their king, who was called Cres, was responsible for the greatest number of the most important discoveries made in the island which contributed to the improvement of the social life of mankind.[94]*
>
> *One of the Cretans, a prophet of their own, said, "Cretans are always liars, evil beasts, lazy gluttons. This testimony is true. Therefore rebuke them sharply, that they may be sound in the faith.[94]*

An analysis of the name Kres through a Sumerian lens suggests a link to KIRIS (see page 221) or perhaps KIR which can also be read as GIR. The names of both Crete and Greece come to mind. KIR/GIR, symbol of the fish, is discussed in chapter 20. It's interesting to note that the name of the people is associated with lying through the above biblical reference, most probably a reference to a Greek prophet called Epimenides who was said to have lived around the 7th century BC.

> *Cretan: Old English Cretense (plural), "natives or inhabitants of Crete, from Latin Cretanus (singular); see Crete. They were proverbial in ancient times as liars; compare Greek noun kretismos "lying," literally "Cretan behavior,"*

17

The Sun, the Lion, and the Pyramid

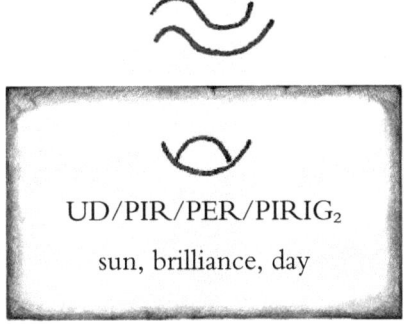

UD/PIR/PER/PIRIG₂

sun, brilliance, day

UD is given as 'day, heat, summer, sun' 529 times at the earliest Uruk IV period, 3350 to 3200 BC. It bears a striking resemblance to the Egyptian hieroglyph Akhet which is commonly understood to mean 'horizon' or 'mountain of light' and forms part of one name of the Great Sphinx in Egypt: Hor em akhet.

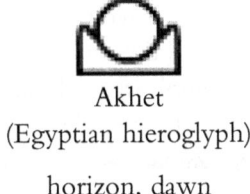

Akhet

(Egyptian hieroglyph)

horizon, dawn

Sumerian PIR or PER, another phonetic value of the sun symbol, is the origin of the word 'pyramid' and of Greek Perseus, whose mother was imprisoned in a bronze chamber to prevent him from being born. It was Zeus, in the form of a shower of gold, who penetrated both chamber and mother. See the adventures of Perseus in a new light thanks to the alchemical aspect of Zeus on page 168. Zeus was said by the Greeks to be the son of Hermes.

> *Pyramid: 1550s (earlier in Latin form piramis, late 14c.), from French pyramide (Old French piramide 'obelisk, stela,' 12c.), from Latin pyramides, plural of pyramis 'one of the pyramids of Egypt,' from Greek pyramis (plural pyramides) 'a pyramid,' apparently an alteration of Egyptian pimar 'pyramid.'*

According to the lexical lists, the phonetic form PIR stems from a combination of PI and IR/ER.

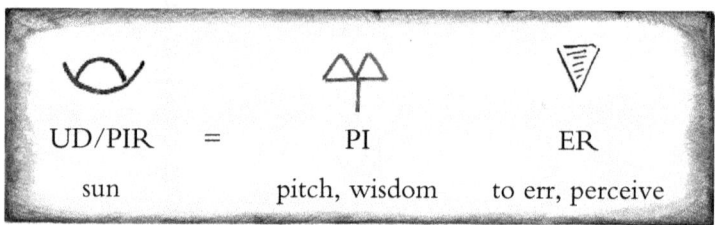

PI

PI is given as 'to deduct' 5 times. 'To expand', 'reason', 'plan', 'wisdom', and 'understanding' are also given for that early period. PI refers to perfection in all domains; musical, mathematical, or the written word. From the two given meanings of deduction and expansion, the essential idea of PI as the symbol of adjustment to make perfect is apparent. Sumerian scribes copying from damaged tablets would add the two symbols HE-PI, a hole in the pitch, to indicate that there was a break and thus an imperfection in the work.[95] Pitch is the word I favour for the symbol. It would have had a more general sense at its origin, broader than 'musical', extended to resonance.

> *Pitch: 1520s, Meaning 'act of throwing' is attested from 1833. Meaning 'act of plunging headfirst' is from 1762; sense of 'slope, degree, inclination' is from 1540s; musical sense is from 1590s; but the connection of these is obscure.*
>
> *Perfect: early 15c. alteration of Middle English parfit (c. 1300), from Old French parfit 'finished, completed, ready' (11c.), from Latin perfectus 'completed, excellent, accomplished, exquisite,' past participle of perficere 'accomplish, finish, complete,' from per 'completely' (see per) + combining form of facere 'to make, to do' from PIE root.*

The PI symbol varies, sometimes resembling a pair of rabbit or dog ears, or as two vertical lines sticking up above SAG, the (human) head, occasionally resembling a geometrical shape of two equal triangles with the radius of an invisible circle pointing downwards and, on other tablets, appearing to take the form of a tuning fork, although the two prongs seem a bit too far apart for that – perhaps a touch of wishful thinking. Here below two examples[96]:

PI is the third symbol of the Tree of Consciousness and Knowledge where it represents 'knowledge'. An example of PI used in a musical context is found in the proverb cited below[97]:

There is cause and effect in the above proverb. PI, the pitch, corresponds to or becomes AN, sky and lightness; a particularly 'joyful' note or pitch will have the effect of lifting a horizontal form, a roof, skyward. PI with EL, the notion of purity of sound, appears in another long Sumerian proverb and again in *The Story of Sukurru*. Given as 'his heartstrings stretches' in line 35, the literal translation would be 'the pure pitch' that provokes extreme emotion. See KI-EL on page 87 for EL.

ER/IR
ER has the given meaning 'smell' but also 'to go' and extended by me as 'to wander'. ER fits into this picture of a pyramid, of perfection, and perhaps of sound, by broadening 'smell' to 'sense', 'to experience' encompassed in the overall meaning 'to perceive', from PER, the sun and pyramid. See page 195.

> *Err: c. 1300, from Old French errer 'go astray, lose one's way; make a mistake; transgress,' from Latin errare 'wander, go astray,' figuratively 'be in error,' from PIE root*
>
> *Perceive: c. 1300, via Anglo-French parceif, Old North French *perceivre (Old French perçoivre) 'perceive, notice, see; recognize, understand,' from Latin percipere 'obtain, gather, seize entirely, take possession of,' also, figuratively, 'to grasp with the mind, learn, comprehend,' literally 'to take entirely,' from per 'thoroughly' (see per) + capere 'to grasp, take,' from PIE root.*

The Lion or Lioness

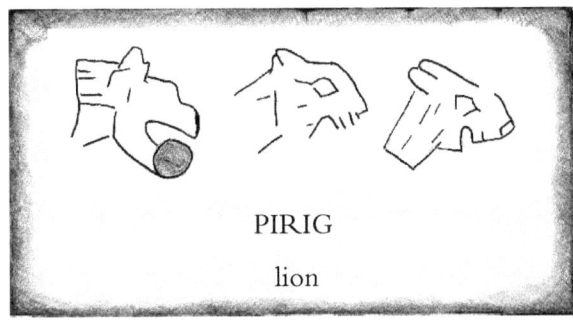

PIRIG

lion

PIRIG is given as 'lion' 12 times and once as 'strength'. The symbol, a head and gaping mouth, perhaps a lioness since there is no obvious mane, appears in photos on 24 tablets at the Uruk IV period, ca. 3350 to 3200 BC. Above are three examples[98] copied from the tablets, the first with a round mark stamped at the level of the mouth. In some later examples, the mouth is turned very much towards the ground with a strangely prominent eye turned to the sky.

The sun symbol UD/PIR, also having the phonetic value $PIRIG_2$, is related through that sound to the Sumerian 'lion' from the earliest period. That gives a most intriguing threesome; the sun, the lion and, for both, the first syllable of the pyramid. An entry for PIRIG in the lexical tablets gives it opposite its three components: PI-RI-IG:

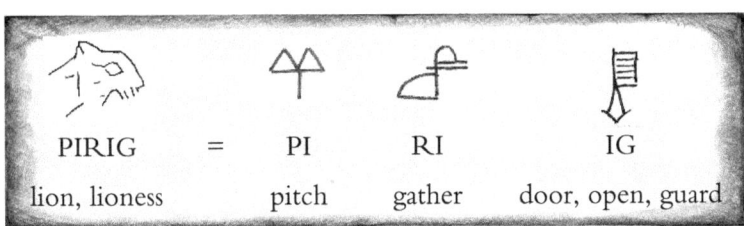

PIRIG	=	PI	RI	IG
lion, lioness		pitch	gather	door, open, guard

PI with RI give 'peri', origin of Greek peri-. See page 112 for 'meter'. The distance around a circle, the circumference, corresponds to its perimeter. PE-RI is also discussed in chapter 19. PI as 'musical pitch' with RI as 'gather' indicate a connection between Greek peri- and a gathering of sound, perhaps a combination of notes, a harmony, birdsong.

> *Peri-: word-forming element meaning 'around, about, enclosing,' from Greek peri (prep.) 'around, about, beyond,' cognate with Sanskrit pari 'around, about, through,' Latin per, from PIE root.*
>
> *Pre- : word-forming element meaning 'before,' from Old French pre- and Medieval Latin pre-, both from Latin prae (adverb and preposition) 'before in time or place,' from PIE *peri-*
>
> *Prior: 'earlier,' 1714, from Latin prior 'former, previous, first;' figuratively 'superior, better;' as a noun 'forefather; superior rank;' comparative of Old Latin pri 'before,' from PIE*

PIR, the sun, and PIRIG, the lioness, lie at the origin of pyr-, pir-, 'pre-' leading to words like 'prior' and 'primordial', a suffix conveying the most ancient of times. This also sits well with the first syllable of Prometheus, whose name is said to mean 'forethought'. See chapter 11.

IG/IK is given as 'door' 8 times, as 'open', and 'to guard' but also intriguingly 'to be available' and 'at hand'. This is the inversion of KI, the 'place' or 'key'. PI-RI-IG might translate to 'of the pyramid or perimeter to guard (the door)'. The lion guards the entrance. The lion or lioness is on hand, guardian of the sun. Below is another detail from the Narmer palette with an image that corresponds particularly well to symbols RI, the bird, with IG, the door.

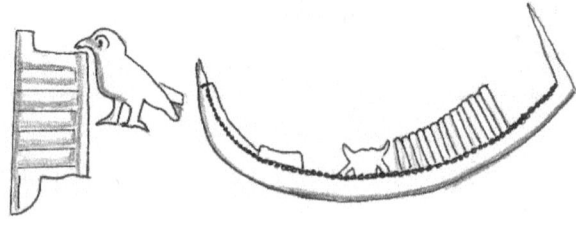

With all of the above, my thoughts have long since turned to Egypt, to the Giza plateau, its pyramids and to the great Sphinx, the stone lion. The symbols mentioned here appear on clay tablets that are proven to have existed in the 4th millennium BC. If all the dating is correct, they precede the supposed date of completion of the Great Pyramid by the pharaoh Khufu by hundreds of years. This said, there is nothing in this analysis that can prove beyond doubt that the Sumerian texts referred to structures past or present at Giza - even if I am convinced that this was the case. But neither can it be said that the information here is born of wishful thinking.

There is another PIRIG lion symbol which has a small sun symbol integrated, further demonstrating the ties between the two. It takes the phonetic forms PIRIG$_3$/UG/UK and is given with the added meaning of 'fury' at 2500 BC. UG/UK can be linked to the following etymologies, never forgetting that the letter 'O' is non-existent in the Sumerian dictionaries:

> Oct-, word-forming element meaning "eight," from Greek okta, okt-, from PIE root.
>
> Oculist: "eye doctor," 1610s, from French oculiste (16c.), from Latin oculus "an eye" from PIE root.
>
> Occult: 1530s, "secret, not divulged," from Middle French occulte and directly from Latin occultus "hidden, concealed, secret," past participle of oculere "cover over, conceal," from assimilated form of ob "over" (see ob-) + a verb related to celare "to hide," from PIE root *kel- "to cover, conceal, save."

The existence of an etymological link between 'oc' and 'ob' is suggested in the above. Yet the sounds are quite different and 'ob' more likely stems from Sumerian UB, the pentagram symbol, which has meanings including 'corner' and 'recess'. My interpretation of the above etymology is that the 'oc' of 'oculus' stemming from the lion symbol might be a reference to the gaze of the Sphinx towards the rising sun. But it might be that there is a link between UG, the lion-sun symbol and UB/UP. See pages 264 and 265 for Latin operculum and the link to PER.

There is yet another PIRIG, this one appearing on the CDLI photos with its mouth gaping over symbol ZA, 'sound', 'noise', 'bead' or 'four'. It has the phonetic forms AZ/AS/AZA/ASA. AZ might thus represent a combination of sun, lion, and sound. Note that this is the inversion of ZA.[99]

PI-RIG

A couple of lexical entries for PIRIG give PI with RIG:

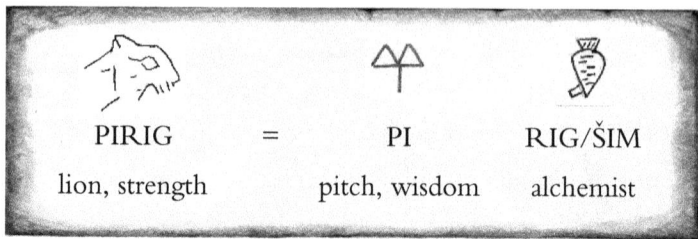

| PIRIG | = | PI | RIG/ŠIM |
| lion, strength | | pitch, wisdom | alchemist |

RIG is the brewer of beer discussed in chapter 15. In the context of PIRIG, the fiery lion or lioness, the combination might represent the perfecting or perfection of the alchemical process.

> *Rig: late 15c., originally nautical, 'to fit with sails,' probably from a Scandinavian source (compare Danish, Norwegian rigge 'to equip,' Swedish rigga 'to rig, harness'), though these may be from English; perhaps ultimately from PIE *reig- 'to bind.'*

What could be the connection between ŠIM, the alchemist, and the rig, the sailing equipment of a ship? It might come from the notion of enabling movement, the mast, ropes, sails and all the equipment enabling the lifting of the ship to the sky: the mutation of ingredients in the alchemist's pot, the brew that is necessary in order to take flight in a celestial ship. Looking for RIG in the lexical entries threw up just one breakdown, lodged in the centre of a longer word and as expected: RI-IG, the bird and the door.

There is a bird by the door of the Narmer palette, next to the celestial bark. See the illustration on page 188. Perhaps just coincidence but RI with IG gives 'the bird who guards or opens the door'. And it looks like the Narmer ship had a bull – and perhaps even a reed façade – on board.

There are also birds surrounding the rigging of Odysseus' ship on the famous Greek Siren vase in the British Museum, a detail of which was used to illustrate *The Story of Sukurru* (see chapter 15). That is the ship named the Clay Eye, from the symbols ŠI-IM that led to ŠIM that lead to RIG…

18

Hermes and the Crystal Heresy

There is no obvious agreement amongst scholars past or present on there being just one original Hermes with the additional title Trismegistus, meaning 'three times great'; it has been suggested through secondary sources that there were three:

> *There were three Hermes. The name Hermes is a title. (...) he whom the Hebrews called Enoch, whose name in Arabic is Idris. The Harranians declare his prophethood.*[100]

The later Greek god Hermes is generally understood as the deified form of the original Egyptian figure who would also have been Egyptian Thoth. The following quote, with its reference to alchemy, gives an overview:

> *... the first man who spoke about the science of this art was Hermes, the wise man and Babylonian who moved to Egypt...and about the Art he wrote a number of books... He observed the specific and spiritual properties of phenomena and his knowledge of the art of alchemy was substantiated by his investigation and observation. He also knew about the making of talismans and wrote many books about them...Hermes wrote about the stars, incantations, and things incorporeal (pneumata)...*[101]

Over the millennia, a mountain of confusing information has been amassed on the subject of Hermes Trismegistus and his writings, known as the Corpus Hermeticum. There have been many theories about who he was, if he even existed and when - enough to make your head spin. I prefer to cut to the chase and stay with the essential subject which is Sumerian as the founding language. Hermes is the central piece of the puzzle connecting some of the other names that figure in this book. Hermes was documented in ancient texts dating to the beginning of our era as the prophet of the Sabians of Harran. That point is important since it constitutes an ancient link between the people of the region in northern Mesopotamia and the Giza plateau in Egypt. It should also be remembered that the Sabians had their home at a very short distance from Gobekli Tepe. This short quote from the 1st century AD offers a fascinating clue, the possibility of a unique pagan culture stretching back over many millennia:

> *In a book of the Sabians called Al Hatifi...are ascribed to them wonders of incantation, enchantment, knots, pictures and pendants... and images of animals cut on stones... This book which is lost, deals with magic.*[102]

My suggestion is that Hermes Trismegistus is one central figure, one great wisdom teacher, who may or may not have been followed by similar figures, given the same epithet out of respect and because they carried out a similar mission. Did he originate in the region of Harran? The study here concentrates on the name itself. For the rest, we shall see – once the original language of that figure has been identified, who knows where it might lead?

The following is the etymology found on Etymonline:

> *Hermes: son of Zeus and Maia in Greek mythology; Olympian messenger and god of commerce, markets, and roads; protector of herdsmen, travelers, and rogues; giver of good luck, god of secret dealings, and conductor of the dead. from Greek Hermes, a word of unknown origin.*
>
> *Hermetic: 1630s "dealing with occult science or alchemy," from Latin hermeticus, from Greek Hermes, god of science and art (among other things), who was identified by Neoplatonists, mystics, and alchemists with the Egyptian god Thoth as Hermes Trismegistos "Thrice-Great Hermes," who supposedly invented the process of making a glass tube airtight (a process in alchemy) using a secret seal. Hence, "completely sealed" (c. 1600, implied in hermetically).*

If Hermes was such an important figure in Egypto-Greek mythology, to my knowledge it has not yet been recognised anywhere that he was already renowned in Sumerian writings. The officialised translations of Sumerian literary texts give many names along the way but not that of Hermes. To succeed in injecting him into the history of Sumer would be the equivalent of a metallic giant hurling boulders into an ocean. It would create unprecedented and all-engulfing waves, a historical tsunami. Nevertheless, it's more than time to resuscitate the Great Magician through the analysis of his name, to give him his rightful place in the common histories of Mesopotamia and Egypt and to rediscover something of his essence through the earliest writings that we possess. But first, a few points to ponder:

Hermes gave his name to stone artefacts called 'herma' that once bordered roads and were supposed to act as his substitutes in bringing luck to travellers. Apparently, the earliest form of them was simply a pile of stones onto which passers-by would add a pebble here and there. It's written that oil was also poured to anoint them, but no reason given for that. Versions of the herma seen in museums today are large rectangular blocks of stone with a carved head on top, presumably that of Hermes, and on some - very strangely - male genitals carved in bas or high relief onto the appropriate area of an otherwise unadorned block. No attempt was made to carve the rest of the body.

Greek Hermes had a good number of attributes, including the winged sandals, the talaria mentioned on page 174 (from TAL, the bird), that served him well in his role as messenger of the gods.

> Herald: 'messenger, envoy,' late 13c. (in Anglo-Latin); c. 1200 as a surname, from Anglo-French heraud, Old French heraut, hiraut (12c.), (...) from PIE root.

Hermes is also well-known for his magical wand, the caduceus or kerykeion, a staff with two interlocking snakes and a pair of wings at the top. A Mesopotamian origin has been suggested for that image.[103]

HER

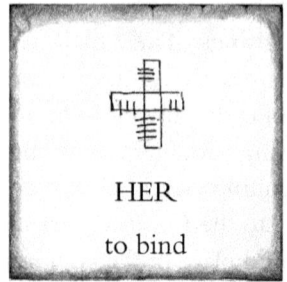

HER

to bind

There is no better place to begin the grand task of breathing new life into the great Hermes Trismegistus than to consider the Sumerian symbol with the phonetic value of HER and HIR. Its appearance and meaning provide an intriguing point at which to begin. HER is given as 'to bind' 405 times. Unfortunately, there are no early photographic examples of it on CDLI. Above is a copy from a handwritten list of symbols discovered on tablets found during the excavations at Ur in the 1930s. It was published in 1935 under the reference UET 2^{104} by the epigraphist, Reverend Eric Burrows. This is the only hand-drawn example of HER that I have so far been able to find. Although it only dates back to the ED I-II period of 2900-2700 BC, what is exciting is the numbering on it; 4 strokes on the lower section while number 3 is repeated on the left and top, and 2 is given on the right. It may be that the scribe was lazy and threw in a few strokes at random, slightly crossing the outer lines, to indicate the binding. I'm not referring to the Reverend who, I daresay, took great care in the copying of it. I don't think it's the case. The strokes look neatly done. Unfortunately, nothing can be ruled out or confirmed until there is at least one more example available from the same or, dare I hope, an earlier timeframe when the symbols were not already veering towards cuneiform abstraction. Fingers crossed.

HER/HIR is broken down in the ancient lexical entries in two ways. The sound originates with HE_2-IR/ER and HI-IR/ER. That is why it's possible to read the symbol of the cross as either HER or HIR:

a)

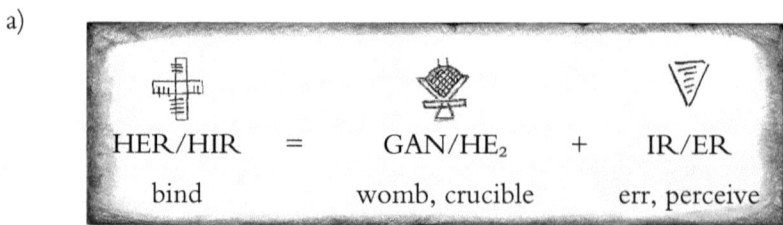

HER/HIR = GAN/HE_2 + IR/ER

bind   womb, crucible   err, perceive

b)

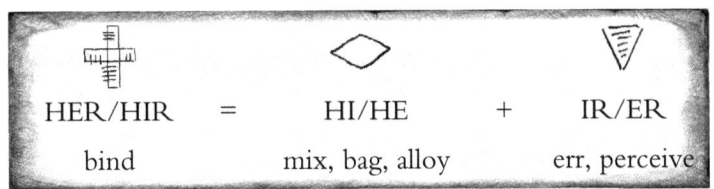

HER/HIR	=	HI/HE	+	IR/ER
bind		mix, bag, alloy		err, perceive

GAN, mentioned in the first chapter as the Matriarchal womb, can also be understood as the entrance to the Milky Way and as the alchemist's crucible. With one lexical entry giving GAN/HE$_2$ in first position and the other giving HI, the connection between the two is obviously the mixing of elements in the crucible. GAN is, if not a synonym, closely linked to HI, founding symbol of 'hymen' amongst others. See HI as an element of MEHIDA on page 117.

ER, also discussed in the context of PIR/PER, is given as a form of the verb 'to go' 7 times at 2500 BC. The Platonic character, Er, sits well with the notion of perceiving and experiencing something that is beyond common comprehension. Did Plato use Er as a name because he knew it to be the symbol for wandering and experiencing? Did he use it intentionally because he had knowledge of more ancient writings? At this point in the study, the answer seems obvious to me. You must decide for yourself.

The story of Er appears in the final section of Plato's Republic. It's told by Socrates to Glaucon:

> But in what manner or by what means he returned to the body he could not say; only, in the morning, awaking suddenly, he found himself lying on the pyre. And thus, Glaucon, the tale has been saved and has not perished, and will save us if we are obedient to the word spoken; and we shall pass safely over the river of Forgetfulness and our soul will not be defiled.[105]

Er went through the process of death and re-emerged to tell the tale; a moralizing story about the choices made during life and their effect on future reincarnations. This concept corresponds to the two possible breakdowns of HER to GAN-ER and HI-ER, a return to and a wandering inside the cosmic matriarchal womb. ER is also source of Greek Eros, with final UŠ, Sumerian symbol of virility.

> *Eros: god of love, late 14c., from Greek eros (plural erotes), "god or personification of love," literally "love," from eran "to love," erasthai "to love, desire," which is of uncertain origin.*

HI-ER, HE-ER, HE-IR, HI-IR
Quite a lot of words take their source here. A few examples:

> *Hierophant: 'expounder of sacred mysteries,' 1670s, from Late Latin hierophantes, from Greek hierophantes 'one who teaches the rites of sacrifice and worship,' 'one who shows sacred things,' from hieros 'sacred,' from PIE root.*
>
> *Hierarchy: from Greek hierarkhia, from hierarkhes 'leader of sacred rites, high priest'*
>
> *Hieroglyph: from Greek hieroglyphos*
>
> *Here: Old English her 'in this place, where one puts himself; at this time, toward this place,' from Proto-Germanic pronominal stem *hi- (from PIE) Cognate with Old Saxon her, Old Norse, Gothic her, Swedish här, Middle Dutch, Dutch hier, Old High German hiar, German hier.*

HI-ER gives the origin of Greek hieros and hierogamy, the concept of sacred sexuality and rituals linked to fertility found in 'hieros gamos'. Note the use of HI, partial origin of 'hymen' and HE_2/GAN for the womb.

HER/KIRID/KIRIS/KEŠ₂

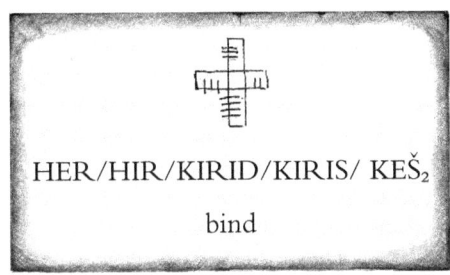

HER/HIR/KIRID/KIRIS/ KEŠ₂

bind

The symbol of the bound cross is also given as KIRID, KIRIS and KEŠ₂ among other phonetic values. The most commonly cited in academic texts is KEŠ₂, with lexical entries under that phonetic value taking up nine pages of the ePSD site. It must be said that the act of binding found in this symbol could have taken many practical forms from weaving of cloth to insulating buildings, waterproofing boats or tying up prisoners. There is also the notion of creating a boundary around an object or place that might explain the large number of entries in a pragmatic fashion. But there is more to this cross than meets the eye. It's the manifestation of a boundary that goes beyond earthly considerations.

There are quite a few collocations to be found in the old texts and lexical entries for the various phonetic values. I generally refer to the symbol as HER on the understanding that, whatever the sound of it, the image remains the same. At the same time, HER is very closely related to if not a synonym of symbol EZEN which is discussed on page 231. All this to say that it isn't possible to analyse everything or take every form and collocation into account. That is why this section focuses on the breakdown of the main phonetic values of each symbol, the resulting symbols with their earliest given meanings and the etymological possibilities of each.

I have tried to keep this analysis as clear as possible, but, from that apparently straightforward cross of HER, there emanates an interlocking web of symbols and meanings. Individually, they are fascinating but, from time to time, it's useful to stand back and look at the whole. That's why a family tree of the symbols has been included on page 212. The analysis is divided into two main sections for the alternative phonetic values attributed to HER:

HER/KIRID on p.198 and HER/KIRIS on p.221.

HER/KIRID

The lexical entries opposite KIRID lead to a mysterious place. KIRID breaks down to KI-RI-ID (RI-ID shown to be the breakdown of RID on another list):

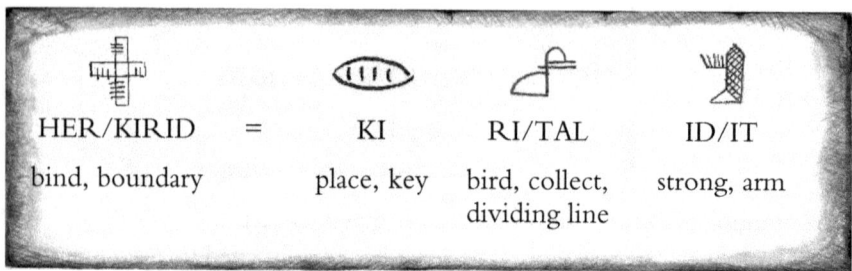

RI-ID associated with KI, the place, might translate to 'Place of the bird with a strong wing'. Strong might be the adjective for the bird and its talons. ID or IT has the meaning of an arm or wing. The association of talon and wing perhaps indicates an emblematic bird, strong in every respect. The Place of the Mighty Bird.

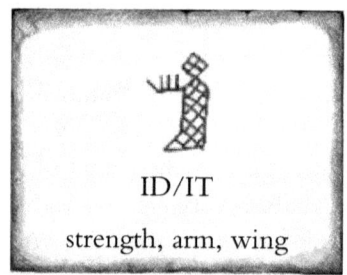

Above is a particularly detailed rendering of ID copied from the drawings of proto-cuneiform script done by German archaeologist Adam Falkenstein in 1936[106]. It appears to be a combination with the basic ID as a cross-hatched DU, foot symbol. There might be an IB feather protruding to the left and at the tip a LU, sheep and light, symbol perhaps indicating four directions or meant to symbolise the moon.

In *The Story of Sukurru*, ID appears several times as the 'strong arm' of KAL, which is a symbol linked to time and personified as the lamassu, the stone bull man who sports an impressive pair of wings. The name 'lamassu' is taken from the Assyrian phonetic value ascribed to the cuneiform version of the original

KAL symbol. ID and KAL appear twice together on lines 63 and 110, giving 'the strong arm of the lamassu' or 'the strong wing of the stone bull man'.

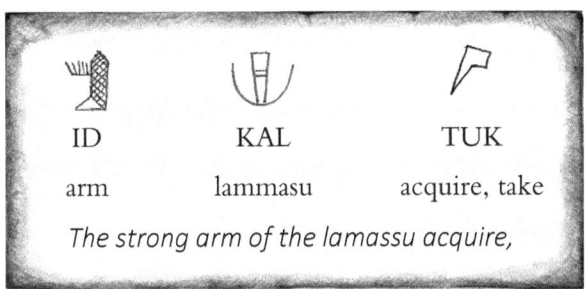

ID	KAL	TUK
arm	lammasu	acquire, take

The strong arm of the lamassu acquire,

Line 110 appears in the context of the orders given to Noah for the waterproofing of the ark. KAL is the unfortunate figure who will be left behind with the promise of becoming the leader – once the ark has left. It's quite clear that there's a sense of idiocy and clumsiness involved in the actions of the character, but that's the humour of it; never forgetting that the lamassu figurine, a reclining bull, was buried by the front door of Mesopotamian homes, apparently to bring luck. Perhaps it didn't always work.

Ides: 'middle day of a Roman month,' early 14c., from Old French ides (12c.), from Latin idus (plural) 'the ides,' a word perhaps of Etruscan origin.

Calends: c. 1200, 'a day as reckoned back from the first of the following month' (as fourteenth calend of March = February 16th), from Latin kalendae 'first day of the month' in the Roman calendar. See Calendar

Calendar: This is from calare "to announce solemnly, call out," as the priests did in proclaiming the new moon that marked the calends, from PIE root.

RID

RI with ID is the breakdown of RID/MES, the seal. Working backwards from the name Hermes also leads to symbol RID/MES:

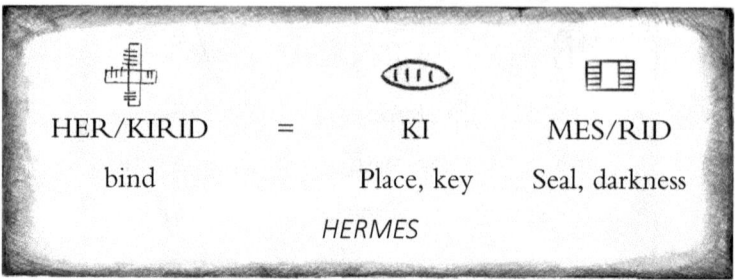

MES

Symbol MES is given as 'cylinder seal' and 'sealed tablet' 12 times from 2500 BC. A cylinder seal and a sealed tablet are not the same. Cylinder seals are small, round artefacts made of hard stone. They were carved to form impressions when rolled over damp clay and a hole was sometimes pierced through to allow for a string to be threaded, the seal to be worn around the neck. But if 'sealed' is the adjective and 'tablet' the noun, I take this to mean that one or more tablets were hidden from view or that they were hermetically sealed. The only other solutions would be that this description is an error or that it's a formula used only by academics, a classification to which I am not privy.

Between HER 'to bind' or 'bound' and MES which is the seal, there can be no doubt that we are sliding sideways into the domain of the Great Hermes, passing through the Magician's boundaries.

MES is given 7 times as 'hero' and 'manly', presumably an attribute of Hermes. Heroe is just one more Greek word of previously unknown origin.

> Hero: late 14c., 'man of superhuman strength or physical courage,' from Old French heroe (14c., Modern French héros), from Latin heros (plural heroes) 'hero, demi-god, illustrious man,' from Greek heros (plural heroes) 'demi-god,' a variant singular of which was heroe. This is of uncertain origin; perhaps originally 'defender, protector' and from PIE root

MES is given as 'blackness', 'black spot', and 'black wood' 6 times at the same period. Collocated with prefix GEŠ/GIŠ, the tree or wood, MES is given 9 times as 'tree'. GIŠ is the most recurrent symbol of the entire language, understood to be the prefix for all words relating to wood. In *The Story of Sukurru*, it's the first symbol of the Tree of Consciousness and Knowledge.

MES appears over several pages in the lexical entries, broken down in two ways: as ME-ES/IS or ME-EŠ₃ (ME-AB). Although it isn't listed as one of the versions of MES, I will add ME-EŠ as a third possible combination. There is no obvious reason for it to be left out of the phonetic values here.

a) <u>ME-ES/IS/GES/GIS/ GIŠ</u>

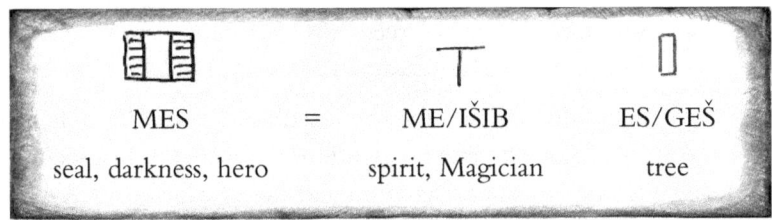

MES	=	ME/IŠIB	ES/GEŠ
seal, darkness, hero		spirit, Magician	tree

As phonetic IŠIB, symbol ME is given as 'sorcerer', 'magician' and 'spell' along with various 'priests' 7 times. ES and IS are phonetic values of GEŠ/GIŠ, translating the above to 'Magician of the tree'. ME combines with TE to signify measurement (See ME-TE on page 112), giving 'measurement of the tree'. ME is found numerous times with GIŠ in the lexical entries, usually as GIŠ-ME.

Unwinding the syllables and symbols from HER and KIRID has revealed MES at the first level and the ME-GIS of Trismegistus at the second level. It has led to a sealed tablet, a hero, to a dark place, to spirits and spells, a magician, a measure, and to a tree...which in turn leads to other similar sounds:

> *Tree: Old English treo, treow 'tree' (also 'timber, wood, beam, log, stake'), from Proto-Germanic *trewam (source also of Old Frisian tre, Old Saxon trio, Old Norse tre, Gothic triu 'tree'), from PIE root.*
>
> *Three (and tri-): Old English þreo, fem. and neuter (masc. þri, þrie), from Proto-Germanic *thrijiz (source also of Old Saxon thria, Old Frisian thre, Middle Dutch and Dutch drie, Old High German dri, German drei, Old Norse þrir, Danish tre), from nominative plural of PIE root.*

GEŠ breaks down to GI with EŠ in the lexical lists:

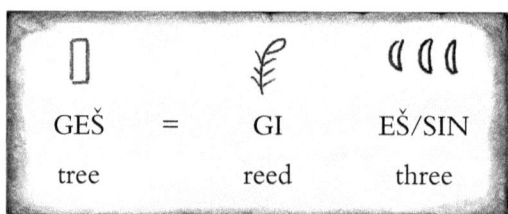

GEŠ	=	GI	EŠ/SIN
tree		reed	three

How many branches does it take to turn a stalk into a tree? Surely at least three. In *The Story of Sukurru*, line 58 mentions the reed, GI, in a section that is an obvious reference to the preparation and use of cannabis. KA-NA-AB gave Persian kanab. (See page 167.)

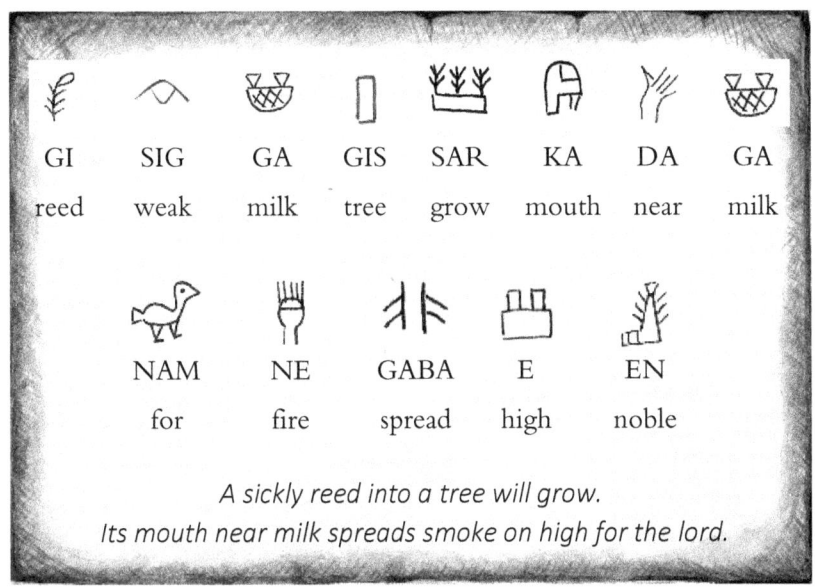

A sickly reed into a tree will grow.
Its mouth near milk spreads smoke on high for the lord.

And a further breakdown of HER/KIRID into KI-RI-ID will add our bird, RI/TAL, along with its claws, its talons, and its collect/release skills into the mix. The bird has always been in the thick of things where trees are concerned. See TAL in the chapter on Greek Talon.

b) <u>ME- EŠ₃/AB</u>

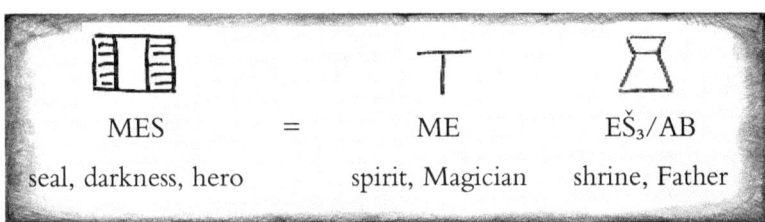

This time the combination stems from ME with AB, the father figure who is also the ocean and underground water. It might translate to the 'spirit of the father' or even to 'the measurements of the shrine given by an ancestor' if the ME-TE combination is considered. See page 19 for AB, the gully inspector. See page 285 for AB-GAL, the Great Father, where ME is integral to his epithet.

c) ME-EŠ/SIN

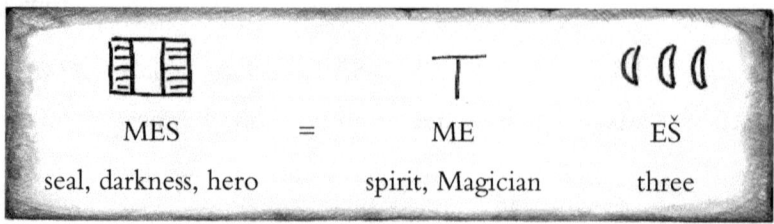

MES	=	ME	EŠ
seal, darkness, hero		spirit, Magician	three

Finally, in the analysis of the MES of HER-MES, there remains the phonetic value MEŠ, from the two symbols ME and EŠ. With ME-EŠ, Hermes Trismegistus becomes complete. At this level, we find the 'three' of 'Three Times Great' hidden in the 'mes' of Hermes. ME-EŠ might translate to 'the three spirits', 'the three spells' or 'the Magician/Magic of the Three'. This combination appears at the end of an enigmatic section, on line 268 of *The Story of Sukurru* where it was translated to *the spirit of the three*. See page 156.

MEŠ is not given as being related to MES, the sealed tablet, despite the obvious connection through both ME and the sound IS/ES/IŠ. MEŠ shows up on ePSD only as ME-U.U.U (shown here above). However, ME also has the phonetic value of MEŠ$_2$ and is combined with EŠ on numerous lexical entries. Also see page 219.

EŠ/SIN
three

If I were overly purist, I would not allow myself to mention that phonetic SIN, the number three, is symbolic of the three phases of the moon and the three ages of humanity, and that this Sumerian symbol is the origin of the name of the moon god Sin. It can also be found here hidden inside the name of Hermes through EŠ. It all comes down to the difference between an S and a Š… May readers of this decide for themselves.

GES-HER

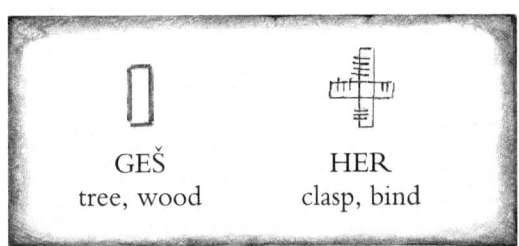

It's noteworthy that a similar situation occurs for GEŠ, the tree, where the phonetic value GES is the only form to be left out of the numerous possible pronunciations of the symbol. For that reason, the Arabic name for Giza, El-ges-her, cannot be entirely matched to its Sumerian origin without the risk of finger-pointing. IS and ES are alternative phonetic values for GIŠ/GEŠ/GIS, but GES is not given. Nor does GES correspond to any other symbol, which might have been a reasonable explanation for the situation and led me to leave all mention of this coincidence to one side.

Concerning El-ges-her, the two last symbols that correspond, in my view, to this name can be found together in various Sumerian writings and on the lexical lists. However, they are translated as the uninspiring 'hair clasp'. Presumably, that is the result of GEŠ as the prefix 'wooden' and HER/KIRID as 'clasp', with four examples given at the late 2000 BC mark. If GES is taken as noun, it might translate to the 'binding or boundary of the tree'. That description is somewhat reminiscent of the Hittite images showing T-shaped pillars bound in thread or cloth. But there is no evidence of GEŠ as anything other than wood.

MES/RID

Our word 'rid' is used only in the negative sense of getting rid of something unwanted these days, but it appears to have had a more positive connotation of freeing or releasing in the past.

> *Rid: c. 1200, 'clear (a space); set free, save,' from a Scandinavian source akin to Old Norse ryðja (past tense ruddi, past participle ruddr) 'to clear (land) of obstructions,' from Proto-Germanic *reudijan (source also of Old High German riuten,(...), from PIE root.*

Do the words 'read' and 'riddle' have their origins here? That would be appropriate too; KI-RID as 'The Place of the Riddle'. The phonetic form also appears as RIT which might relate to 'writ' and 'writing'. The Place to Read. The Key to the Writing… The Key to Writing in Riddles…

> *Write: Old English writan 'to score, outline, draw the figure of,' later 'to set down in writing' (class I strong verb; past tense wrat, past participle writen), from Proto-Germanic *writan 'tear, scratch' (source also of Old Frisian writa 'to write,' Old Saxon writan 'to tear, scratch, write,' Old Norse rita 'write, scratch, outline,'*
>
> *Rite: early 14c., from Latin ritus 'religious observance or ceremony, custom, usage,' perhaps from PIE root.*
>
> *Riddle: 'A word game or joke, comprising a question or statement couched in deliberately puzzling terms, (…) The first element is from Proto-Germanic *redaz-, from PIE root.*
>
> *Read: Old English rædan (West Saxon), redan (Anglian) 'to advise, counsel, persuade; discuss, deliberate; rule, guide; arrange, equip; forebode; read, explain; learn by reading; put in order' (related to ræd, red 'advice'), from Proto-Germanic *redan (...), from PIE root.*

With KI in first place of KI-RID, it might be considered as the key to reaching the sealed tablet, the key with which to read it or them. Both place and key are exciting finds.

MES/KIŠIB

Finally, MES has another phonetic value, KIŠIB, leading to yet another set of intriguing results:

a)

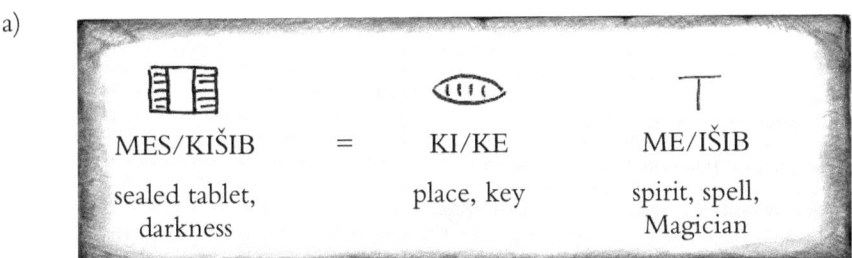

This time the combination is that of KI before ME. Looking back to the other results containing ME, it becomes possible and even reasonable to translate this hidden element, the MES of Hermes as:

- Magician of the Tree

- Magician of the Shrine

- Magician of the Three

KI-ME or KE-ME can be read as the Place of the Magician, a dark enclosed place, sealed within the confines of HER. KE-ME can also be read as The Magical Place, a title that is reminiscent of John Anthony West's documentary series 'Magical Egypt'. Because, of course, that is where the symbols of Hermes have long since taken us, to Egypt and to the work of a great Magician. KE with ME appear together on several tablets at the Uruk III period, 3200-3000 BC, one of which shown here below[107]:

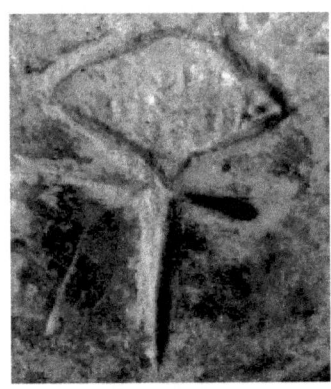

Kemet is the name given by the Greeks to ancient Egypt and is said to mean 'Black Land'. If an absolute link were to be made between the Sumerian and Greek with that meaning, then it would need to be the symbol KE with MI. Symbol MI, completely different in form from ME, has the meaning 'black'. I decided to look for both versions on the ancient lexical tablets. KE and MI don't appear side by side although they appear there within longer phrases and there is some evidence that MI and ME are sometimes interchangeable. However, KE-ME is found three times alone and in the correct order opposite the following combination:

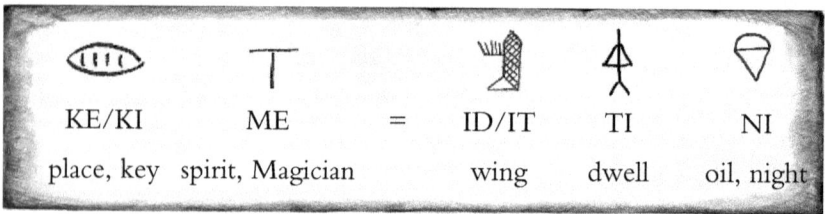

KE/KI	ME	=	ID/IT	TI	NI
place, key	spirit, Magician		wing	dwell	oil, night

It's not difficult to imagine that either ID/IT alone or a combination of IT with TI might be at the origin of the final consonant of Kemet. It's equally evident that there is an element of 'blackness' in NI which has the given meaning of 'oil' 728 times. I translated both MI and NI to 'night' in the context of *The Story of Sukurru*. (Nyx is the Greek goddess of night.) The original symbol MES is also given as 'blackness'. This might be intended to convey the secrecy, the hermetic quality of the whole. It might equally refer to a real place sealed in darkness. Although it would be nice to narrow the options down, with NI there might also be a direct reference to oil that is being used, perhaps as a lamp in the darkness, perhaps to anoint stone. Another symbol, ITI, based on UD, the sun, but with vertical lines sprouting above it, is given as 'moon' in Sumerian dictionaries.

One interesting translation that can't be ignored if we are truly standing on the sacred land of Egypt and at the foot of the Great Lion is Kemet as the 'Place of Magical Measurement' and, if my evaluation of IT/ID is correct, measurement of time by means of the moon.

See ME-KI on page 90.

MES/KI-ŠI-IB

Another way of dissecting KIŠIB is given just once on the lexical tablets:

b)
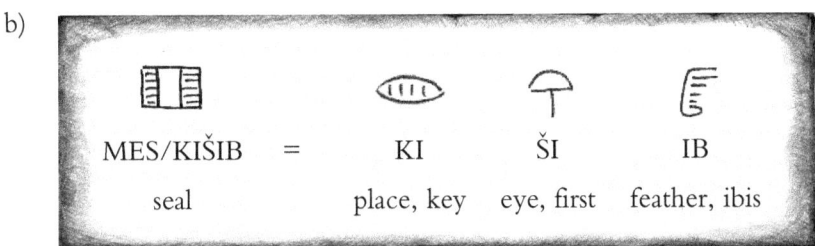

This breakdown introduces two new symbols into the equation. ŠI is the all-seeing eye of ŠIM, both bird and alchemist. See chapter 15. It's given 8 times as 'eye' and 134 times as 'first, earlier, front, face'.

IB resembles a bird's unfurled wing but can also be seen as an individual feather, a meaning attributed in light of its presence on line 40 where IB is given in opposition to NA, the weight of stone (see page 152). I even went so far as to translate it to 'ark' on line 111, a decision made long before I began the present study and one that I stand by. IB is given as 'oval' 29 times. Thoth, the Egyptian birdman, is pictured on numerous temple walls and papyri. He is understood to be a god of the moon, bringing knowledge of the measurement of time. The ibis, reflected in Sumerian symbol IB, Feather of Truth, is found on line 40 of *The Story of Sukurru*, and is central to the ceremony of the weighing of the heart. In Egyptian lore, Thoth is central to that ritual. Thoth is the ibis and IB. IB is enclosed in the heart of MES. Thoth is within Hermes.

Below is one of the rare occasions where the etymology of a Greek name is said to take its source from the Egyptian language and from a word with a quite different sound.

> *Ibis: stork-like bird, late 14c., from Latin ibis (plural ibes), from Greek ibis, from Egyptian hab, a sacred bird of Egypt.*

The Greek version of the sacred bird's name has its origin in the Sumerian IB, a direct trace of Thoth, the ibis-headed Egyptian figure, inside the multi-layered name of the Great Magician, Hermes Trismegistus. There have already been references to a mighty bird with RI/TAL and this is confirmation. This combination might translate to 'Place of the Feathered Eye' or 'Place of the Eye of the Ibis'. That doesn't negate Egyptian 'hab' as a name for the same figure.

ME/ IŠIB/ ŠIB

Following on from KI-ME, another way of finding the ibis character of Thoth but with the bonus of an extra symbol is directly through the lexical entries for IŠIB:

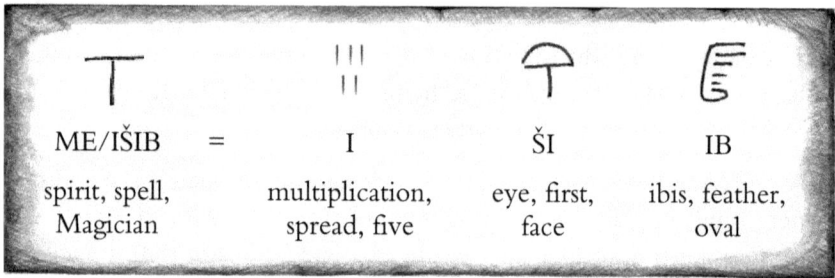

This time the symbol I, already mentioned as the original expression of the Fibonacci sequence on page 10, is found within the symbol ME which is found inside the MES of Hermes. This is an organic book that reads inwards and outwards, possessing dimensions that would surely drive a prescriptive grammarian quite mad. The symbols are all keys but to what?

HERMES TRISMEGISTUS

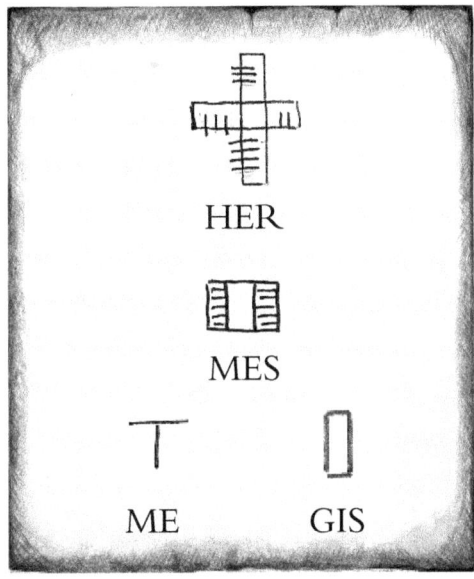

This is more than a name. It's a message from the most ancient of times, from the Great Magician himself. There are three layers to the hermetic puzzle, the second contained in the first, the third contained in the second:

Here is the original key, intended to demonstrate the mindset that must be employed on the clay tablets if we are to recuperate something of their original meaning; hermetic only to those who are unwilling to abandon conventional methods and make the leap of faith into a world generated by the Great Magician's name.

Deep within the name of Hermes is encoded the symbol that represents the Fibonacci sequence. I is the essence of ME, one third of IŠIB, the magic, the spreading eye of the ibis. It indicates the 'harmonic design', as John Anthony West calls it, of the fabulous Temple of Karnak at Luxor. Emanating from the deepest level of the name, the root and the harmony of everything, organic balanced growth begins in the heart of Hermes; An ever-expanding spiral carried up and out by means of the magic, possibly translated as the spirit vessel, that also sits at the centre of this code.

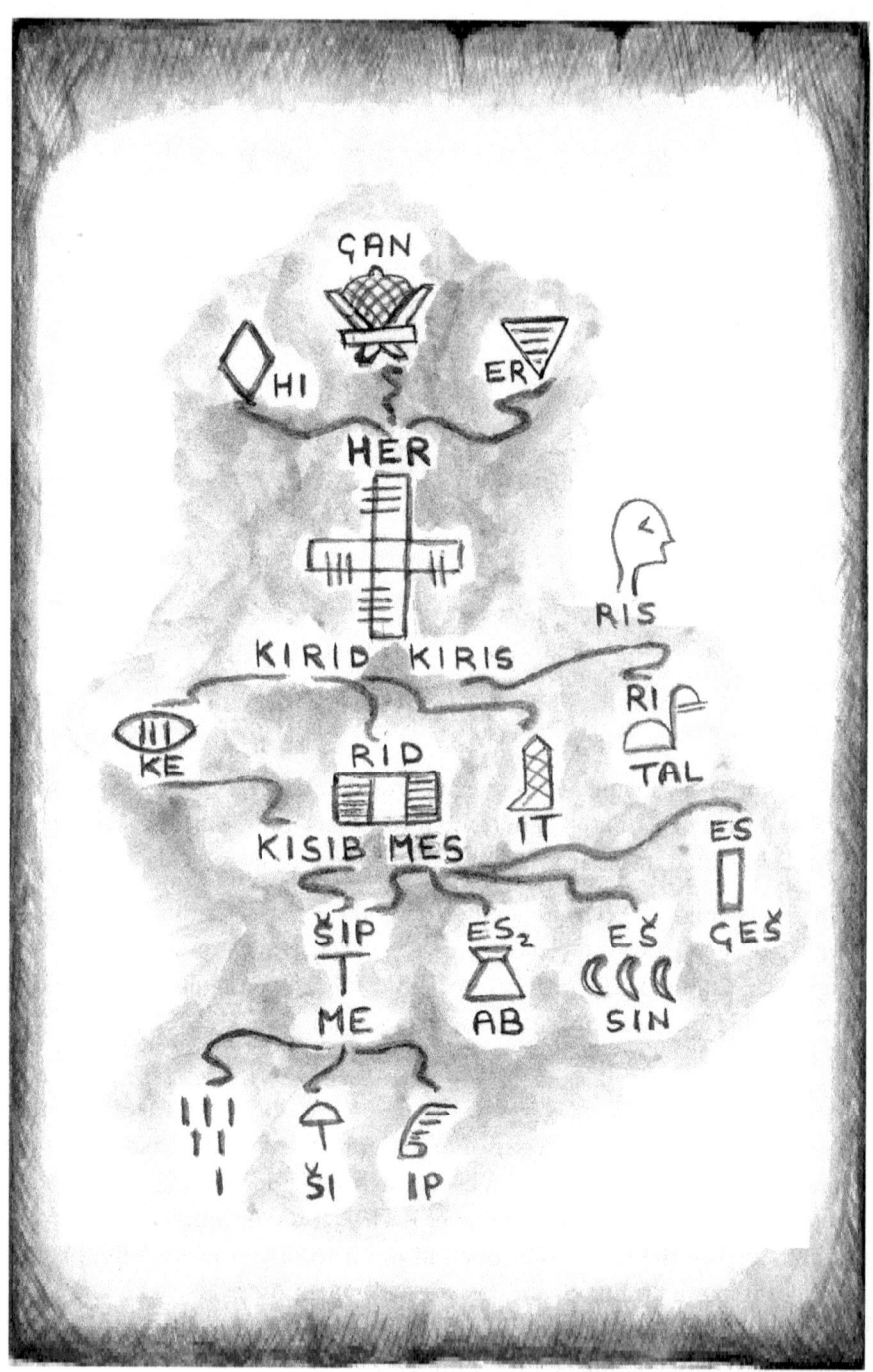

From Ship to Navel

Visit the Great Pyramid of Giza and, after climbing the narrow passageway to the King's Chamber where you can at last stand up straight, examine the famous granite box before you turn around and face back towards the low entrance. Don't forget to stop and consider the lone T inscribed on the interior side of the lintel stone there. Then, when you have had your fill, go down and round to the southern side and to the Museum where the Pharaoh's ship is exhibited above the rectangular pit in which it was discovered.

There are seven boat pits in all close to the Great Pyramid, with remains of boats found in only two. Three of them form a separate group because, contrary to the rectangular pits on the southern side, they are considerably larger and oblong. They are shaped like ships and all three lie on the eastern side of the Great Pyramid. Contrary to Khufu's ship, there is no obvious way of dating them. Wood can be dated but not stone.

IB, the feather, translated in *The Story of Sukurru* to 'feather', 'cloud' and 'ark' in three different contexts, can also be read as IP. The importance of this phonetic value hit home at a very late stage in the writing of this book. But, when it did, all the elements, the loose strings hanging down from the cosmos suddenly began to spiral and to weave – as they had done more than once since this journey began. IB/IP is an element of ŠIB/ŠIP which, in turn, is one phonetic form of ME, the magic. KI and ŠIP are the two elements of KIŠIB which, in turn, is one phonetic form of MES, the sealed tablet. A new way to consider KE with ME:

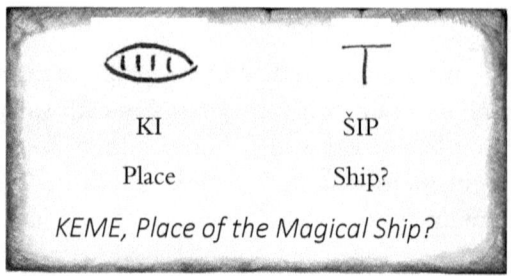

KI — ŠIP
Place — Ship?

KEME, Place of the Magical Ship?

Ship: Old English scip "ship, boat," from Proto-Germanic *skipa- (source also of Old Norse, Old Saxon, Old Frisian, Gothic skip, Danish skib, Swedish skepp, Middle Dutch scip, Dutch schip, Old High German skif, German Schiff), "Germanic noun of obscure origin" [Watkins]. Others suggest perhaps originally "tree cut out or hollowed out," and derive it from PIE root.

Nothing in the Sumerian dictionaries relates symbol ME/ŠIP directly to a ship. The argument that a magical ship should be read into this symbol is made, first and foremost, based on the exactitude of the sound. In the same way that ME is at the origin of 'me', (given in Sumerian dictionaries as 'to be'), ŠIP is the source of 'ship'. Both words are imbued with the magic of the Tau and have preserved their integrity - in the same way that Khufu's ship made of noble cedarwood survived millennia in its stone tomb next to the Great Pyramid.

Looking around for elements to further support this realization, I found that 'keme', from proto-Turkic, in the languages of Kazakhstan and Kyrgyzstan translates to 'ship'.[108] In Turkish, the word became 'gemi'. I would contend that etymological dictionaries can't explain either of the words 'me' and 'ship' in a more – or even equally – well-substantiated and logical manner.

Returning to KIŠIB/MES (from page 204 onward), it becomes possible to consider its underlying symbols in a new context:

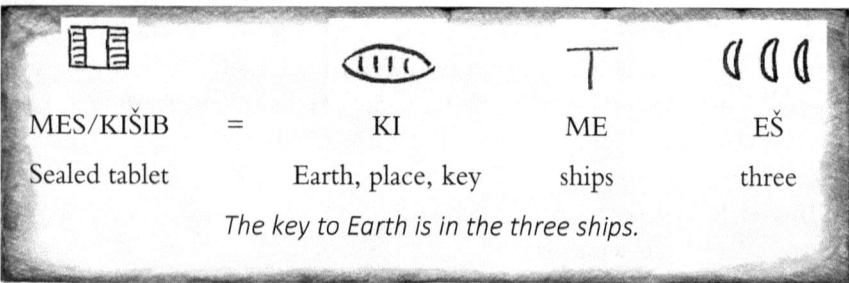

MES/KIŠIB = KI — ME — EŠ
Sealed tablet — Earth, place, key — ships — three

The key to Earth is in the three ships.

KI-ŠI-IB (page 209) led to the eye of the ibis. IB was shown to be the Feather of Truth on line 40. In Egyptian lore, the role of judge in the weighing of the heart falls to Thoth, the ibis figure. IB is both the feather and the ibis. I repeat myself, but all in a good cause.

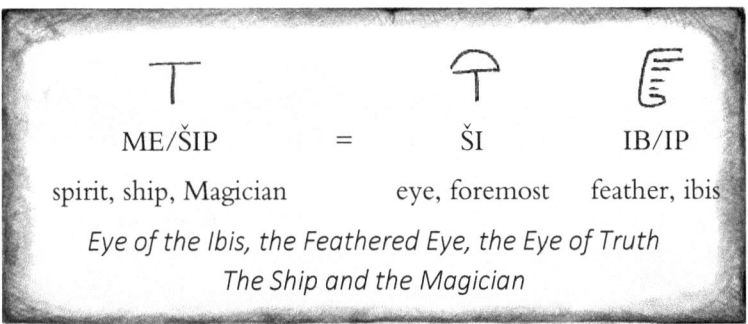

ME/ŠIP   =   ŠI   IB/IP

spirit, ship, Magician   eye, foremost   feather, ibis

Eye of the Ibis, the Feathered Eye, the Eye of Truth
The Ship and the Magician

The eye of Thoth, ŠI-IB/IP, becomes ŠIB or ŠIP, taking on the T-shaped form mentioned extensively here and in previous chapters. By association and verified through all the above findings in the lexical entries, the eye of Thoth is ME, symbol of the measurement of everything. The I of IŠIP, another phonetic value of ME, is the unfurling, the spreading of the wing. Thoth is the Magician to be found at the heart of HER-MES.

In Chapter 10, Signs of the Magician, the link was shown between the T-shape and the position of the third eye or pineal gland, particularly through the example of lines from *The Story of Sukurru* where ME appeared between two ŠI, 'the spirit between the eyes'. See page 105. Origin of the Tau, it represents the pineal gland in the same way that the painted dot on the forehead of a Hindu does; as an external symbol. The 'eye' of Egyptian Thoth goes straight to the source, showing the physical shape of the 'stone' that is the pineal gland. This is not an original theory. It has long been suggested by others and, in that it's verifiable at a glance, I'm happy to refer to it here.

The ship is an other-worldly vessel. In Egyptian lore, it is the 'solar barge' and the much-illustrated eye that appears as a protective symbol on the prow of ships (see page 166) is known as the Eye of Horus, but it also appears in some images as that of the sacred cow, Hathor. Note that I make no attempt to relate the names of Horus or Hathor to Sumerian IB. Deciphering the Egyptian hieroglyphs is not within my remit. In *The Story of Sukurru*, there is a direct reference on line 131 to the harnessing of the ship by the sun, which triggers the impressive cursing scene lasting for the next ten lines.

> *Then, the day, the sun...rising before the noble frame,*
> *the sweetly swaying vessel its rope seizes.*

Referring back to pages 17-18 and to line 44 of *The Story of Sukurru*, the pagan character who will be tied to the ship's mast for his task as spirit (NAM ME) must not be forgotten in the context of the cosmic ship of the Magician. It might just as well translate to either *'in order to become the spirit'* or *'for his task as Magician'* where NAM is 'fate' and NAM-ME the *'magical bird'* on the rigging of the ship. At this point, a new layer of meaning can be added to the all-important T-shaped symbol ME. Not only does it serve as a symbolic reminder of the third eye, the spirit that is 'me', particularly when sandwiched between two examples of ŠI, the eye, but it is embodied in the ship's mast.

There are three examples of ŠI-ME-ŠI in *The Story of Sukurru*. The first comes on line 43, preceding the reference to the pagan, where it was translated in context as the 'central beam'. Pan will be tied to the mast to prevent him from playing his pipes. In another story, no doubt originating from that Sumerian source, it will be Odysseus, the Homeric figure (whose name begins with OD/UD, symbol of the sun), who will be tied to the mast of his ship to prevent him from succumbing to the siren song. Without a mast, impossible to capture the spirit wind. Without the spirit, the magic, there will be no sailing, either earthly or cosmic. It is impossible to over-emphasize the importance that sailing vessels of all kinds had in the ancient world. The images and relics of them abound, not least in dynastic Egypt. Here below the T-shaped beams in an Ancient Egyptian sailing scene discovered in a tomb at Giza[109]:

NA and ME, Stone and Ship, Navel and Naval

The obscure origin of the word 'navel' was mentioned on page 78 in the context of Gobekli Tepe. The importance of the navel stone - Greek omphalos - in ancient times is well documented. On page 99, I mentioned the possibility that stone circles, the Irish keel and the ubiquitous KL sound were references to a ship's keel, and even suggested that the original ark of Noah is represented at Gobekli Tepe in its animal-laden stone circles.

Although the navel is not recognised as part of the following grouping, there is an etymological link between 'ship' and 'nave' through Latin navis. Etymological dictionaries refer to a PIE sound that is given as 'nau-':

> PIE root 'nau-': the hypothetical source of/evidence for its existence is provided by: Sanskrit nauh, accusative navam "ship, boat;" Armenian nav "ship;" Greek naus "ship," nautes "sailor;" Latin navis "ship;" Old Irish nau "ship," Welsh noe "a flat vessel;" Old Norse nor "ship."
>
> Nave: "main part of a church," 1670s, from Medieval Latin navem (nominative navis) "nave of a church," from Latin navis "ship" from PIE root.

Thus, the sacred place that is a church can be assimilated to a ship according to the etymological dictionaries. Consider the form of a church nave with its side aisles, an aerial view, the form of ME. Where did the shape originate? Does anyone know? Look back to the three massive ship-shaped boat pits carved out of stone on the eastern side of the Great Pyramid of Giza. Look considerably further back to the stone navel of Turkish 'gobek' and Gobekli Tepe. Remember the Irish keels and the many examples of stone-laden burial sites taking the form of ships. Ships, symbolic or real, were sacred.

Sumerian NA, the stone, is the source not only of the word 'navel' but also nautical words, all things naval. NA is the stone of the dodo, the flying bird that doesn't fly. NA is the flying stone on which the story is told in NA-RI, the narrative. NA is the stone of the wild bull of destiny in NA-AM, a bird called NAM who is the Simurgh – NA-NAM, weight of destiny! - the lofty bird who is the reflection of self (see chapter 14, The Bird of Prophecy). NA-ME, the magical stone, the Magician's stone, the stone and the ship, the ship that is made of stone, the stone that is a ship...

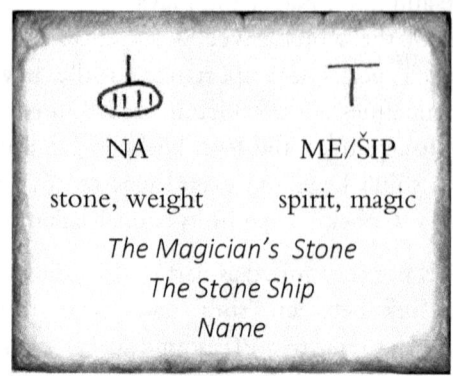

NA-ME is given as 'somebody' once at an early period and again 14 times after 2500 BC. NA appears with ME numerous times in the lexical entries. Sumerian NA-ME gives the origin of English 'name':

> Name: Old English nama, noma "name, reputation," from Proto-Germanic *naman- (source also of Old Saxon namo, Old Frisian nama, Old High German namo, German Name, Middle Dutch name, Dutch naam, Old Norse nafn, Gothic namo "name"), from PIE root.
>
> -ship: word-forming element meaning "quality, condition; act, power, skill; office, position; relation between," Middle English -schipe, from Old English -sciepe, Anglian -scip "state, condition of being," from Proto-Germanic *-skepi- (...) from PIE root.

Line 20 offers one of 5 similar phrases using NAM-MU in this manner. See page 117 for MU/MEHIDA:

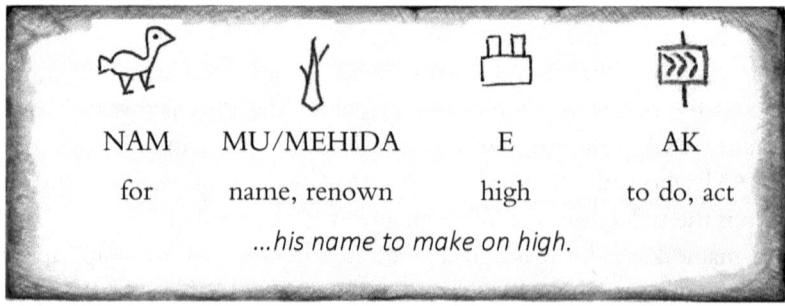

Three Ships

After visiting the Khufu Boat museum, wander back to the eastern side of the Great Pyramid and, if you can get past the camels and their owners, find the massive pits. They differ in shape from that of the Khufu boat pit on the southern side. They may well be from a different era.

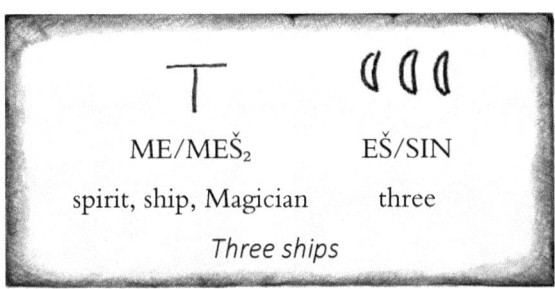

ME-EŠ appears numerous times in the lexical lists, and with MEŠ$_2$, another phonetic value of ME. The combination appears on line 268 of *The Story of Sukurru*. Also see pages 204 and 214.

What is the significance of those three stone ships seemingly arriving from the east to the Great Pyramid of Giza, two placed alongside its eastern façade and the third docked before it at a skew angle parallel to the causeway? And what of that popular Christmas carol 'I saw three ships come sailing in...'? The song refers to the three Magi who appear in one biblical text[110], also arriving from the east, birthplace of the sun, bringing their gifts of frankincense, gold and myrrh to the baby Jesus, to the Christ. They follow a bright star, of course. Everyone knows that story. But how old is it and where did the idea originate? Did the three ships of Egypt arrive at the same time or in three different sets of circumstances? Are the stone imprints in the Giza plateau a reminder of the arrival of three wise men bearing gifts, perhaps bringing their knowledge at times of great catastrophe? See GIR, the fish, on page 271. Or are they part of a highly sophisticated message, perhaps important elements in a map?

The ultimate Sumerian link with Egyptian Thoth and the Giza plateau is through KE-ME, the magical place of the ship, Kemet, ancient name of Egypt, all of it, all of them found in the depths of HER-MES which is the NA-ME, the name and the stone ship of the Magician, Hermes Trismegistus, wisdom teacher revered by the inhabitants of Harran. How old can this riddle be? Readers of this must decide for themselves. Take your time. Take the

219

time to return to the King's Chamber of the Great Pyramid and to reconsider the T carved into the middle of the lintel stone. The 'chalking of the doors' is carried out today as an Epiphany or 'Three Kings Day' ritual. Crosses interspersed with the initials of the three kings are inscribed over doorways by practising Christians as a blessing. The origin of it is unknown.

Above are two photos taken inside the King's Chamber in difficult circumstances. The very fact of showing an interest in the carved letter brought a guide with his group scurrying over to comment on the graffiti above. Within seconds, a new group began to arrive from underneath the lintel stone, taking their time to stretch after the cramped climb. As the room became more crowded and it became increasingly difficult to take a photo in that dim place without someone's shadow getting in the way, we hurried to get it done. Nevertheless, the T can just be seen, and I saw it for myself; as I remember it, neater, broader and deeper than other markings on those granite walls and unattached to any other lettering, slightly left of centre and at eye level. On one hand, it is very different in style and execution to the graffiti above. On the other, it is far from resembling a hieroglyph. It's different. Is it significant? I hope to be forgiven for mentioning it here because I can't prove that it is anything older or more important than a very neat, isolated piece of graffiti from the 19th century. But it is not impossible that it was carved there at an earlier time as the mark of a more ancient tradition, perhaps by Saint Anthony of Egypt himself. (See pages 114, 236 and 238.)

HER/KIRIS

Returning to the phonetic values of symbol HER, the lexical entries for KIRIS show:

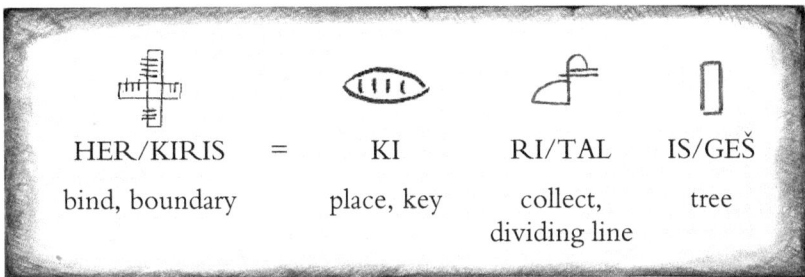

These are all symbols that have already appeared in the analysis of KIRID. This time, the RI/DAL/TAL bird is still central to the name as it was with KIRID, but GEŠ, the tree, takes the place of ID, the wing or strong arm of time.

KI with RI, Place of the Bird, give the origin of Greek kyrios 'ruler, lord,', Greek kyriakon 'of the Lord', for houses of worship, and Kerykos, the herald. Greek Hermes was said to be the messenger and herald of the gods. There are quite a few more possibilities:

> *Keryssein 'to proclaim, to cry (as a herald),' from or related to keryx 'herald, messenger,' a word of uncertain origin, perhaps from PIE root.*
>
> *Chrism: 'oil mingled with balm, a sacred ointment consecrated and used in Church rites,' (...) from Greek khrisma 'an unguent, anointing, unction,' from khriein 'to anoint,' from PIE root.*
>
> *Chrestomathy: 'collection of literary passages' (especially from a foreign language), 1774,(...), from Latinized form of Greek khrestomatheia 'desire of learning; book containing selected passages,' lit. 'useful learning,' from khrestos 'useful' (...) from PIE root.*

> *Crypt: early 15c., cripte, 'grotto, cavern,' from Latin crypta 'vault, cavern,' from Greek krypte 'a vault, crypt' (short for krypte kamara 'hidden vault'), fem. of kryptos 'hidden,' verbal adjective from kryptein 'to hide,' which is of uncertain origin.*
>
> *Chyrso-: before vowels chrys-, word-forming element meaning 'gold, gold-colored,' also sometimes 'wealth,' from Latinized form of Greek khrysos 'gold,' which is usually said to be a Punic (Semitic) loan-word (compare Hebrew and Phoenician harutz 'gold')*

In words that combine a messenger, Keryx, the notion of oil used to 'anoint', Chrism, and the link to useful learning through Chrestomathy, among others, it's not difficult to discern the direct relationship that has always existed between Sumer and Greece, between Sumerian HER and Greek Hermes. That said, I find no mention of gods in this Sumerian name. The symbol AN doesn't show up at all. But the reputation of Hermes as herald is confirmed.

KIRI is a sound that is found in two versions of symbol HER, pointing to the importance of the sounds 'kir' and 'kiri' in relation to the emblematic figure. .Hermes Kriophoros is one of his Greek titles. It's said to derive from a bizarre story in which the hero saved the city of Tanagra by circling the place with a ram, or possibly a lamb, wound around his shoulders. Kriophoros means the 'ram-bearer'. The close resemblance between Greek khrysos meaning 'gold', the story of Hermes Kriophoros and his ram, along with the symbol HER and its phonetic value KIRIS lead in the direction of another strange Greek story, that of the golden fleece. It is not beyond the realms of possibility that this is the sheep of LU, in other words a 'golden light' to be associated with Hermes. (See page 11 for LU.)

According to The Forge and The Crucible[111], on the ancient Indonesian island of Java, the smith was a much-venerated figure working in a mysterious context who bore the title 'Kris-smith'. It's worth noting that kris is also the name given to a type of dagger.

> *Guess: c. 1300, gessen "to infer from observation, perceive, find out; form an opinion, judge, decide, discern; evaluate, estimate the number, importance, etc. of," perhaps from Scandinavian (compare Middle Danish gitse, getze "to guess," Old Norse geta "guess, get"), or from or influenced by Middle Dutch gessen, Middle Low German gissen "to guess,"*

Here's an amusing theory for the origin of the word 'guess'. First, it must be noted that 'guess' was not always what it is today. The idea of risk and conjecture, opinion-forming based on nothing solid comes to mind. But it was once synonymous with 'to perceive', 'to judge' or 'to estimate' of numbers or the importance of something. Guess had a more sober, worthy connotation than we give it now. There was an element of serious consideration that has been lost. The etymological dictionaries don't know the real origin of the word. They too are guessing in the modern sense of the word. I see no reason not to suggest that 'guess' comes from Sumerian 'ges'. At the very least and at this late stage in the book, it can be said that the suggestion is grounded in more than unsubstantiated opinion. It is possible that 'guess' derived from GI and EŠ, the three reeds, that it was a 'tree', related to 'three', of some sort, a wooden instrument, rectangular, small or long that served for measuring, for guessing in the ancient sense of the word. Perhaps it was the instrument that Egyptian Thoth is seen holding up in many images.

KI-RIŠ/RIS

Finally, mention must be made of the combination that, no doubt, forms part of the overall pattern even if it isn't found in the lexical entries currently available to us. KI-RIS gives 'the Place of the Head':

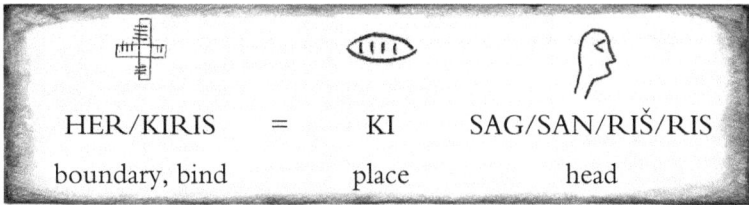

HER/KIRIS	=	KI	SAG/SAN/RIŠ/RIS
boundary, bind		place	head

Given as 'head', 'person' and 'capital' 317 times at the earliest period, the image doesn't leave much doubt. But, as we know by now, there is always much more than superficial knowledge to be gleaned from the old symbols.

This is an alchemical reference. Also see page 149 for a reference to the head in relation to Gobekli Tepe.

> *The names of the Philosophers who spoke about the art: Hermes, Agathodaimon and many others... They are remembered for making the head and the perfected elixir.* [112]

Two lexical entries combine SAG with RI, the bird, and EŠ, three or thirty, both of which already present in the analysis of HER-MES on page 212 but not previously shown as linked one to the other:

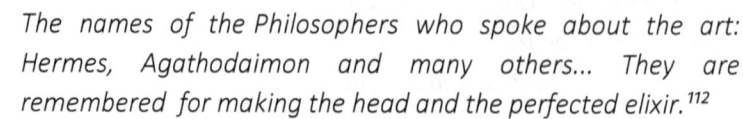

SAG/RIŠ	=	RI/RE	EŠ
head		bird, gather	three, thirty

The three birds on the mast of the Greek Siren vase come to mind as do the thirty birds of The Conference of the Birds (see page 170):

> *Rise: Old English risan "to rise, rise from sleep, get out of bed; stand up, rise to one's feet; (...), from Proto-Germanic *us-rīsanan "to go up" (source also of (...) German reisen "to travel," originally "to rise for a journey").*

SAG/RIS is mentioned again in the company of PI on page 294.

HER–RE

There is another collocation of interest to be found in the KIRIS sound associated with our regular visitor, the collector bird, who has taken up residence in the middle of HER. Keeping the same symbols but changing the phonetic values of them from HER to KIRIS and from RI to TAL:

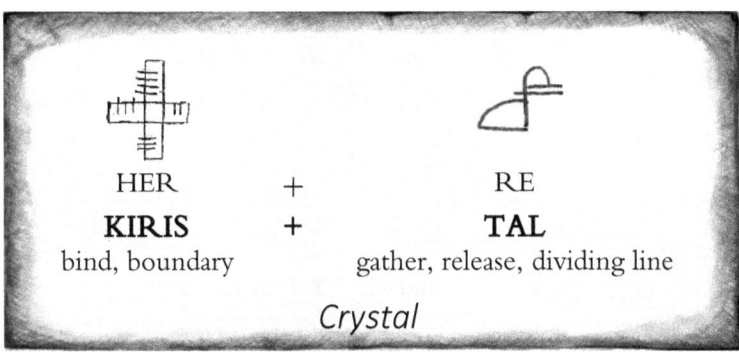

HER	+	RE
KIRIS	+	**TAL**
bind, boundary		gather, release, dividing line

Crystal

At the risk of repeating myself and to make the explanation crystal clear, TAL, the bird distinguished by its claws, is present as RE/RI within two phonetic forms of HER; KIRID and KIRIS. TAL also appears separately but collocated with the symbol HER/KIRIS.

> *Crystal: formerly also cristal, and, erroneously, chrystal, Old English cristal 'clear ice; clear, transparent mineral,' from Old French cristal (12c., Modern French crystal), from Latin crystallus 'crystal, ice,' from Greek krystallos, from kryos 'frost,' from PIE root.*
>
> *Heresy: 'doctrine or opinion at variance with established standards', from Latin hæresis, 'school of thought, philosophical sect.' The Latin word is from Greek hairesis 'a taking or choosing for oneself, a choice, a means of taking; a deliberate plan, purpose; philosophical sect, school,' from haireisthai 'take, seize,' middle voice of hairein 'to choose,' a word of unknown origin.*

There is an intriguing proverb or riddle where the two appear together, here below with one possible translation[113]:

A measure taken that all divides but collectively binds, a troublesome measure will be.

As with the majority of the earliest Sumerian texts, composed of riddles and wordplay, it can be understood in more than one way. There is the obvious meaning of the bad rule of law. But, if we consider that this refers to the hermetic teachings, that it is perhaps one of the very earliest elements of those texts, then we look a little closer.

On the ETCSL site where this proverb has been reproduced, symbol HER is given as KEŠ₂, and is presented in capital letters while the rest of the proverb is shown in lower case. As I understand it, the proverb was inscribed on a tablet in the Old Babylonian period. The abstract cuneiform style of writing (transliterated in lower case) of those times was used for it except for that one symbol KEŠ₂/HER which retained something of its pre-3000 BC, pictographic form (typed in capitals). That was a significant choice on the part of the scribe even if we can't know exactly what was meant by highlighting the symbol in that way. The 'proverb' tablets date to somewhere between 1900 and 1600 BC, but, of course, that says nothing about the original creation of the texts. The HER symbol was found on much older tablets. I suggest that the scribe was copying text from a considerably more ancient source and that the intention was to make the meaning of it plain for readers by using contemporaneous abstract cuneiform while retaining only the most sacred of the original images.

I have added the noun 'boundary' into the mix for the above illustration of HER because it's useful to bear in mind that this symbol, generally given as 'bind', is a cross that can be understood as marking a particular place and that it is the origin of the word 'here'. It corresponds to all the mythologies concerning Greek Hermes in his boundary-breaking role as messenger to the gods, to boundary stones that are associated with dividing lines, to the boundary-signalling herma mentioned on page 193, and to the binding of stones mentioned in several other sections.

AL, symbol of the alchemist's bellows, is mentioned in chapter 15, Shaman and Alchemist, and in chapter 16, Talon, the metal robot. 'All' is not listed as a meaning of AL in Sumerian dictionaries. But then neither is the bellows. See pages 165 and 177.

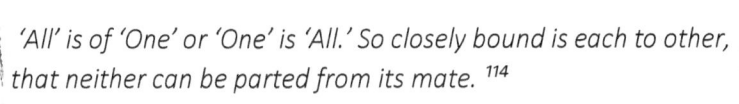

'All' is of 'One' or 'One' is 'All.' So closely bound is each to other, that neither can be parted from its mate. [114]

This excerpt from a hermetic text dated to the 2nd century AD has distinct echoes of the Sumerian proverb. Add a touch of humour, a soupçon of wordplay and multi-layered meanings. If any doubts were lingering, it becomes increasingly obvious that the language of Hermes Trismegistus was that of the early Sumerian symbols.

In Basque, the isolated language of a region shared between France and Spain, 'herri' is given as 'town', 'people', 'country' and herriko as 'town hall'. Perhaps there is no connection at all with the HER-RE/RI central to the proverb, but both suggest a gathering together to make decisions for a community. The origins of the Basque language have been studied by experts from different perspectives and all have come to the same conclusion. It has no relatives. Like Sumerian, that's just the way it is.

The proverb on page 226 implies a rule of law. But is it earthly or cosmic? Is the measure a law and could GIG, given as 'sick' or 'troublesome' 43 times, be the source of 'gigantic'? Collocated with GA, it was translated to Ga's giants on line 255 of *The Story of Sukurru*.

> *Giant: c. 1300, 'fabulous man-like creature of enormous size,' from Old French geant, earlier jaiant 'giant, ogre' (12c.), from Vulgar Latin *gagantem (nominative gagas), from Latin gigas 'a giant,' from Greek Gigas (usually in plural, Gigantes), one of a race of divine but savage and monstrous beings (personifying destructive natural forces), sons of Gaia and Uranus, eventually destroyed by the gods. The word is of unknown origin, probably from a pre-Greek language.*

If HER-RE can also be read as KIRIS-TAL with the combined meanings of binding and crystal, we are looking at another layer of meaning.

HER-RE = KIRIS-TAL = Crystal

Crystal is an element in nature, found as infinitely small particles in rocks, in granite or as stand-alone rock; rock crystal, quartz crystal. Those who want to better understand the geology and science must look it up for themselves. Those who know it all already, please bear with me. I'm not about to copy huge swathes of information from internet. And yet, it's necessary to touch on the subject here because it's at the heart of a mystery; that of the obfuscation of the Sumerian language and of an ancient school that I choose to call the Crystal Heresy; a school grounded in hermetic knowledge, an alchemical, philosophical understanding that had no place for man-made gods.

Crystallization is the coming together of indeterminate matter to form just one. It fits well with the quote from the Asclepius[115] above. The phrase 'crystal clear' is applied as qualitative adjective to show that an idea or substance is exceptionally plain to see or to see through - not at all the case when I first encountered HER and RE.

A piece of rock crystal formed into a lens and somehow dated to around 750 BC was found in Iraq in the 19th century. Today, the Nimrud lens sits in the British Museum. The following is part of the description of it given on the museum's website:

> It could certainly have been used as a crude magnifying glass, with a focal length of 12 centimetres from the plane surface. Over the years it has been examined by a number of opticians (e.g. Gasson 1972), many of whom believe that it was deliberately manufactured as a lens. However, although this piece of rock crystal has been carefully ground and polished, and undoubtedly has optical properties, these are probably accidental. There is no evidence that the Assyrians used lenses, either for magnification or for making fire, and it is much more likely that this is a piece of inlay, perhaps for furniture. [115]

The Nimrud lens may or may not have been used for magnification in ancient times. The fact is that it had been ground into a neat round form, and that it had optical properties…that it was held up to someone's eye during the making and after, during the inspection. Did they then notice those properties and imagine the services, other than ornamental, that such material might provide? How could that not be the case? That the properties of the Nimrud lens were accidental is a matter of opinion. Another quality of crystal that can be exploited is the production of energy. Piezoelectricity is produced by mechanical exertion on certain solid materials, of which quartz crystal. A prefix of Greek origin, 'piezo-' indicates the mechanical force which can be understood as a squeezing, a tightening of the material.

> Direct piezoelectricity of some substances, like quartz, can generate potential differences of thousands of volts.
>
> The efficiency of a hybrid photovoltaic cell that contains piezoelectric materials can be increased simply by placing it near a source of ambient noise or vibration.[116]

It is interesting to note, in this context, that symbol HER/KIRIS is given as 'to squeeze', 'to tighten', and particularly 'to bind', this last appearing 405 times at 3000-2500 BC.

The concept of tightly binding crystal to create an electrical charge becomes increasingly compelling when the TAL of 'crystal' is taken into consideration. As I have mentioned a few times now, this is the bird that has several names: RI, RE, TAL and DAL. It's a direct relative to, if not the same bird as, the Idigna bird of the Taurus mountains whose alternative name is DALLA (see chapter 13). They are both related to Greek Talus, also known as Talon (see chapter 16). Claws and nails have copiously played their part in ancient myths. The metaphor of a bird in flight, it's talon clutching prey, would be a valid one for a force exerted on a crystalline stone. RE/RI is the 'collecting' or 'gathering' of that force but is given 10 times at the earliest period with a range of evocative meanings of which 'to release' and 'to imbue'. With GEŠ, the wood, it is also a beam and a dividing line. With its common partner, the water symbol, RI becomes the collecting and the releasing of a flow (with the presence of a dividing line between the two): RI-A.

> Re-: word-forming element meaning "back to the original place; again, anew, once more," also with a sense of "undoing," (...) from Latin re- "again, back, anew, against," "Latin combining form conceivably from Indo-European (...)

HER = EZEN

As mentioned at the beginning of this chapter, a search among the photographs on the CDLI site for an example of symbol HER/HIR/KIRID/KIRIS at 3000 BC or earlier comes up empty. The earliest versions date to 2900-2700 BC. For quite some time, I relied on two images I had found; a computer rendering given on the CDLI proto-cuneiform sign list, and another computer-printed example shown on *L'Ecriture Cunéiform*. I write this without having seen one single original HER on a clay tablet from anywhere in the Uruk periods between 3350 and 3000 BC. However, there is another symbol closely related to and even basically the same as HER which can and must be taken into consideration in the investigation into the origin of Hermes:

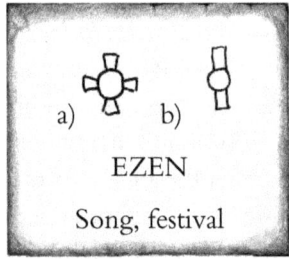

EZEN

Song, festival

EZEN/EZEM is given as 'festival' 291 times and once as 'sing'. 'Sing' is given a further 138 times at the later 2000 BC period.

In the pictographic lists of *L'Ecriture Cunéiforme*, EZEN is given alongside what appears to be a depiction of HER minus the cross-hatching, presumably an indication of the 'binding' and the only difference between them shown there. They appear together under the same reference 301. EPSD gives the two symbols HER and EZEN separately, while CDLI shows images of symbol EZEN on tablets at the earliest period but only seven much later tablets as the abstract cuneiform image of HER – given there as HIR.

EZEN is found numerous times in the lexical lists opposite or next to KIRID and other phonetic forms of HER. With all of those sources citing a link or even synonymity, there can be no doubt that EZEN is an essential element in this investigation.

HER appears on line 18 of *The Story of Sukurru* where it was translated to 'binder'. It appears again as HER-HER-RI on line 245. EZEN, with symbol

KASKAL at its centre, appears as UBARA in the refrain of *The Story of Sukurru*, the epithet of a ruler. See lines 7, 74, 77, 144, 147, 277 and 278. UBARA also appears on line 32 of the Sumerian King List where it is translated '*In Šuruppak, Ubara-Tutu became king*'. It is possible that there is much more to be gleaned, particularly as UBARA appears in the King List at the moment of a great flood, but is also followed by KI, possibly the suffix of a place name, on a couple of tablet fragments from the 2nd millennium BC where the translation goes '*the year UBARA was restored*'. See notes 18 and 19. At the time of the translation, not having penetrated the deeper levels of meaning, I conformed to the existing version of UBARA as a ruler. Another version of EZEN is given as BAD$_3$ with symbols AN or BAD at its centre. BAD$_3$, given 50 times at the earliest period as 'wall', is found twice on line 231.

EZEN appears on line 208 of *The Story of Sukurru*, introduction to the ritual of the three offering baskets. I gave it as a 'festive song' in that context. The pictogram varies but it takes the form of a central round shape with four protrusions, sometimes just two as shown above (b). It would be convenient to suggest that symbol EZEN is the image of the place where a festival or, more significantly, a ritualistic chant is to be added into the mix of the piezo-electrical machinery hypothesis that is gathering pace here. What does seem beyond coincidence at this stage is the phonetic similarity between EZEN and Greek piezein, the pressure.

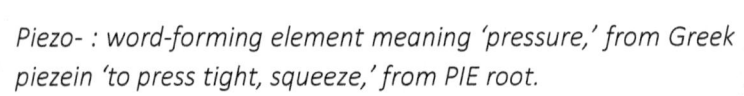

Piezo- : word-forming element meaning 'pressure,' from Greek piezein 'to press tight, squeeze,' from PIE root.

EZEN on the lexical tablets is broken down as either I or E with ZE or ZI and EN or IN:

a)

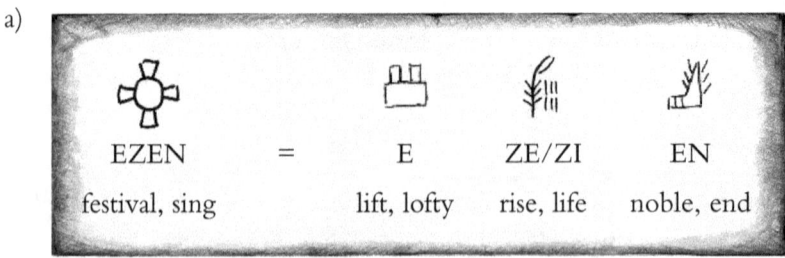

EZEN	=	E	ZE/ZI	EN
festival, sing		lift, lofty	rise, life	noble, end

232

b)

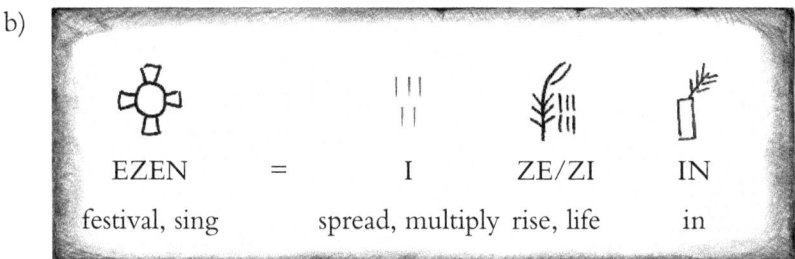

EZEN	=	I	ZE/ZI	IN
festival, sing		spread, multiply	rise, life	in

The presence of I once again, demonstrating a spiral modelled on nature and thus a fundamental symbol of life, is noteworthy in the context of energy creation.

ZE/ZI is given as 'to issue; to levy, raise, muster, to swell, to expand, to rise' 29 times at 3000-2500 BC on ePSD. It's given as 'to tear out; to break, destroy, to be troubled, to erase' 51 times, and 'right, to be right, true, loyal' 26 times at the same early period. It's also given as 'life' 64 times. Altogether a hyper-active sign.

ZE is the origin of Greek Zeus which goes someway to explaining the energetic nature of it. Given as father of the god Hermes in Greek mythology, ZE is the root to which is added Sumerian UŠ, the suffix designating Greek male names. Zeus was the very active god of the sky, with a thunderbolt and an eagle among his belongings, so perhaps all the definitions above can be justified by his presence. Except of course that here we are looking at a time thousands of years before he was to be born into Greek mythology. Zeus was Sumerian and yet, like Hermes, he is not named in any of the literary translations. How did that happen?

What we know about him from the Greek stories is that, as a baby, he was exchanged for a stone and hidden in a mountain cave so that his father, Kronos, wouldn't find him. A lot of noise, music and singing, a din was made to hide the sound of the baby crying. We know that Kronos (Father of Time) swallowed the stone thinking that he was eating his own child; a strange idea but the Greek myths are all strange. Zeus grew up thanks to this noisy stratagem and, amongst other feats, went on to attack his enemies, the Titanes, by throwing boulders at them. There is a lot more to be said about Zeus, but I am interested only in force, in sound, and in stones. A lot of rock throwing was done in those times. I suspect that Zeus knew quite a bit about Greek piezein and singing too.

> *Energy: 1590s, 'force of expression,' from Middle French énergie (16c.), from Late Latin energia, from Greek energeia 'activity, action, operation,' from energos 'active, working,' from en 'at' (see en- (2)) + ergon 'work, that which is wrought; business; action,' from PIE root.*

EZEN appears frequently on tablets at the Uruk IV and III periods in the company of EN, a symbol that is given as 'noble' but which I have also translated as 'end'. My reasons become obvious in *The Story of Sukurru*. One of them is that EN is the inversion of NE, 'fire' and 'renewal', becoming the end that is renewed. Round and round, EN-NE-EN-NE. See chapter 19 for more on this pair.

If EZEN is the source of Greek piezein, it would be reasonable to expect PI to be the first syllable of it although the two do not appear together in the lexical entries. PI is discussed in the context of the pyramid where it's shown to be the first syllable of PIR/UD, the sun.

PI is the musical pitch or perfect resonance, while EZEN provides the chant. The ZI of EZEN is the lively element causing to rise, both Zeus and Greek zeo, the bubbling (see page 168). Let's add into the mix that Slovakian for 'song' is 'piesen' or 'pesem' while Sumerian EZEN can also be read as EZEM or ESEN. There is alchemy at work.

> *Essence: from Latin essentia 'being, essence,' abstract noun formed (to translate Greek ousia 'being, essence') from essent, present participle stem of esse 'to be,' from PIE root.*

We find the origin of crystal in KIRIS with TAL and its direct link to 'pressure' and 'squeezing'. We find Greek piezein, in PI with EZEN, sources of sound or resonance. They are all, except for PI, directly linked to HER, the binding and boundary, and to Hermes. The suggestion of electricity generated by some form of resonance and pressure is the direction in which the crystal of Hermes continues to turn. And if we are being energetically nudged, then it surely couldn't be for the sake of a tiny diamond in a Swiss watch or a piece of quartz for some small gadget. It must be a stone of much greater force, of a far-reaching effect. If used to create useful energy here on

Earth in times so ancient that we have lost the knowledge of them, what other evidence might there be?

There is no trace of a collocation between PIR/UD and MEŠ in the lexical entries. It would have allowed an interpretation of Greek pyramis as PIR-A-MEŠ/MIS, adding the number three to the definition and allowing us to consider the possibility of three pyramids. But hey-ho! We don't always get what we want and none of the lexical links made in this book are born of wishful thinking. And we do have Hermes, now a thoroughly Egypto-Sumerian hero. Still, the combination is intriguing. This is how it might (but does not) appear:

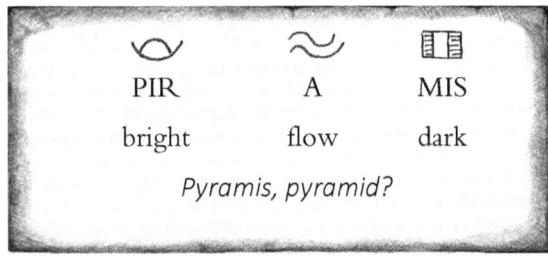

Hermes and pyramis appear to have their final syllables in common. They share the symbol ER through HI-ER and PI-ER with the given meaning 'to go', and my offerings of 'to wander', 'to err' and 'to perceive'. So what is flowing in the centre of the pyramid between darkness and light? And what did Plato know when he wrote the strange story of Er?

Cairo in January 2019 (the strange event that led me to the stone ships).
At the entrance to the Great Pyramid of Giza, we found ourselves stuck behind a young Polish woman who was alone and tetanised with fear at the idea of climbing up through the narrow tunnel. She was gripping the wooden railing tightly and moaning 'I'm going to die'… We started encouraging her and, eventually, accompanied her to the King's Chamber where she spent some time staring back at the hole she had just arrived through while we went to the 'box'. After a few minutes, she came over, tapped me on the shoulder and asked, 'Did you see the carving?' She led me back to the entrance and pointed out the inscribed 'T' that can be seen on the lintel stone, slightly left of centre. It's not something that really stands out. It's not begging for attention but it's quite plain. For some unexplained reason, she assumed that it would be of interest to me and she was right. See page 220.

T, the form that became Greek Tau, is arguably the most important symbol in the Sumerian language. I mentioned on page 114 that it's also found on a lintel in the south of France as the Tau symbol of the Order of Antonins, the medieval healing monks, followers of the great Abba, Saint Anthony of Egypt.

I thanked Martha from Warsaw profusely with a garbled explanation of why her courageous climb had been so important to me and that was that. We took a couple of photos and went back down. We didn't see the friends who had, inexplicably, left her to visit the place alone. I can't help thinking there was nothing coincidental, the fact that she stayed next to the entrance to the King's Chamber, that she found it important to take those few strides across the room to fetch me back and point out that symbol. Why? I have an opinion. Readers must decide for themselves.

19

The Sator Templar Connection

High up on the wall of a steep gorge carved by waters flowing down from the Pyrenees mountains, and just a few kilometres from the village of Rennes le Chateau as the crow flies, sits a large natural cave accessed by a flight of narrow steps. The place served as a hermitage from the 14th century until about 1930. Today, it can be visited by anyone who doesn't suffer from vertigo. Rows of wooden benches facing an image of Jesus on the cross furnish the place, suggesting that it is still in use. At the far end of the cave, just behind the crucifix that serves as centrepiece or altar, is a large murky pool of water, result of infiltrations through the rock.

Rennes le Chateau, a village in the Aude region of France, is at the centre of a well-documented mystery dating from the 19th century, and brought to public attention in the best-selling novel, *The Da Vinci Code*. Grounded in existing tales about the area and the strange behaviour of a village priest, the suspicion that he had found a treasure, threaded with an intriguing but fabricated theme about a bloodline from Jesus, the storyline of the book was irresistible. Add into the mix that the region was once that of the mysterious Cathars, a religious movement of uncertain origin, perhaps linked to the equally mysterious Knights Templar, persecuted into extinction by the Catholic church in the late Middle Ages. *The Da Vinci Code* is a fiction and most people enjoy a thriller when they get the impression that something real lurks below the surface of it. And there is indeed a mystery in that region. It's less well known but very real.

It wasn't the size or strange atmosphere of that gully cave that caused me to catch my breath. It was the sight of a large rectangular carved stone placed to the right of the steps leading to the altar there. The carving on the front of the stone seems too fresh to date back to the 14th century, but the eerie head perched on top with its staring eyes and gaping mouth looks extremely ancient. Apart from the fact that the carved stone, a Sator square, might be perceived as out of place in a religious environment, what surprized me the most was the unique manner in which it had been designed.

What was a Sator square doing here inside a cave on the sheer cliff face of the Gorges of Galamus? Whoever chose that stone and its text must have been an uncommon monk. Whoever drew the template for it and gave the order to place it there was someone in possession of unusual knowledge. It's true that the cave is called the Hermitage of Saint Anthony, a tribute to the monk of Egyptian origin. (See page 114). Was it done in the 14th or early 15th century when it's said that the place was first inhabited? It may be that the stone we see today is a replica of something older, too damaged to remain, too precious to be left uncopied. Who knows how far back its history goes? That has always been my feeling about the text of *The Story of Sukurru*. The dating is only good for the clay. It proves nothing about the story imprinted on it.

There are two unusual stories attached to the caves of the Galamus Gorges.[117] There is the recorded tale of two men, Albert Foncay Map and Marie-Bernard Brauge, who, in 1597, decided to climb down through a large hole that was once open inside it somewhere. Map came back out with horrendous wounds and died three weeks later, delirious, apparently terrified, and incapable of explaining what had happened either to him or to his colleague who never reappeared. The entrance to that hole has long since been covered over.

Another more recent enigma concerns strange unexplained lights seen and filmed at night hanging in the sky close to the entrance to the cave. Be that as it may, this section is concerned only with the most unusual standing stone that remains unremarked and rarely photographed. It has a unique version of the Sator square carved on it.

The Sator square, also called a magic square and sometimes the Templar square, is a riddle. Because it has been found in various locations having no connection with each other, at different times in history, it's quite well documented. The earliest known version was found painted onto a wall in the ruins of Pompei in Italy and, for obvious reasons, easily dated to around 79 AD. But it also exists scratched into church walls as far away as England at much later dates. There is no knowing how old the first example might have been, except that it must, again for obvious reasons, post-date the introduction of the Phoenician alphabet, perhaps around 1200 BC. Whether we consider its presence at Pompei or in a cave near Rennes-le-Chateau in the 14th century AD, it's origin and the meaning of it remain unknown. The only method by which we might attempt, if it is at all possible, to determine the origin of the Sator square is by solving the riddle.

As I said, the cave where this version of the Sator-Templar square is displayed sits within the Gorges of Galamus in the Pyrenees mountains of France. At the bottom of that gully lies the river of the Eagles. Above is the mountain range of the Crows. The names are evocative of the mysteries contained in age-old mythologies. The setting corresponds to those places where the energies of the cosmos fuse. And the Sator square smacks of the kind of game played by the riddle-loving scribes who wrote *The Story of Sukurru* and the many Sumerian proverbs. They were not the only signs that led me to sense an ancient challenge waiting silently to be taken up by someone versed in the old symbolic language…

Those were my first thoughts but my second was that it couldn't have anything to do with Sumerian, a language devised long before the emergence of the first alphabet. The Sator square has been studied many times over and attacked in every obvious way, excluding Sumerian of course. It takes an alphabet to compose a riddle of that kind. The square can be described as a palindrome, apparently written in Latin; the words on it read in all directions, from top to bottom and from left to right or vice versa. By the way, the PAL of palindrome comes from Sumerian PAL, also BAL, meaning 'to turn', 'to rotate':

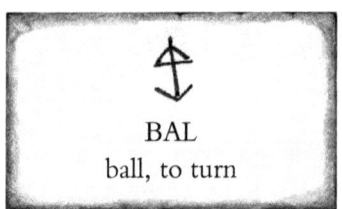

BAL
ball, to turn

Given 503 times as 'to turn over, to rotate, to cross', with GIŠ as qualifier, it was once the wooden spindle of the weaver, the tool that served to wind the clew of wool, the spindle that served to whack a drunken man, the spindle of the cosmic Matriarch, the pole on which the planets whirled… KA, the word, with BAL, the turning, indicates the moment in history when the Sumerian pictograms were spun around to eliminate all knowledge of their profound significance and make them nothing more than abstract signs. But the sounds persisted….KA-BAL. That was the time to which the story of the Tower of Babel refers; no sudden event but a gradual wearing down, a millennia-long obfuscation of everything there is to know about our original worldwide pagan roots.

> *Palindrome: 'line that reads the same backward and forward,' 1620s, from Greek palindromos 'a recurrence,' literally 'a running back.' Second element is dromos 'a running' (see dromedary); first is palin 'again, back,' from PIE root.*
>
> *Ball: 'round object, compact spherical body,' also 'a ball used in a game,' c. 1200, probably from an unrecorded Old English *beal, *beall (evidenced by the diminutive bealluc 'testicle'), or from cognate Old Norse bollr 'ball,' from Proto-Germanic *balluz (source also of Dutch bal, Flemish bal, Old High German ballo, German Ball), from PIE root.*

The attempt to find a sentence by reading the Sator square from top left to bottom right is well documented but the result is lacklustre and, in my opinion, unconvincing:

SATOR AREPO TENET OPERA ROTAS.

The farmer Arepo works with a plough.

The most obvious similarities with Latin lie in TENET from 'tenere' meaning 'to hold' and RUTAS from 'rota' which gave us words relating to 'rotation'. These are words that have been recognised in past studies of the riddle, but the sentence has no real meaning and, in my opinion, borders on ridiculous. Why would anyone have bothered? AREPO, resisting all attempts at translation, has been transformed into a name. That is more than reminiscent of some Sumerian translations. If it is impenetrable, it must be the name of a person, a monster or, better still, a god.

Each line comprises five letters. Considering them as elements of monosyllabic words, representing phonetic forms of Sumerian symbols, allows for a number of alternatives, with the possibility of at least three words in every direction. For example, SATOR could be dissected as SA-TOR or as SAT-OR.

The first question is where to begin. It may not correspond to our cultural expectation of a 'normal' sentence from top left to bottom right or even the opposite of that, from bottom left to top right. After all, it's a puzzle. The most obvious place to begin (to a lover of the Sumerian mindset that is) is in the middle.

ENE

Whichever way it turns, the choices are E with NE or EN with E which correspond to three Sumerian symbols:

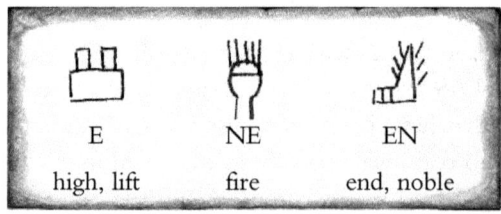

Sumerian E-NE, without any obvious reason apart from this enigma and line 33 of *The Story of Sukurru* shown below, is given as 'game' and 'play' around 2000 BC. It's also found as 'pleasure'.

EN-NE-E might translate to 'the fiery noble to lift' where the most usual noun-adjective-verb order is respected. But it isn't the only possibility. It might also indicate a central or topmost fire, one that is at the end of something. See the given etymology of 'energy on page 234.

Line 33, comprising 12 symbols, makes use of E-NE and NE-E. This is the first part:

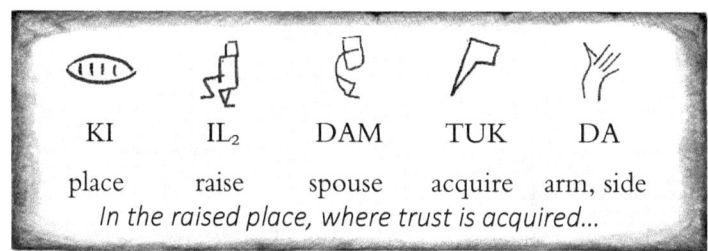

KI	IL₂	DAM	TUK	DA
place	raise	spouse	acquire	arm, side

In the raised place, where trust is acquired...

DAM is given as 'trust' 6 times and as 'spouse' 977 times. As always, there were choices to be made in the translation. 'Trust' took precedence over the more obvious 'spouse' because of context. There was the inference of the hero being in a situation conducive to trust which, of course, is what marriage is all about...but not only. Without wandering too far from the subject in hand, it is interesting to note the cultural revelation: contracts were agreed at a raised place. The line continues:

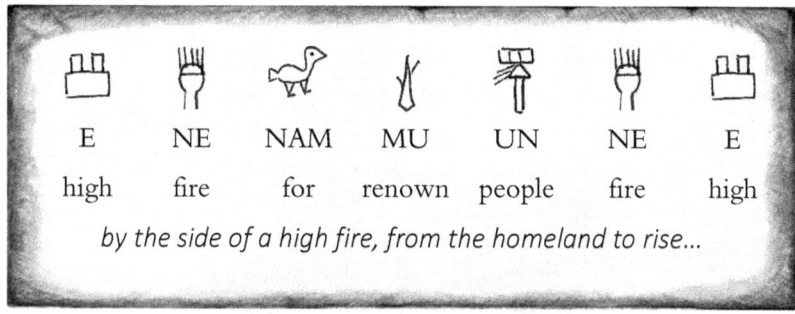

E	NE	NAM	MU	UN	NE	E
high	fire	for	renown	people	fire	high

by the side of a high fire, from the homeland to rise...

Thanks to NAM, we understand that there was a purpose to the first section. This was a scene of seduction, but the underlying story was that of a hidden whispering voice telling the hero what should be done. The purpose here is not to refer to similarities with other stories. The point of mentioning line 33 is to show how E-NE and NE-E were mirrored and obviously intended to convey a sense of climax, a high fire. It might be said that a vow was taking place for the renown of the land. In context, it must also be read as the 'high fire' of a pair of lovers.

E is used as 'lofty' in *The Story of Sukurru* when it occurs as adjective with characters there, including the lofty camel. Whatever the choice, it refers to height. EN, the end, is the inversion of NE, the new. E has an extra meaning of 'chick', discovered thanks to a translated proverb. This is the new-born of the phoenix, risen from the flames.

> *New: Old English neowe, niowe, earlier niwe 'new, fresh, recent, novel, unheard-of, different from the old; untried, inexperienced,' from Proto-Germanic *newjaz (source also of Old Saxon niuwi, Old Frisian nie, Middle Dutch nieuwe, Dutch nieuw, Old High German niuwl, German neu, Danish and Swedish ny, Gothic niujis 'new'), from PIE root.*

The EN, central to this puzzle, has the given Sumerian meanings of 'lord, ruler, master' while in Greek it means 'one'. EN has already been discussed as the central symbol in the name Enki (See pages 34-35) where it can be understood as a point of contact between sky and Earth. It might also be the origin of the character known as Enoch, who was taken up into the sky.

EN-NE is also the origin of Greek Ennead, number nine. There is a high fire, a powerful energy at the centre of the Sator square. It recalls the central founding symbols of the cross that is HER: HI-ER and GAN, the alchemy, the cosmic womb, and Greek hieros, filled with the divine, holy.

The strange head carved onto the top of the Galamus Sator stone was carved in high relief onto a diamond-shaped background strongly resembling the HI of HI-ER, that together form the origin of HER, the binder and the boundary. With his tongue hanging out, a characteristic of Greek Orpheus whose decapitated head hangs around the neck of Athena, he certainly doesn't look ecstatic. The head also calls to mind the experience of those men who climbed down into the hole in that cave at the end of the 16th century.

PERI-

Moving out to the second range of letters, it becomes more useful to assume that there are two outer circles or squares and a core to the palindrome. This one surrounds the core. The most obvious Sumerian origin of this circle or square is, of course, PER, the sun and pyre.

PER was discussed in detail in chapter 17 along with its two founding symbols, PI and ER. Another way of looking at the line gives:

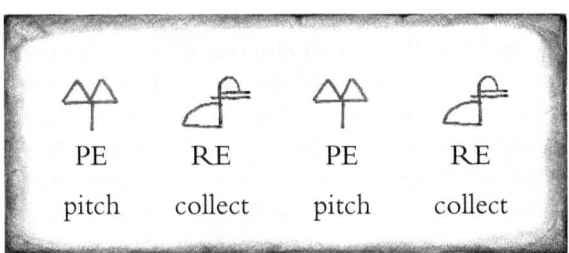

245

PE and RE, curving twice around the central point, can be written PI-RI, PE-RI, or PE-RE. They all give the origin of Greek PERI-, perimeter as mentioned on page 187, the enclosure. Together and in motion around the central fire, these four symbols resonate as they turn. The effect is like that of EN-NE. They are self-perpetuating. Replace phonetic RE by its all-important value TAL and find PE-TAL or PE-DAL:

> *Petal: 1726 (earlier petala, 1704), from Modern Latin petalum "petal" (17c.), from Greek petalon "a leaf; leaf of metal, thin plate," noun use of neuter of adj. petalos "outspread, broad, flat," from PIE root.*
>
> *Pedal: 1610s, "lever (on an organ) worked by foot," from French pédale "feet, trick with the feet," from Italian pedale "treadle, pedal," from Late Latin pedale "(thing) of the foot," neuter of Latin pedalis "of the foot," from pes (genitive pedis) "foot," from PIE root.*

TENET

There is more to be said about the form of the Sator enigma that sits in the cave above the river of the Eagles. It's different from the other known examples of the palindrome, unique in that it visibly integrates two Sumerian symbols. It was thanks to the Galamus Gorge carving that a connection to the far older civilisation of Mesopotamia became evident and that is why it caught my attention more than any other example of the Sator square. The T of TENET is more than phonetic TE. It's also the Sumerian T-shaped symbol ME, symbol of the Magician. Notice that it appears directly in relief against the chipped stone rather than carved into a smooth surface like all the other letters. And it appears on all four sides facing inwards towards the heart or the summit of the enigma. That difference in form and direction from all other known examples of the riddle gives the clue that we must look at the whole thing as more than two dimensional, and that it must be considered as a pyramidal form.

ME-TE has been mentioned more than once; I can't repeat often enough that these two combined are the founding symbols of the measurement of everything in existence and origin of the metre. The evidence of extremely ancient knowledge encased in this Sator square is confirmed by the form of the nose and eyebrows on the grimacing head above it. These are the exaggerated facial features that can be seen on artefacts around the world, all with a common understanding, a reference to a spirit world, to the pineal gland, the third eye, to magic and to Hermes. See the stone masks of Gobekli Tepe on p.107. Consider also that the rectangular Galamus stone with the strange head has the same form as Greek Herma boundary stones discussed on page 193 or the figure on the Egyptian Narmer palette, and that its wide-open mouth is indicating sound or a passageway. Consider that the head has been curiously carved, integrated into to the diamond form of HI, the mixing of alloys, the passage of souls and of curses. See HAR on page 42.

The Greek word 'tenet' has the same meaning as the principal symbol of Hermes, HER, the binding and the holding. It is also reflected in Sumerian TE, the tethering, a cord stretched between two crosses:

> Tenet: 'principle, opinion, or dogma maintained as true by a person, sect, school, etc.,' properly 'a thing held (to be true),' early 15c., from Latin tenet 'he holds,' third person singular present indicative of tenere 'to hold, grasp, keep, have possession, maintain,' also 'reach, gain, acquire, obtain; hold back, repress, restrain;' figuratively 'hold in mind, take in, understand,' from PIE root.

And the crossed form of the two Greek tenets on the Sator square can be said to amalgamate the cross of Sumerian HER, the T-shaped forms of ME, and the connection of two points found in TE. There is nothing coincidental. A connection exists between Sumer, Hermes and the Galamus version of the Sator Templar riddle.

Looking at it from this perspective, as an aerial view of a pyramid, convex or concave, the four sides converge onto a flat top or bottom where the N of EN has its place. At the centre of each side of the pyramid the words TEN and NET create four stairways leading up to or down from the platform. We might equally be in a pit, at its heart, looking upwards to the sky.

The two crossed TENETs break down to symbols TEN-ET. Phonetic NET doesn't exist as a symbol, although NIT, phonetic value of UŠ, the symbol of masculinity, is probably of consequence. We are left with TE-NE-ET, TE-EN-NE-ET, or TEN-ET. As TE and TEN are two phonetic forms of the same symbol, that leaves just four to consider here:

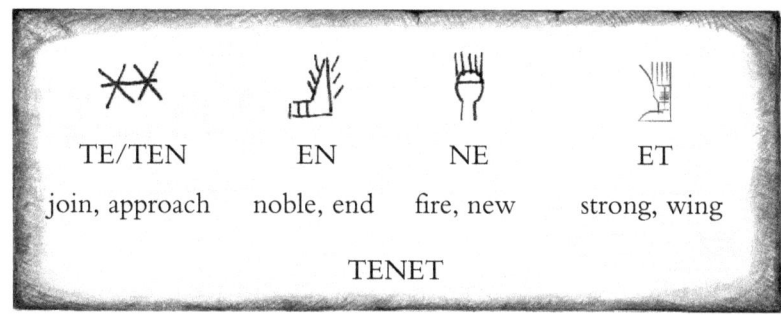

TE is given as 'foundation' 5 times and 'membrane' once, with further later translations as 'skin, layer, film'. TE-ENE-ET might translate to 'fire (in the middle) tethered by the strong wing'. This central cross indicates a structure that is securely founded and forming a protection on all four sides. Two strong wings are crossed and binding. A net has been formed around a form of energy. A different example of ID/IT/ET is shown here, apparently formed from the foot, DU, combined with the upward waving hand or arm, possibly ŠU or DA.

> *Net: Old English net 'netting, network, spider web, mesh used for capturing,' also figuratively, 'moral or mental snare or trap,' from Proto-Germanic *natjan (source also of Old Saxon net, Old Norse, Dutch net, Swedish nät, Old High German nezzi, German Netz, Gothic nati 'net'), originally 'something knotted,' from PIE root.*
>
> *Tent: c. 1300, 'portable shelter of skins or coarse cloth stretched over poles,' from Old French tente 'tent, hanging, tapestry' (12c.), from Medieval Latin tenta 'a tent,' literally 'something stretched out,' noun use of fem. singular of Latin tentus 'stretched,' variant past participle of tendere 'to stretch,' from PIE root *ten- 'to stretch.' The notion is of 'stretching' hides over a framework.*

The four central points of the four sides of the Sator square have been pegged out, the foundations laid. This is reminiscent of the Egyptian ceremonies carried out at the placing of temple foundations, a ritual known as 'stretching the cord' apparently to ensure the astronomical alignment of the building.

The lexical entries inform us that TEMEN, one phonetic value of TE, is to be found opposite these three, where symbol TE is repeated within itself:

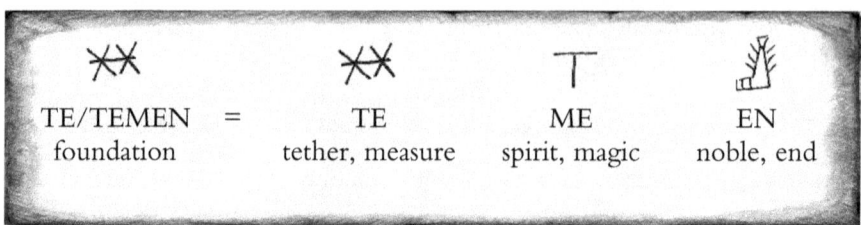

Note the given meaning of TEMEN. The spirit and the magic of ME exist in a hidden layer of TE. ME lies both within and next to TE. They are inseparable. For what it's worth, in etymological dictionaries, 'ten-' is given as a PIE root of words related to 'stretch'. We are tending towards something. Something is 'tendu', French for 'stretched'.

> Temple: "building for worship, edifice dedicated to the service of a deity or deities," Old English tempel, from Latin templum "piece of ground consecrated for the taking of auspices, building for worship of a god," of uncertain signification. Commonly referred to PIE root *tem-.
>
> Templar: late 13c., from Anglo-French templer, Old French templier (c. 1200), from Medieval Latin templaris (mid-12c.), member of the medieval religious/military order known as Knights Templars (c.1118-1312).

Sumerian TEMEN gives the origin of Greek temenos which means 'a sacred area surrounding a temple', and source of our word 'temple'. This logic also applies to the temple of the human head.

The place within the temenos, the heart of the temple, was called the hieron, a name that takes us back to HER and to the lexical entry of HI-ER.

Another word related directly to the temple and element of the Sator square is found here: from PE-RE, the peribolos which is the court surrounding the temple and enclosed by a wall.

250

> Latin temporalis "of time, denoting time; but for a time, temporary," from tempus (genitive temporis) "time, season, moment, proper time or season," from Proto-Italic *tempos- "stretch, measure," from PIE root.

There is an obvious linguistic connection between 'temple' and 'temporalis'. TE-ME can be understood as measure of both place and time.

Sumerian TEMEN, having the given meanings of 'foundation' and 'layer', is also found as TEN, another phonetic form of TE. TEN is shown on all four sides of the Sator square.

> Ten: Old English ten (Mercian), tien (West Saxon), adjective and noun, from Proto- Germanic *tehun (source also of Old Saxon tehan, Old Norse tiu, Danish ti, Old Frisian tian, Old Dutch ten, (...), from PIE root.

What importance should be given to the evidence that the number ten is integrated into the puzzle? If we consider that EN-NE is 'nine', origin of the Greek Ennead (line 206 translated to 'the fiery lord' and line 207 translated to 'nine'), then the notion of a game or a hidden message that combines symbols with numbers, concerns the dimensions of a temple and the measurement of time takes shape. See ZAG for a reference to 'four' on page 254. Also, the ancient Greek number system transforms TEMEN (T=300, E=5, M=40, E=5, N=50) into 400.

> Nine: Old English nigen, from Proto-Germanic *newun (source also of Old Saxon nigun, Old Frisian niugun, Old Norse niu, Swedish nio, Middle Dutch neghen, Dutch negen, Old High German niun, German neun, Gothic niun 'nine'), from PIE root.
>
> Ennead: 'group of nine things,' 1650s, from Greek enneas (genitive enneados) 'group of nine,' from ennea 'nine' (see nine).

To conclude this section on TENET, the cross of the Sator square, TE-EN-NE-ET, can be read backwards or forwards, to right and to left. At the centre is the force, the energy, a back and forth between EN and NE, the fire, the end and the renewal. On all sides, the tether of the strong wing. They are fitting symbols for a self-sustaining power, an unending source of energy, a machine. But also, without a doubt, a temple, a Temple of the Sun.

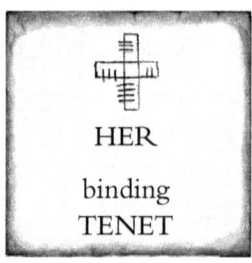

HER

binding
TENET

N x N = double N = ZAG

The other Sumerian symbol that appears more discreetly but clearly on the Galamus carving is ZAG, represented in the uppermost and central square of the pyramid, the N of EN and the N of NE. They cross and combine into ENE. Where all the letters are in their normal vertical position, N should appear just once as in any modern crossword puzzle and that is how it appears on other examples of the Sator square. But not here. The two ENs on the Galamus stone combine but, in the right light, both appear, one upright and the other upside down. They combine to form a bow on the uppermost place of the pyramid from an aerial perspective.

ZAG

shoulder, to tie

The given meanings of ZAG are 'arm' and 'shoulder' 216 times. It's also given as 'border', 'boundary', 'district' and 'limit' which is quite fascinating in light of the function of the Greek Herma stone, the myths related to Hermes, and the given meaning of HER. ZAG is also given once as 'nose rope', another equally interesting finding in the light of the Narmer palette and Prometheus. See the image on page 128. And, of course, Sumerian ZAG at 3350-3200 BC is over two thousand years older than the first examples of alphabetical Phoenician and over three thousand older than the earliest example of the Sator square.

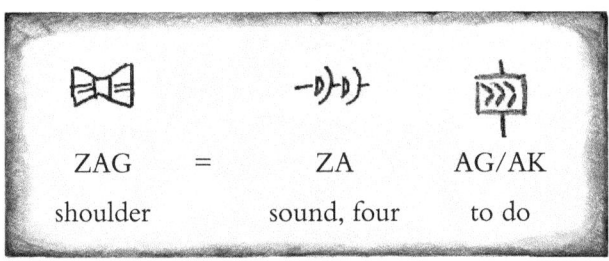

There are two voluminous and comparatively unusual lexical entries for ZAG opposite the ZA-AG combination. I haven't attempted to reproduce them here, but their existence is noteworthy. These two might translate to 'four sounds to make' or just 'sound to make'. ZA is given as 'bead' and 'gem' 18 times at 2500-2000 BC which is consistent with the notion of a shoulder tie or bow that might be clasped and decorated with jewellery. There are several different forms, one of which I have copied above. Some look like the tiny cymbals of a Greek sistrum. Another form is simply four strokes and almost identical to $LIMMU_2$, meaning 'four'. The word 'sound' is not given but is understood in combinations with other symbols. ZA is also the ancient solfeggio name for B flat. When I was looking for that link between ZA and sound, (and for what it's worth) I came across the following post on the NASA website:

> *Astronomers in England have discovered a singing black hole in a distant cluster of galaxies. ... (...) The sound waves coming from it are in the form of a single note, so rather than a song it is really a drone. Using the piano keyboard's middle C note as a reference point for the middle of the piano key music range, Fabian's team determined the note is a B -flat.*[118]

N x N = M = EME

This is the final clue to the Sumerian origin and message of the Galamus Sator square. The inverted Ns come together not only to form ZAG but also the letter M. Thus, we find either N or M as the central letter of the enigma. In the Greek numeral system, M has the value of 40. Replacing ENE (EN-NE) with EM-ME, the spirit wind (see page 256), gives the phonetic form EME. The corresponding symbol is a combination of KA with ME:

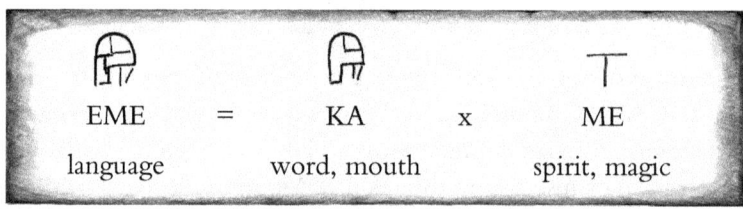

EME   =   KA   x   ME

language   word, mouth   spirit, magic

EME is given as 'tongue, language' 178 times from 2500 BC. EME with GI, the reed or staff, is given 21 times at 2500 BC as 'Sumerian language'. To find this very lightly veiled reference to the Sumerian tongue at the centre and, according to perspective, at the summit of the Galamus Sator square allows the final piece of this puzzle to fall into place and to confirm, if there was still any doubt, the very real link between Sumer and the Galamus Sator square. Note that M appears plainly according to the angle at which it is viewed. Also note that it doesn't appear at all on other versions elsewhere. This is a very special Sator enigma, the key to all others.

EME is the voice of the Magician or the magical word. If we continue to understand ME as the symbol of measurement, combined with KA, the word, it becomes everything that needs to be said about measurement and magic. Eme is also the ancient Greek word for 'me' which brings us full circle to symbol ME, the original T-shaped symbol and to the Tau.

The Rope, the Sail, and the Ship

A final point on EM-ME, the wind and the spirit. They appear twice together in *The Story of Sukurru*. On lines 124 and 126, they were translated in context to:

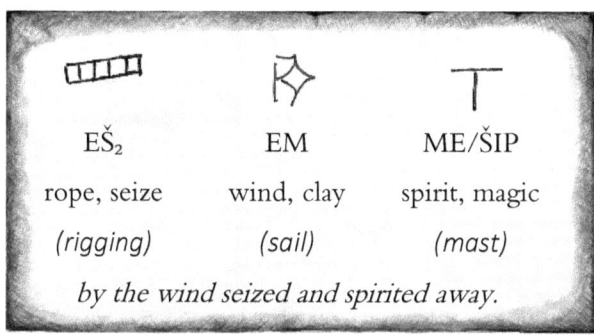

The above three symbols together evoke elements of the cosmic ship not only from the context in which they are found in that story, but through the old pictograms themselves; EŠ₂ is the image of the rope and has the given meaning of 'to seize'. EM/IM looks suspiciously like a sail hanging from a beam and has the given meaning of 'wind'. The T-shaped mast of ME to which the pagan flute-player of *The Story of Sukurru* will be tied (see pages 17-18) represents the 'ship' (see page 214).

Whoever first created the elements of this language did so at least partially within the context of navigation, and a relatively advanced large-scale form of it. This is clearly not the stuff of woven coracles and paddles on Mesopotamian rivers. And it has considerably more in common with Homeric tales than with those primitive sheep traders who have, until now, been credited as the only source of the pictographic pre-3000 BC forms of Sumerian.

EZEN

The Sator square without its outer ring takes on the shape of Sumerian EZEN, the 'song' and 'festival' with its four external pegs. As previously mentioned, EZEN is more than a sibling of symbol HER. EZEN is generally given at the earliest Uruk IV period as a circle that has four rectangular attachments – like the Ts of TENET. Visually, its core could be understood as symbol KIL with four pegs added to it.

Below are three examples of EZEN on tablets from the Uruk IV period. The left-hand example has symbol EN at its centre, providing the most complete symbolic equivalent of the Sator square[119]:

  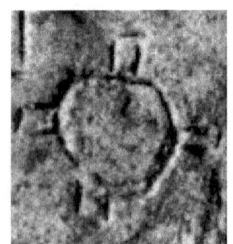

SATOR

Step away from the core of the ENE 'game' and from its immediate periphery, to look, from a safe distance, at the outer circle. It becomes necessary to replace letter 'O' non-existent in the Sumerian dictionaries with 'U', a cosmetic gesture with no harm done.

This is the ground plan. At the centre of each of the four sides, the T indicates ME-TE, the measure and the foundation, the pegs that hold the tent in place. But clearly it isn't meant as a static pyramid. It served a purpose. The imperative form of ROTAS, rotate, in this outer circle indicates that this is where the machinery is set in motion.

> *Rotation: 1550s, from Latin rotationem (nominative rotatio) 'a turning about in a circle,' noun of action from past participle stem of rotare 'turn round, revolve, whirl about, roll,' from PIE root.*
>
> *Roll: early 13c., 'rolled-up piece of parchment or paper' (especially one inscribed with an official record), from Old French rolle 'document, parchment scroll, decree' (12c.), from Medieval Latin rotulus 'a roll of paper' (...), from Latin rotula 'small wheel,' diminutive of rota 'wheel' (see rotary).*

Words indicating both the movement of the wheel and regret expressed by 'to rue' come from Sumerian RU. Why would there be a link between the two? A story of passing time, marked by the circling of planets, and some event that will give cause to 'rue the day'? It's one of our lost stories. Perhaps it will come to light again one day. RU appears as 'to rue' on line 272 when the lofty camel gets its revenge. Camels, known as 'water-hearts', don't joke around.

RU is mentioned once as 'weapon'. 'To lay down', 'to impose', 'to release', 'to fall', 'to drop' are some of the meanings given for earliest period.

> *Rue: 'feel regret,' Old English hreowan 'make sorry, distress, grieve' (class II strong verb; past tense hreaw, past participle hrowen), from Proto-Germanic *khrewan (source also of Old Frisian riowa, Middle Dutch rouwen, Old Dutch hrewan, German reuen 'to sadden, cause repentance'); in part, blended with Old English weak verb hreowian 'feel pain or sorrow,' and perhaps influenced by Old Norse hryggja 'make sad,' both from Proto-Germanic *khruwjan, all from PIE root.*

It's also the origin of the French word 'roue', the wheel from Latin rotas. The wheels of the Sator square are about to be set in motion.

> *Saturn: Old English Sætern, a Roman god, also 'most remote planet' (then known), from Latin Saturnus, originally a name of an Italic god of agriculture, possibly from Etruscan.*
>
> *Saturate (v.) 1530s, 'to satisfy, satiate,' from Latin saturatus, past participle of saturare 'to fill full, sate, drench,' from satur 'sated, full,' from PIE root.*

In this outer perimeter of the Sator square, it might just be Saturn, the planet, also considered to be Kronos, Father of Time, who is linked to circular movement and to the imposition of that movement thanks to RU in ROTAS. Greek Saturn/Kronos generally devours his children but eats a stone in place of Zeus who has escaped. He is eventually forced to spit them all up, stone included. Greek Talus throws boulders at passing sailors and Greek Hermes is buried in piles of stones that are thrown at him. The projection of stones is a bad habit, but a common theme in the mythologies, a binding thread. Let's hope that the release of the Sator machine doesn't lead to more of it.

TAS and UR are two phonetic values for the same symbol, both dog and lion. Imagine that the outer circle can be rotated in both directions, clockwise and anti-clockwise in the manner of a Rubik cube. SAT becomes TAS when turned anti-clockwise or read from right to left. In this way, there are two dogs or lions to be found in SAT-UR, three turns to the left for TAS and two to the right for UR, the two animals facing in opposite directions.

Otherwise, SAT is one phonetic value of KUR, the mountain, and, with UR, reads 'the mountain and the dog', or 'the mountain of the dog'. An additional point concerning phonetic value KUR is a lexical entry showing the following breakdown:

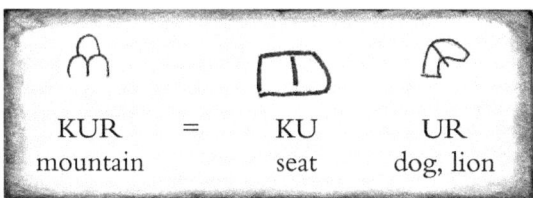

This translates to 'seat of the dog/lion' or perhaps a 'seated dog/lion'. It is only those who haven't studied, even superficially, the Egyptian pyramids and the Great Sphinx of the Giza plateau who will need me to add that the dog in question – who sits or rather lies beside three mounds in SAT-UR – mirrors the image of Anubis lying across a casket, represented here by the rest of the square, but also, with TAS-UR, the two guardian lions lying back to back on the Sphinx stele, a plaque said to have been erected by Pharaoh Khufu. It sits between the two front limbs of the Great Sphinx of Giza. Below them, the central element of the plaque looks very much like a labyrinth, a riddle. Of course, there is also the possibility of looking at the above SAT-UR symbols together and seeing there three pyramids behind a lion. Is it a step too far?

RU-TAS, rotation of the dog, wheel of the dog? Whichever way you turn, there are dogs or lions. UR-UR is given 21 times as 'cultic person', 'jackal', or 'caterpillar'!

> *Ur- prefix meaning 'original, earliest, primitive,' from German ur- 'out of, original,' from Proto-Germanic *uz- 'out,' from PIE Aureate: early 15c., 'resembling gold, gold-colored,' also figuratively, 'splendid, brilliant,' from Latin aureatus 'decorated with gold,' from aureus 'golden,' from aurum 'gold,' from PIE root.*

There are several themes that appear from the combinations of SATUR and RUTAS; circular movement, Saturn and time, the notion of saturation, and the dogs who look in both directions. On the Narmer palette, the two lions with their long necks form a circle and end up nose to nose. This calls to mind the Great Sphinx staring at its counterpart, Leo, in the sky.

A few final points

It's also possible to find SA, the string, with TUR, the youth…

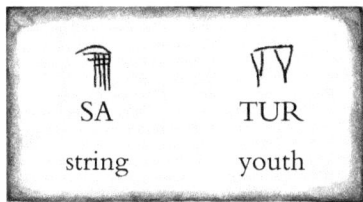

SA-TUR turns up several times in the lexical entries with GIŠ. SA is given as 'string of a bow or musical instrument', 'catgut string' 64 times at a late period. TUR has the given meanings of 'child, son, daughter' 623 times, and 'to be small, to diminish, to subtract' 111 times. It was translated to 'young' in the context of *The Story of Sukurru*. The image appears to be a pair of breasts with milk flowing downwards which, of course, corresponds quite well to the given meanings. However, there is always something more to the symbols and I suspect that it might also be the origin of the word 'tower'. Below are four drawings from the earliest period showing that TUR varies quite a lot, and, in some, a similarity can again be found with that most ubiquitous of forms, KIL, the round or square block.

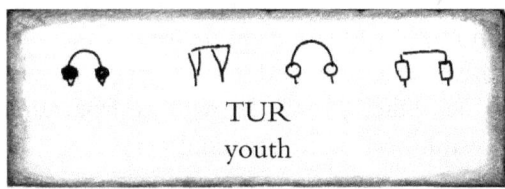

SA with TUR, the string of the musical instrument and the youth, calls to mind the story of Orpheus, the bard who charms wild animals and birds with his music, whose head ends up hanging from his own cord around the neck of Athena. See line 36 of *The Story of Sukurru*. See pages 277 to 278. In *The Story of Sukurru*, TUR MU is (partially) translated to 'young Mu' on line 34. One solution might have been to translate the two symbols to 'the renowned youth'. Given the references to ballads, chords, and hanging from a cord on the next few lines, it surely links to the myth of Orpheus. But it's not easy to disentangle the threads from the chords, remembering that this text precedes every other piece of writing that we possess.

ROTAS

The pins or pegs of the Sator square are represented by the symbol TE-(ME) in the centre of the outer walls.

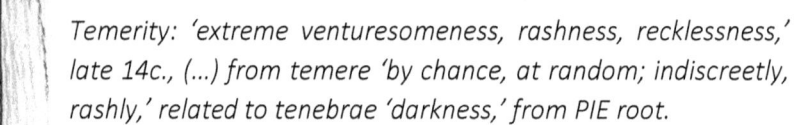

Temerity: 'extreme venturesomeness, rashness, recklessness,' late 14c., (...) from temere 'by chance, at random; indiscreetly, rashly,' related to tenebrae 'darkness,' from PIE root.

Before pulling the pins, move back a pace because now there is nothing to restrain the ancient cogs. A touch of oil perhaps as they begin to turn. The liberated outer circle clicks forward five times, always clockwise. Anti-clockwise would be unlucky...we know this from the cursing stones. SATOR slides forward, over the edge, and down.

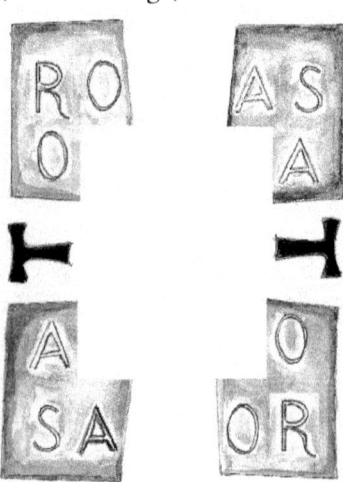

OPERA to APERO

Found on the fourth line down, OPERA has transformed into APERO after five clicks of the outer circle. O-PER, source of Latin operire 'to close' and the 'cover' gives way to A-PER origin of Latin aperire, 'to open' and the 'aperture'.

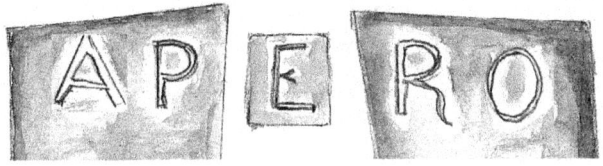

It's not difficult to understand the effect of the rotating wheel. Something has been liberated. Whatever it is, the Sator square is no longer hermetic. Is this what was meant by Pandora's box?

> *Operculum: 1713, from Latin operculum 'cover, lid,' from operire 'to cover, close,' from PIE*
>
> *Operate; late 14c., 'action, performance, work,' also 'the performance of some science or art,' from Old French operacion 'operation, working, proceedings,' from Latin operationem (nominative operatio) 'a working, operation,' from past participle stem of operari 'to work, labor' (in Late Latin 'to have effect, be active, cause'), from opera 'work, effort,' related to opus (genitive operis) 'a work' (from PIE root.*
>
> *Aperture: early 15c., 'an opening, hole, orifice,' from Latin apertura 'an opening,' from apertus, past participle of aperire 'to open, uncover,' from PIE compound.*

A further way of understanding this is to go directly to the origin of the two Latin words and look at the Sumerian symbols. Symbol U is given as 'to sink down', 'to cover', 'to cloud over' 49 times. It has given way to symbol A, the flow. They both relate to PER, the sun. It can either be exposed or hidden.

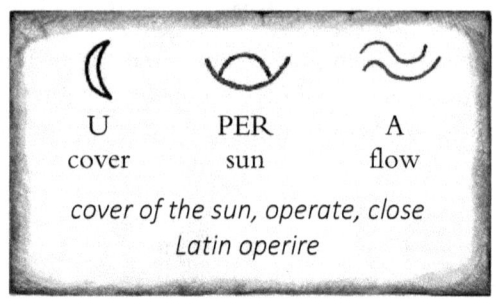

U cover — PER sun — A flow

*cover of the sun, operate, close
Latin operire*

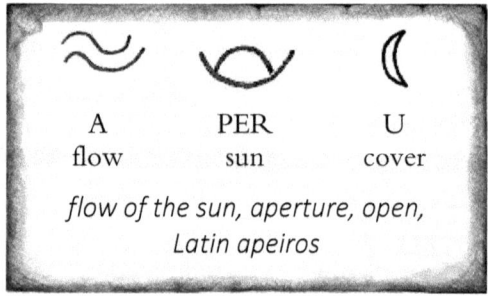

A flow — PER sun — U cover

*flow of the sun, aperture, open,
Latin apeiros*

In order for the combination A-PER to disappear, flow of the sun, and be replaced by U-PER, cover of the sun, or vice versa, the entire outer circle will have to rotate by multiples of five spaces. The Sumerian symbol of spreading and multiplication, I, original symbol of the so-called Fibonacci sequence, is also the number five. (See page 10.) Thus, the rotating Sator square indicates organic growth.

> *Infinite: Latin infinitas was used as a loan-translation of Greek apeiria 'infinity,' from apeiros 'endless.'*
>
> *Everything is generated from apeiron and there its destruction happens. Infinite worlds are generated and they are destructed there again. And he says (Anaximander) why this is apeiron. Because only then genesis and decay will never stop.*[120]

The Movement

The withdrawal of T having released the central fire and the wheels, RO/RU, having been put in motion, a four-pronged pattern emerges from centre out which can be read as NE-RU whichever way it turns. It might be seen as the origin of the swastika pattern and read as rotating fire or fire wheel, one way to describe the sun or any fiery orb:

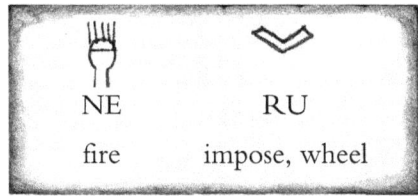

NE-RU appears in ePSD lists as NE.RU with given meanings of 'hostile', 'enemy', 'wicked', 'villainous' and as NERU-GAL opposite 'great evil'. These definitions fit well with the Greek myth of Pandora's box, meant to remain unopened, hermetic because filled with evil spirits. It can also be assimilated to the art of invoking spirits on the condition that they are bound and rendered harmless before interrogation. An unbound spirit jumping from an opened box does not bode well. I would prefer a Magician to be present.

NE-RU is also a term used to indicate that clay formed into a tablet, a brick or a container of some kind has been fired in a kiln and made durable. Compared to the above ominous translations, that is quite reassuring. If some force has been released that results in the firing of clay, it is reminiscent of the clay tablets surviving after being hardened by wildfires that destroyed everything else around them. Knowledge saved by fire.

The Sator Square and the Templar Connection

The SATOR riddle had significance for someone in Pompei in the first century AD, and it was also scratched or carefully inscribed onto walls in various places around Europe as late as the 16th century AD. It was necessarily important to at least one group of people; it seems very unlikely that such a puzzle would have been inscribed in so many different places with such gaps in time if the significance of it and the subject it related to were completely unknown to those who copied it, if they didn't expect others to understand something of its meaning. A visible effort was made to ensure that it wouldn't completely disappear over the course of many generations. But there is another aspect to HER as 'tenet' that has not yet been mentioned; the notion of binding is an essential part of magical procedures linked to the invocation of spirits, and it's destined to prevent harm coming to participants during such a ceremony. Given the association of magic and binding in the Hermes symbol, it's possible that the existence of the Templar/Sator square was the result of its continued use in Roman times as a protective talisman, a binding of potentially unruly spirits, and that full knowledge of its origin was already fading or lost for most of the population – but surely not for everyone.

If a wisdom teacher called Hermes is at the origin of knowledge emanating perhaps from a previous civilisation, why would the information brought to mankind have been subsequently hidden away? Surely it would have been openly available to survivors with copies of the essence of it put into a place considered safe from future catastrophes. Keepers of the knowledge would have been designated and charged with passing the key to future generations in the event of a new catastrophe. Perhaps that is what happened. Perhaps the last catastrophe wiped out the knowledge, wiped out the temple, but left the unlabelled key. And then what? Why was the key not used again, not made public? Does it still exist? In what form? Where is it kept?

Has our civilization missed out on the knowledge once perpetuated in manuscripts, in tablets, or scratched onto walls over millennia? Has the most important piece of information been kept back or destroyed? Did the person who composed the Sator square intend for it to be made and kept public? Did they want or expect its riddle to be solved? If not, why bother? Was the overall alphabetical representation of HER, symbol of Hermes, intended to perpetuate the memory of the name and to make a visual reference to a temple – perhaps even to a temple's dimensions? Was it just a game? A well-known joke? A talisman of forgotten meaning? Or was it the key? I would wager that the Knights Templars were aware that this was the symbol of Hermes

Trismegistus. It might well be that Hermes was their prophet in the Middle East in much the same way that the Great Magician had been that of the Sabians long before. Were they privy to documents on the subject, documents that were never made public?

Graham Hancock in his book *The Sign and the Seal*[121] investigates the theory that the biblical Ark of the Covenant was taken from Jerusalem to Ethiopia. He found multiple examples of the Templar cross in and around Aksum and has also said that, visiting the Church of St. Mary in Lalibela, a building covered in Templar symbolism, he discovered a Sator Square there. The locals had felt the need to keep this particular carving, the significance of which they clearly didn't know, hidden behind a curtain. Were they simply perpetuating an ancient command to secrecy without knowing the meaning of it? If indeed this was an order given by the Knights Templar as the context suggests, it also suggests that the Sator square had a lot more to offer than a play on words, a once-amusing riddle. It existed in the Church of St. Mary as a message for initiates or as a protective talisman and was linked to the Ark of the Covenant, thought to be in safe keeping nearby. Whether the Ark existed and was in Ethiopia or not, the Sator square was understood to be linked to it. That is the important point.

The information in *The Sign and the Seal* by extension infers a link between the Ark of the Covenant, the Knights Templar and that other Sator carving, also relatively well hidden away, but in a French mountain gorge, a region known for its Templar and Cathar presence. Although accessible today, the Galamus Sator stone must once have been visible only to initiates; initiates of what? It is interesting to note that Saint Anthony of Egypt, patron saint of the hermitage, is depicted in several images holding a distinctive T-shaped staff and that the Ethiopian priests also carry a staff of that shape. Is that a common shape for the instrument? Is it a coincidence? Perhaps.

As Graham Hancock explains, the glaucomas and premature deaths of the generations of Ethiopian priests who have guarded the Ark might well result from exposure to its dangerous qualities. That would explain why the Ark was said to have been enveloped in a gold case, a metal that is capable of protecting against extreme levels of radiation. And it raises the possibility that the Templars had knowledge of the existence of a very special stone, a meteorite formed from an unknown metal with properties that might be harnessed while remaining highly dangerous. That stone would have been stored inside the box that became known as the Ark of the Covenant. (See line 47 of *The Story of Sukurru* for mention of MI-NA, the 'black stone'. See page 99.) Perhaps the Sator square was understood to be a protective binding force, guarding against a very real danger.

Returning to the analysis carried out here on symbols HER and EZEN and continuing the journey in Egypt, my theory derived from those symbols that the Great Pyramid of Giza was concerned with the creation of energy isn't new. Although it has long been declared that the original construction was intended as the tomb of Pharaoh Khufu, no mummified body, no obvious commemorative wall decorations were found within it; only an enigmatic rectangular granite box that had been badly damaged, probably at the time when its lid was prised away. Theories about more practical uses involving resonance and uncommon energy sources abound. Greek Perseus, Prometheus and Pandora are all telling a story from different perspectives. The mother of Perseus – notice the PER of pyramid and sun alike - was hidden in a bronze chamber and impregnated by a shower of gold that turned out to be Zeus – another strange myth. The box of Pandora, opened and broken, might be that granite box still guarding its secrets in the King's Chamber, its contents long gone, spirited away. Perhaps it was once used to house a sizable chunk or two of a meteorite, the Pyramid functioning as a source of energy, combining the piezo-electric qualities of the piled-up granite blocks with whatever force emanated from the stone sitting in its midst.

Someone forced their way into the box. I wonder what they made of the contents when the lid finally gave way. Were they expecting a great treasure? Was it just the mummified body of Khufu inside or did they get their hands on a dangerous piece of meteorite? If the latter, was its final journey to Ethiopia? Were there other pieces? Did the Templars, many centuries later, track them down thanks to ancient texts kept secret from the rest of the world? Were one or more brought back to Europe? Perhaps one was dropped down into a gaping hole at the back of a large cave above the Galamus Gorges, a desperate measure to ensure it could cause no more harm. This is all conjecture, of course, but, if there is any truth in it, then the story of the two adventurers who climbed down into the pit, one of whom disappeared and the other who died in terror, should dissuade us from re-opening the door to that hole. Anyway, the vision of the agonized face above the Galamus herma-stone should be enough to discourage anyone from passing that boundary and seeking to know more.

Opera Rotas… or maybe not.

20

Atlantis and the Fish

The clockwise rotation of the five SATOR letters have taken both the mountain, SAT, and the dog, UR, over the cliff and down where they become - SATUR - saturated. Perhaps what follows will seem like a step too far for some. My feeling is that the enigma conveys as much information about the past as is possible in 20 letters and 3 circles. Since we are on the subject of saturation, and at the risk of patience becoming saturated, I will take that extra step off the edge. There might be name-calling and even sinking of reputation, but such is life. Here is my final move on the board of the SATOR game.

- SAT-UR, the Mountain of the Dog slides forward and sinks down.

- SA-AT-UR, where SA is 'net', AT is the oldest reference to Atlantis, and UR is both 'dog' and 'gold'. A fishing net lies around Atlantis, the golden city, the city of the dog. There are a couple of quite different symbols for AT given in L'Ecriture Cunéiforme and elsewhere. Here are three examples:

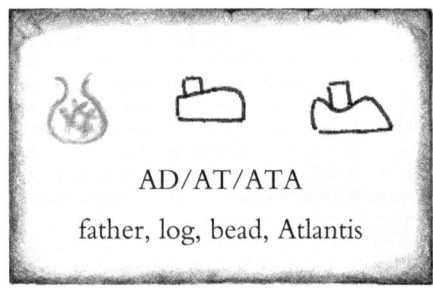

AD/AT/ATA
father, log, bead, Atlantis

AD/AT is given 7 times as 'father' at 3000-2500 BC. Other meanings are not dated. The symbols vary between a fishing net or bag of some kind and something resembling a famous yellow submarine.

269

Below is a portion of a clay tablet from the Uruk III period. It shows an intriguing picture made up of a combination of symbols[122]:

Reading from right to left on this portion of the tablet gives MUN-SU-PAP-BAD-SI-AN-AT-GIR.

- MUN, the symbol in the form of a vessel far right with three vertical strokes, is given as 'brackish', water that has some salt content. It's also given as a type of fish 5 times.

- SU, the small pyramidal form (bottom centre) can mean 'sink' but is also closely linked to ZU, knowledge.

- PAP, above left of SU, is 'to estrange' or 'to wean'. See chapter 1. It can also be read as 'unity of capacity based on a vessel size' according to ePSD.

- BAD directly above PAP has the given meaning 'remote'. BAD is found with BA-AD in the lexical entries. The version on this tablet is unusual in that it has a horizontal line across the top and looks more like a hybrid of BAD with ME.

- SI, the horn, is a symbol of warning and of remembrance with AN, the sky, a close neighbour to its left. SI-AN, remembering the remote sky perhaps?

- The next symbol down is AT or AD, symbol of Atlantis. The etymology of Atlantis is given as Greek Atlantikos, an adjectival form of Atlas and is found in context in Plato's dialogues[123]. The only question is his intention in mentioning the place; Was it a highly detailed but imaginary creation or a veritable historical account? If, as I believe, this Sumerian tablet is also referring to Atlantis, the same question can be raised. It proves the story is more ancient than Plato and thus that he didn't invent it, but is it true?

- The most impressive symbol on this tablet is the great fish called GIR, a cross-hatched version of HA, also 'fish'. Is it meant to be a humpback whale with a particularly impressive tail? The relative size of this symbol indicates that the whole constitutes more than a straightforward text. GIR offers an extremely interesting variety of phonetic values:

GIR/KIR/KIRI

GIR/KIR/KIRI

fish, three times

Pisces

Given 31 times as 'three' and 'to do something three times' at the 2500 BC period, GIR can also be read as KIR:

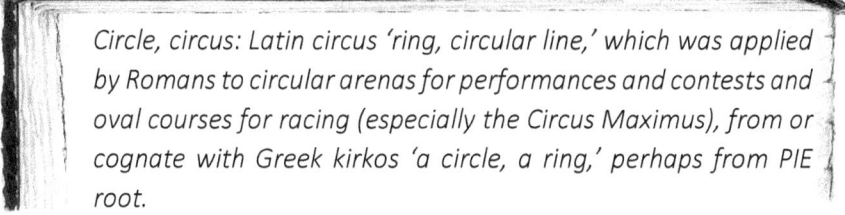

Circle, circus: Latin circus 'ring, circular line,' which was applied by Romans to circular arenas for performances and contests and oval courses for racing (especially the Circus Maximus), from or cognate with Greek kirkos 'a circle, a ring,' perhaps from PIE root.

From it's given meaning and this etymological link, it is not unreasonable to conclude that the great Sumerian fish indicates the presence of three circles.

Plato's account of Atlantis explains that the city was formed of three circular areas, one within the other, and that it ended up deep in the ocean. GIR and KIR make the connection between the great fish and the three circles. In context on the above tablet, AT is directly linked to them.

KIRI, one more phonetic value of the Sumerian fish symbol, provides the bond with Hermes through KI-RI, two of the founding symbols of the KIRIS/KIRID/HER cross thoroughly analysed in chapter 18. It presents a variety of possible meanings: 'in the place to collect', 'the place of the bird, of flight, of the dividing line', 'the place of the eagle's talon', 'the keys to gather', 'from the place to release'.

GIR/PIS/PEŠ
With the phonetic value PIS or PIŠ we find both the Sumerian origin of Pisces through Latin piscis and the source of 'fish':

> Fish: 'a vertebrate which has gills fins adapting it for living in the water,' Old English fisc 'fish,' from Proto-Germanic *fiskaz (source also of Old Saxon, Old Frisian, Old High German fisc, Old Norse fiskr, Middle Dutch visc, Dutch vis, German Fisch, Gothic fisks), perhaps from PIE root *pisk- 'a fish.' Source of/evidence for its existence is provided by Latin piscis.

This can also be linked to the mathematical form known as the Vesica Pisces, the vessel of the fish, where two circles of equal radius intersect in a manner that allows the formation of an equilateral triangle. Of course, I found this information through multiple sources on internet. The third form that results from the intersection of the two circles can be likened to that of a fish.

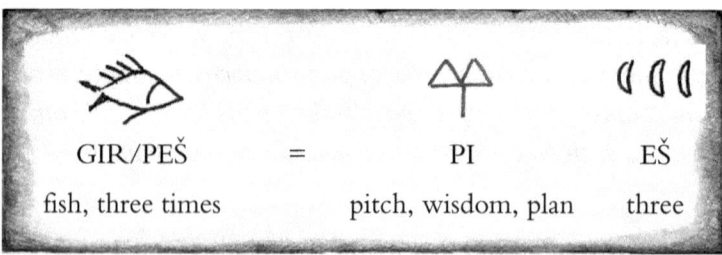

| GIR/PEŠ | = | PI | EŠ |
| fish, three times | | pitch, wisdom, plan | three |

The lexical entries for PIŠ offer a breakdown that includes the number three.

GIR/PUS
This phonetic value leads to the Greek name Poseidon, understood to be the original leader of Atlantis. It brings to mind the three Hermes mentioned on page 191 (ref. 100), and the notion of the wisdom-bringing fish-god who is discussed in chapter 21.

Is Hermes the well-attested fish-god who roamed around dispatching knowledge? Was he represented in fish garb because of the association with Atlantis? Or should we look only for an astronomical link with the constellation of Pisces, the fish? Astronomy is a complex subject not explored here but which certainly plays an underlying role in *The Story of Sukurru*. Line 222 mentions two fish-hands that follow on from SU-SU-SU on line 221. This is the section that mirrors the biblical scene of Noah getting drunk and appearing naked in front of his sons, where SU, translated to 'sink' in that context, takes the form of three pyramids. Read as ZU-ZU-ZU, they become three times 'knowledge'.

Crete, Talos, Atlantis and GIR/KIR
A massive eruption on the island of Thera, now called Santorini and close to Crete, devastated the region in 1646 BC. Both Crete and Greece, names of unknown origin, appear to begin with the GIR/KIR sound. Talos, the metal robot, circled the island of Crete three times every day with his stones. If we consider that KIR, the fish and the three actions, might apply to the region of Crete, then it could be that three events had already taken place there before the eruption of 1646 BC. It's interesting to note that, unlike Pompei, no skeletons were found around the area of the 2nd millennium event, implying that there was ample warning for people to leave. Of course, 'to do something three times' might be completely unrelated to the Santorini volcano. Nevertheless, Talos, menacing and unaware of his own vulnerability, circled the place three times daily with rocks in his hands. Why did he feel the need?

I don't pretend to have solved the mystery of the whereabouts of Atlantis but there is no denying that Talos is attempting to convey something of great importance. He is just one of many figures to be read as metaphor and message. We have either enjoyed the myths of Ancient Greece or found them too confused and out of touch with our world, but they have not faded away. Why would a scribe sit down on an uncomfortable straw-stuffed cushion to write about a metal giant unless there was something more to the story, unless there was a message of interest to be conveyed in a format that would always be repeated... on clay, on papyrus, on parchment, on paper? All the names that appear in Greek mythology should be examined through the lens of the original language; an encyclopaedia waiting to be explored at a new level, hidden in plain sight. We were not supposed to forget that our languages came from that one source.

Atlantis bis

Moving on to another Sumerian artefact, this time a seal impression that has been referenced multiple times in relation to the 'ancient alien' theory in the best-selling books of Zecharia Sitchin. The seal, now held in a Berlin museum[124], became famous for the image interpreted as that of our solar system, including an unknown tenth planet, called Nibiru. The subject gave rise to widespread controversy and heated debate.

Apart from the 'solar system', the tablet has an interesting inscription which has not been translated through monosyllabic Sumerian. There's a translation done by Dr Michael Heiser and published on a site created by him for the unique purpose of proving Zecharia Sitchin wrong, a goal made glaringly obvious in the name: sitchiniswrong.com. He used it to prove the innocuity of the seal, and thus the falsehood of the claim made about Nibiru. All of this inspired me to do my own translation. It's not very long but it's longer than his.

Dr Heiser gives the Akkadian version as '*Dubsiga, Ili-illat, your/his servant*' where Dubsiga is reckoned to be the name of the owner of the seal. My monosyllabic translation uses all nine symbols indicated on his site but takes them back to their earlier forms. It gives the following result:

DUB	SI	GA
tablet	horn	milk

With this tablet, a horn of milk

AN	IL$_2$	LA
sky	raise	hang

to the sky to raise, to hold

AT	ARAD	SU
Atlantis	saying	sink

and, like proverbial Atlantis, sink!

By this tablet, that a horn of milk be raised and, like proverbial Atlantis, sunk!

Long before Plato's mention of it, people far and wide were aware of the fate of Atlantis. It was an age-old theme that had become a saying, a joke. The tablet's inscription can be understood as a toast, raising a glass or, in this case, a horn in remembrance of the event. SI, the horn, is given as 'to remember' although with no dating. Was it really milk? Who knows?

The medium on which it was first engraved, a carved stone cylinder seal, was used to form an imprint on moist clay. We're told such items were meant as a personal signature, bearing the name of the owner and worn on a rope around their neck; Hence Dr Heiser's conclusion that three of the symbols comprised a name, that the message was unimportant, and that Mr Sitchin was wrong. Perhaps there is another explanation. Perhaps it was more of an emblem, not giving the name but where the wearer's identity was somehow inferred by it. Perhaps it was an insignia, a cylinder seal worn by members of an elite club. How can we know? Another pint of beer, barman. How many stamps do I owe?

There is another important aspect to consider. I've come across the collocation of AD with GI_4, the whirling reeds, more than once, including on line 38 of *The Story of Sukurru* where they were understood as a reference to the sinking of Atlantis. AD is given as 'bead' and as 'log' although without reference to numbers or timeline. AD with GI_4 is not only a reference to the round city of Atlantis sunk in the mud below the rustling reeds but also to the adamantine cylinder seal, the bead or log, sinking into and turning in the clay. Every time the cylinder seal was rolled, it would have been understood as an act of remembrance.

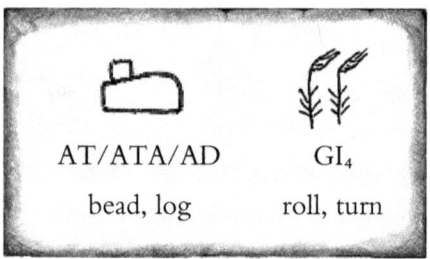

AT/ATA/AD — bead, log
GI_4 — roll, turn

There is something bittersweet in that realisation. Either it was a way of celebrating the disappearance of a domineering ruler, a gesture that revelled in their ignominious end at the bottom of the ocean, or it was an act filled with nostalgia for a golden age that had disappeared. From the light-hearted tone of the Sumerian lines, some amusement was likely found in the comparison. Perhaps it was already too distant a memory to inspire a great deal of nostalgia – already age-old in the 4th millennium BC.

AD/AT appears just once in *The Story of Sukurru* on line 38:

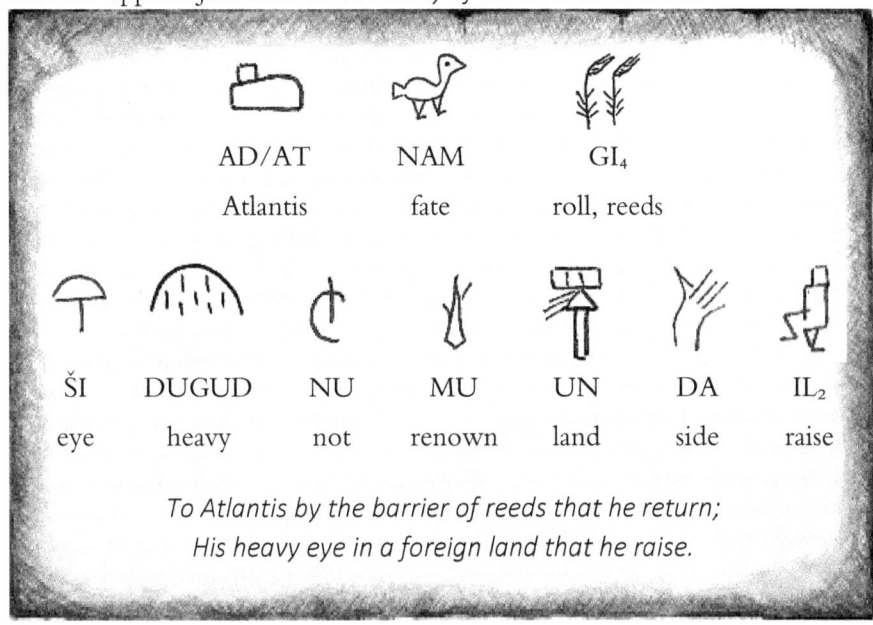

The deciding factor was that useful bird of fate, NAM, conveniently lodged between AD and the rolling reeds. The heavy eye is also a pointer if it is considered – logically – as a reference to AD and considered with the given meaning of 'bead'. In this reference, it's the ocular globe and brings another Greek myth into play, the story of Atlas.

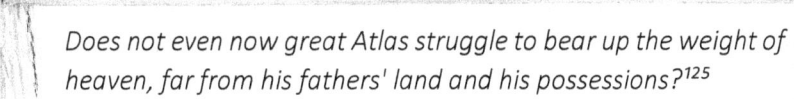

Does not even now great Atlas struggle to bear up the weight of heaven, far from his fathers' land and his possessions?[125]

Of course, it is possible to contend that the Sumerian version on line 38 refers to Atlas and, therefore, not to Atlantis. My suggestion is that they are either one and the same, or rather that AD, also given as 'father', is an epithet of the leader of Atlantis because that was the name of the place. In fact, both AD alone and AD-DA (proximity to AD) are given at the earliest period as 'father'. See page 284.

This section, particularly from lines 36 to 38, raises huge possibilities that can only be mentioned superficially in this context. In the original version of *The Story of Sukurru*, I offer further proof that the symbols on those lines fit into the intriguing story of the sinking of Atlantis while reflecting the much later Greek stories. There is question of a lying fox, NAR/LUL, who is also a musician. See page 66. Again, this smacks of the Greek myth of Orpheus, charmer of wild animals and stones, who caused offense and was killed by women. Line 36 links to a lolling head with its prominent tongue hanging on a cord around the neck of Greek Athena in numerous images but also found in other parts of the world – including on the back of an excavated Easter Island statue. They may well be part of that same mystery.

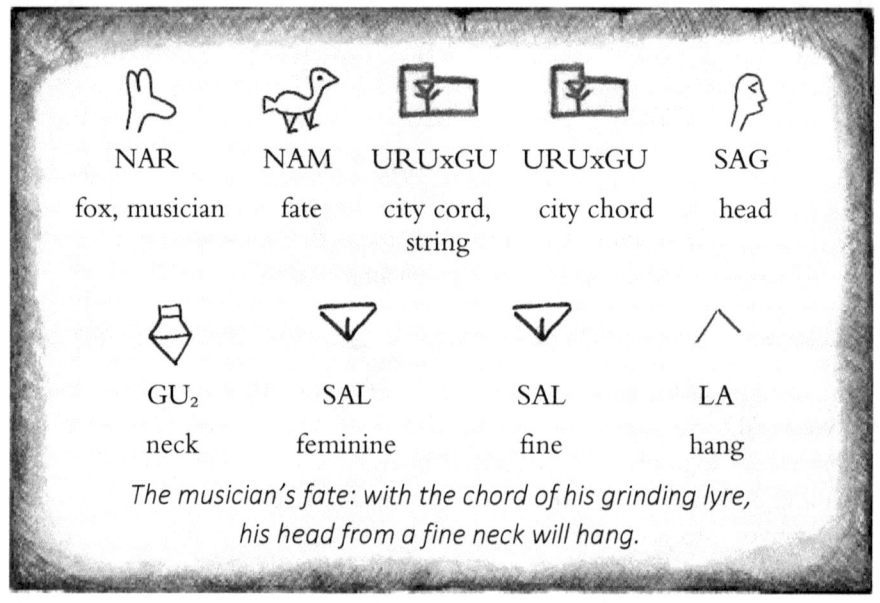

The musician's fate: with the chord of his grinding lyre, his head from a fine neck will hang.

> *Of the combatants on the one side, the city of Athens was reported to have been the leader and to have fought out the war; the combatants on the other side were commanded by the kings of Atlantis.*[126]

At the same time, URU, symbol of the city mentioned twice in line 36, might be the source of Greek Eurydice, wife of Orpheus, lost to him in the underworld. ERI is one phonetic value of URU. Plato's two accounts of Atlantis in the Timaeus and Critias date to around 350 BC. It has been pointed out that, through his explanation of the Egyptian source for information on Atlantis, it becomes possible to situate the sinking at around 9600 BC, a date that calls to mind the existence of the Gobekli Tepe site.

21

The Sky to Know the End

How to conclude in a way that is meaningful? How to weave all the silver threads and multi-coloured beads together into a material of worth, a better understanding of our most distant past, a new coat of iridescent beauty? I have drawn some conclusions from working on the text of *The Story of Sukurru* and subsequently learning more about the Sumerian language during this investigation. There can be no doubt that a highly sophisticated thought process underlay the so-called primitive symbols. The material offered in this book is further proof of something that was laid out as plainly as possible in *The Story of Sukurru*. Is it just the tip of a truly mind-blowing iceberg? I believe it is. At the very least, it's food for thought, a feast even.

The Galamus Sator Square is unique in that it brings together so many pieces of an age-old puzzle: St. Anthony of Egypt is present there in the dedication of the place by its hermit inhabitants. A reference to Greek Hermes and to boundaries is present in the distinctive Herma stone on which it is displayed. The symbol of the Tau is present there – as it is in the King's Chamber at Giza. This is the emblem of the followers of St. Anthony and, multiplied by four in a unique style, in all likelihood refers to the origins of the Templar cross. The Galamus Sator stone has siblings in many places, not least of which the Church of St. Mary in Lalibela, Ethiopia, through which it can also be connected to the Order of the Knights Templar. Finally, and most importantly, the Galamus Sator square links all of the above to the original sacred Sumerian tongue and to a mysterious temple.

I can't pretend to have pierced all the mysteries of the Sumerian language. But I can offer this. Sumerian was a code used to convey a wisdom of magical proportions, origin of the Corpus Hermeticum that is known today through much later Latin translations. And it is difficult to believe that nobody was aware of the existence and contents of the Sumerian texts before our era. The versions that we have in hand today were buried for thousands of years in sand, but who's to say that no other tablets, no other texts from the same family on whatever medium had not been preserved and transmitted elsewhere?

We read in the history books that most if not all manuscripts from past civilisations have been lost along the way, leaving huge gaps in our knowledge of our own history, gaps that have been filled by the musings of later generations. The great library of Alexandria in Egypt centralized a massive number of works from far and wide, all of which were lost over time, perhaps in war or in fire. The details are vague. Before that, the Assyrian king Ashurbanipal had amassed a legendary number of works, most of which were destroyed by fire in 612 BC. Destruction of records, voluntary or not, has turned us all into amnesiacs and prepared the ground for those who would control the past.

In the same way that I feel an urgency to relay the contents of this book as far and as wide as possible, that the evidence contained in it be safely transmitted, I can't help thinking that a group of like-minded people refused the idea that Sumerian wisdom be allowed to disappear under the sand or in any other manner. If that is true, knowledge of the texts did not re-emerge in the 19th century AD. It was always available to a few. Scribes would have worked on, elucidated and copied the riddles, rendered them in alphabetical form through the Phoenician times, but also kept copies of them in their original symbolic form. The Sator square is indicative of that being the case. What was found in Iraq was just one stash of tablets, copies of others that had long since been read, digested and kept as relics in musty cupboards. The priceless collections of selfish hoarders? Where are they?

It must be that the most important coded texts went underground at the time when abstract cuneiform writing became the norm, that they were exploited and that elements of them have since been put forward as new discoveries; a knowledge-laundering process. I might point to the Fibonacci sequence in that context although without proof of any intent to deceive. After all, the original mathematicians were long gone. There was no-one cheated out of anything except perhaps their 'name to spread on high' in the process of re-discovery.

This is where it all began, with the unwisely dubbed 'primitive' symbols of Sumer – remnants from an earlier civilisation, the language that was used to teach the new generations how to survive and thrive. Hermes is at the heart of it. His very name indicates the place at which to start pulling on the thread.

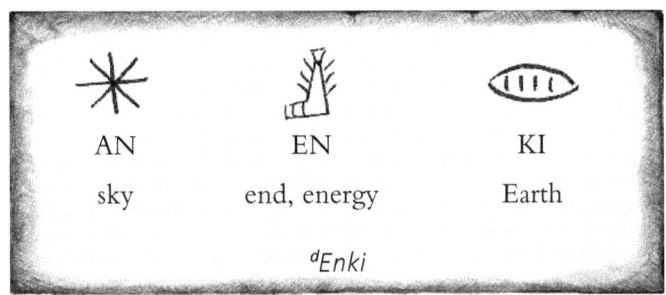

It's time to make amends, to resuscitate Enki/Ea, give him his birth name and his rightful place in the centre of things. I would hope that anyone who has read this far will be able to look at the breakdown of his name and draw their own conclusions. Remember the hermetic nature of Sumerian HER, like a set of Russian dolls where the largest must be opened first and lines are read from middle out. The most precious part is in the middle, safe-guarded, the magical end of a long thread between Earth and sky.

EN, the symbol that translates to both 'end' and to 'noble', is the topmost point of a tower and represents a form of energy there. As discussed in a previous chapter, EN-NE, centre of the Sator square, is the fiery combination of death and rebirth. It is also the number nine (the Ennead), enveloped by four times the number ten.

EN became Enoch rising to Sky-End, to a place called Anen and beyond.

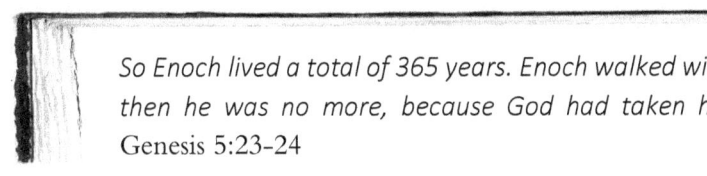

So Enoch lived a total of 365 years. Enoch walked with God, and then he was no more, because God had taken him away....
Genesis 5:23-24

EN is most likely Idris, mentioned in the Qu'ran and assimilated with Enoch. Although ID is not found with RIŠ/SAG, the sage, in lexical entries, all three symbols are encased in the name of Hermes; ID, RI and IS.

George Smith wrote the following concerning Ea:

> he is lord of the sea or abyss; he is the lord of generation and of all human beings, he bears the titles lord of wisdom...It has been supposed that... he was the Oannes of Berosus. [127]

Hermes Trismegistus, the Great Magician, is the correct name for the figure who appears on many Mesopotamian seals, with flowing waters and fish emanating from his shoulders. EA is a reference to his temple, and he can also be seen on certain Kassite seals as the personification of that place. EN is a manifestation of his powers. He possessed the knowledge to bring down the Great Bull, its horns to touch the soil, its force somehow overcome and exploited by the fiery Lion; The bull and the lion, manifestations of the MANA[128], the two forces, set in motion within his temple. There are many images of a bull brought down either by man or by a lion in Mesopotamia. I would suggest they are all metaphors for ancient knowledge of a very real source of energy, the mechanism of which has been lost. But there is another point to consider in matters of EN and Hermes Trismegistus: EN is the Greek word for 'one' while Sumerian dictionaries give it as 'lord, master, ruler' at the earliest period.

Hermes possessed the cord of ME-TE, the magician's measurements encoded in the building of the pyramids of the Giza plateau, also symbolized by the nose-rope of Prometheus shown on the Narmer palette. He was either a survivor or the heir to a preceding civilisation, the fish-god known as Apkallu or Oannes, carrying with him a bag of magic tricks; Carrying the 'ME of Enki' as past translators have called them, presumably without understanding the full implication of that word ME.

There are several names that trip quite easily off the tongue in relation to the earliest beings of the Sumerian myths. Oannes and the Apkallu are those of the mysterious wisdom teachers who came out of the sea to help mankind get back on its feet after a great catastrophe. Adapa is another, understood by some to be connected to the Apkallu and by others to belong to an independent myth. Nevertheless, Adapa is situated, according to four tablet fragments, at the earliest times as a fisherman and son of Ea, the water tower. The following are brief summaries of my findings:

Adapa

> *The contents of the four tablets may be here summarized as a clue to their contents, which in the translation alone may not always be clear upon the first examination.*
>
> *No.1 Adapa or perhaps Adamu, son of Ea....*

The above is a quote from *Cuneiform parallels to the Old Testament*[129]. The reader is offered a summary in the author's own words of a translated version of four fragments of clay tablets, three of them discovered in the remains of the Library of Ashurbanipal and another found in Egypt. Fortunately, and unlike most Sumerian translations, the book also gives a transliteration of the original symbol. The name is shown there as A-DA-PA. If this is Sumerian PA, it has another phonetic value, MU_6, which would explain why the author hesitates between Adapa and Adamu, particularly if he was looking for parallels with the Old Testament name Adam. It can be argued that, given the number of phonetic values acquired by some of the original symbols, it's not always difficult to choose what you're looking for. The only way to be sure of one's findings is to be sure of the form of the original symbol, preferably from more than one example, and then to study context, an interconnection of symbols over several lines of text that does not in its globality amount to gibberish or to an isolated myth with very little rhyme or reason. I don't know what King Ashurbanipal in the 7th century BC understood those symbols to mean or if he read them as the name of Adapa, son of Ea, but, since re-translating *The Instructions of Shuruppak*, I personally have become slightly sceptical.

I found just one trace of 'adaba' in *L'Ecriture Cunéiforme*. That is given opposite the symbol LU_2, man, with symbol BAD attached. It appears only at around 2000 BC. Nothing at an earlier or later date, which is unusual for any symbol. A phonetic value of the same two symbols given as ADDA with the meaning 'corpse' is found on ePSD. There is also mention of Adapa in the translation of a proverb, where the corresponding transliteration comes from symbols A-DA-BI, a strange match and not a useful one – apart from demonstrating that translators find phonetic Adapa in differing combinations of symbols. Surely they can't all be right. The case of Adapa demonstrates the importance of knowing which symbols underlie each translation. That is where the meaning of the aggregated forms can be found.

I was despairing of ever making his acquaintance when I came across a phonetic match between the Adapa of history books and the following combination:

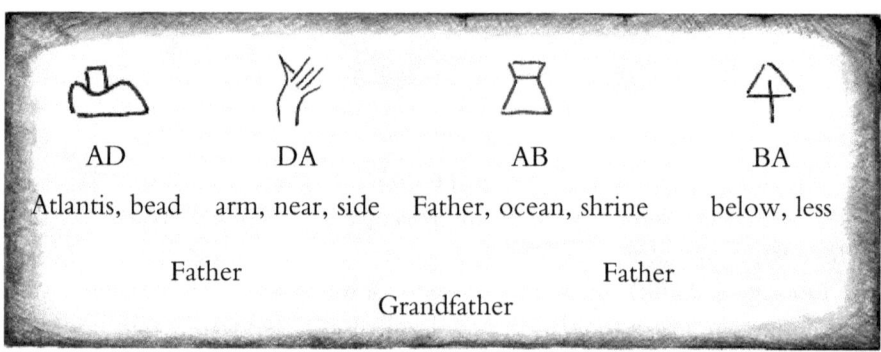

This four-symbol combination is mentioned on the ePSD site as 'grandfather', although without any reference as to dating or quantity. AD-DA is given as 'father' 3 times at the earliest period while AB/ABBA is given as 'father' 5 times. Taken together as AD-DA-AB-BA (where AB is also read AP), the consolidated sound becomes either ADABA or ADAPA, unlikely to be coincidental. There appears to be just one text where these four symbols come together. On line 7 of 'The Marriage of Martu'[130], they were translated to 'grandfather' within the phrase 'I was the grandfather of the holy cedar.' It's interesting to see the title associated with a tree. The translation of AD/AT/ATA to Atlantis is mine. I stand by it. See section 20 for the full explanation.

Of course, it isn't possible to conclude that biblical Abraham, a worthy candidate for the AB symbol, was once the ruler of Atlantis, but the joining together of these four symbols leads to some intriguing interpretations. The least that can be said is that AB has been well and truly associated with AD thanks to the above Sumerian reference, the Great Father with Atlantis. It's also interesting to note that Sumerian AD with DA is given as phonetic Akkadian 'abu'. (See page 16.)

Apkallu

This is another name cited in relation to Oannes, the fish god, and the passing-on of ancestral wisdom. Apkallu is shown as the Akkadian phonetic form of ABGAL which is, in turn, represented visually by the association of symbols NUN and ME. They can be found together on numerous tablets dating to the Uruk III period of 3200-3000 BC with NUN mostly placed directly above ME. The positioning might imply that ME can be read in first place, possibly as a noun and, if ME/ŠIP as 'ship' is added into the equation, the possible interpretations become increasingly intriguing:

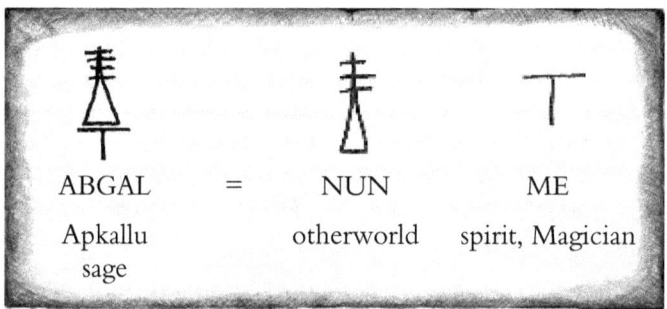

ABGAL is given as 'sage' 18 times at the earliest period. By now, it has become evident that the presence of ME as 'magic' also implies reading it as a capital T and finding there the underlying reference to ME-TE, the measurement, and to TE-ME, the temerity of a figure who might well have been perceived as heroic but perhaps also a little too daring for his own good. This is Prometheus who played with fire. This is the magician who took the bull by its horns. To my mind, all the manhood rituals involving bull-leaping stem from him. If ME is understood as the verb 'to measure', in this context, it will concern measuring the otherworld and be done in an apparently magical manner by leaping into the sky, tossed upwards on the horns of the bull, flying over the head of Taurus.

NUN, which bears some resemblance to the Egyptian hieroglyph 'djed', has some quite unhelpful given meanings. At the earliest period, it's given 12 times as 'prince, foremost, best'. At a much later Akkadian period, it's given twice as a 'metal object', apparently copper. Through association with other symbols and at a late date, there is an element of strength and guardianship that appears to be in play, but overall it's not an easy symbol to explain. In the lexical entries, it can be found as NU-UN, the reason behind my choice of attributed meaning.

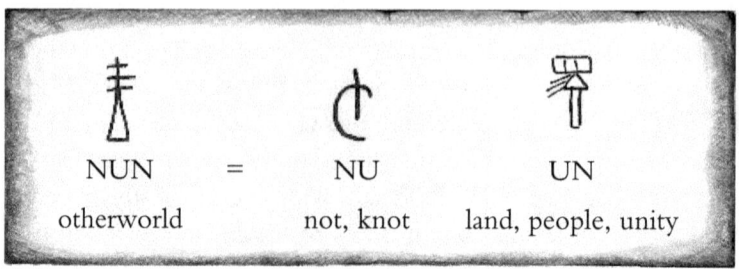

NU, the knot or the negative, and UN, unity, people and land, also given as 'Kalam' (see page 179). In context, it became 'not of the land' and, by extension, I translated it as 'otherworldly'. One method of chasing meaning, if all else fails, is to work backwards from a word of unknown origin:

> *Announce: c. 1500, "proclaim, make known formally," from Old French anoncier "announce, proclaim" (12c., Modern French annoncer), from Latin annuntiare, adnuntiare "to announce, make known," literally "bring news to," from ad "to" (see ad-) + nuntiare "relate, report," from nuntius "messenger" from PIE root.*

Nun or nuun is the fourteenth letter of the Phoenician and Arabic alphabets with the meaning of 'large fish' or 'whale'. With Latin nuntius, the messenger, a large fish-person with a bag of tricks and knowledge of measuring to impart becomes a very possible result of NUN with ME. It might be coincidental, but the truth is that this analysis fits very neatly with the enduring images of Oannes or the Apkallu.

Thus, it appears that AB-GAL, translated to 'Great Father', is a spiritual or magical messenger, not of the land, but perhaps of the ocean and perhaps even an other-worldly messenger. Neither the wisdom-bringing fish god nor the alien in their spaceship first suggested by Zechariah Sitchin can be ruled out by an examination of the symbols involved. Without finding the symbols within a broader context, I have to remain neutral. Nevertheless, ancient references to and images of a fish god as candidate for the 'Great Father' cannot be totally ignored. The lexical entries relating to ABGAL lead to several different associations but the most cited is the breakdown of the later Akkadian version which is Apkallu. This is where they found the name:

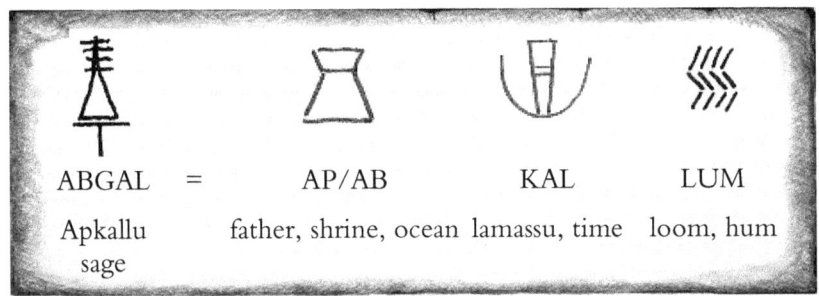

AB and KAL are both symbols of time. It has come to mind more than once that, notwithstanding the possibility that he once lived, the original patriarchal figure given as AB is to be associated with Kronos, also Saturn. KAL is the winged bull man, the lamassu, an amalgamation of astrological symbols and source of 'calendar'. KAL is replaced by GAL, the great, on a couple of lexical entries, giving AB-GAL-LUM, the Great Father and the (cosmic) loom. Add GAL with the meaning 'great' into the mix and it appears that this speaks of the greatness of time, the evidence of an ancient period.

There is no mention of LU, the light and the sheep, in the ePSD corpus concerning Apkallu but that doesn't eliminate the possibility of its existence somewhere, and it is certainly an element of LUM. In the meantime, it seems that the oldest version would have been pronounced Apkallum or Abgallum – if indeed it is to be considered as an epithet. As for LUM being the origin of 'loom', that is entirely my interpretation of it based on the symbol's appearance, of weaving lines, on its obvious and hitherto unexplained etymology, and its use in context.

> *Loom: weaving machine, early 13c. shortening of Old English geloma "utensil, tool," from ge-, perfective prefix, + -loma, an element of unknown origin*
>
> *To loom: 1540s, "to come into view largely and indistinctly," of uncertain origin.*

This is both an earthly and cosmic loom. It's also the origin of our verb 'to loom' with its ominous connotation, which both AB and KAL might be doing here. LUM has another amusing phonetic value; HUM, the hum of the loom. It might give 'the Great Father humming' and carry us further into the realm of Saturn. Does Saturn hum?

> Humble: late 13c., of persons, "submissive, respectful, lowly in manner, modest, not self-asserting, obedient," from Old French humble, umble, earlier umele, from Latin humilis "lowly, humble," literally "on the ground," from humus "earth," from PIE root.

The Baptist

> (...)in whose time appeared the Musarus Oannes the Annedotus from the Erythræan sea.[131]

Oannes is understood to be the name given in Greek by Berosus to the fish-god of the Chaldeans. I found no trace of it. That doesn't mean that the information is wrong but there is no trace in the Sumerian lexical entries of U or UA in collocation with AN, although they do appear side by side on some tablets. In the few lexical lists concerning ABGAL and AP-KAL-LUM, there is nothing that might connect them to Oannes or Iannes. A connection between biblical John the Baptist and the Mesopotamian fish-god has been suggested based on a possibly-second-hand account of the writings of Berosus who is said to have lived in the 6th century BC. It isn't substantiated by the name. The truth of the matter is that there is nothing fully reliable about this information gleaned from later writers claiming to cite from the works of Berosus. Nevertheless, a connection with Sumerian ABGAL, the Great Father, Apkallum and NUN.ME, the magical otherworldly messenger, becomes intriguing via the notion of baptism.

> Baptize: "to administer the rite of baptism to," c. 1300, from Old French batisier "be baptized; baptize; give a name to" (11c.), from Latin baptizare, from Greek baptizein "immerse, dip in water," also figuratively, "be over one's head" (in debt, etc.), "to be soaked (in wine);" in Christian use, "baptize;" from baptein "to dip, steep, dye, color," perhaps from PIE root.

'Baptist' comes from the same Sumerian source mentioned in relation to Babel and Babylon in the first section; BAB which became the name of the admirable Indian stepwells, vav or vaav. As already mentioned, BAB breaks down into symbols BA and AB/AP, origin of abba, the Father, he who has an intimate connection with watery places.

Baptism as 'immersion in water' doesn't necessarily have a religious or even a ritualistic connotation at its origin. It might well have been a manner of describing anything or anyone who disappeared completely beneath the water for whatever reason but then reappeared. PAP...he's gone, PAP... now he's back again. The BAB of ABBA, immersion of the ancestor.

AB-GAL, the Great Father, the Great Ocean, the Great Shrine; Did a man with the skin of a fish ever walk out of the Eritrean sea to bring hope to the world?

The Herald
John the Baptist was a herald. His announcement is said to be that of the arrival of Jesus but, like the far more ancient Hermes Trismegistus, he was generally revered as a wise man and teacher:

> What then should we do?" the crowds were asking him. He replied to them, "The one who has two shirts must share with someone who has none, and the one who has food must do the same." Luke 3:10-11

Working backwards to the Sumerian source, we find MIR given 57 times as 'herald'. It appears at the Uruk III period, ca.3200-3000 BC:

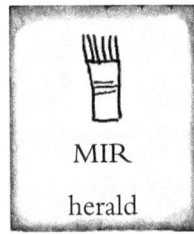

The idea that many, if not all, of the most ancient manmade structures, from standing stones to pyramids, were built to mirror star systems and their movements cannot be swept aside as speculative nonsense. There are obvious advantages to positioning stones or more elaborate buildings in a manner to coincide with the movement of the sun, the moon and the constellations, not least of which to foresee, to herald the seasons for various agricultural tasks. That is one good reason for the words 'mirror' and 'herald' to be closely related, and for a master astronomer to be known as a herald.

> *Mirror: early 13c., from Old French mireoir "a reflecting glass, looking glass; observation, model, example," earlier miradoir (11c.), from mirer "look at" (oneself in a mirror), "observe, watch, contemplate," from Vulgar Latin *mirare "to look at," variant of Latin mirari "to wonder at, admire" (see miracle).*
>
> *Miracle: (...) from Latin miraculum "object of wonder" (in Church Latin, "marvelous event caused by God"), from mirari "to wonder at, marvel, be astonished," figuratively "to regard, esteem," from mirus "wonderful, astonishing, amazing," earlier *smeiros, from PIE root.*

In the lexical entries, MIR breaks down into either MI-IR or ME-IR. MI signifies 'darkness' and 'night. Once again, the T-shaped ME of measurement is in the thick of things and Plato's Er continues to wander.

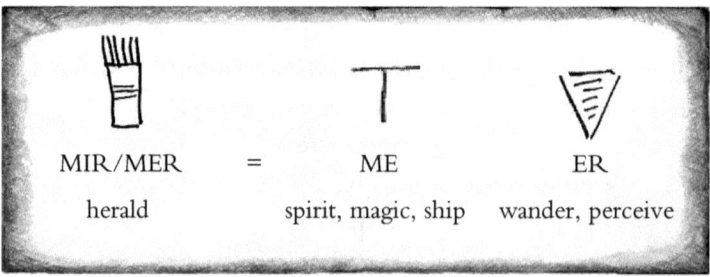

| MIR/MER | = | ME | ER |
| herald | | spirit, magic, ship | wander, perceive |

At least 70 percent of Earth's surface is covered by water. Imagine that dark reflective surface mirroring the rest of our galaxy as we circle around the sun in a constant dance. There is good reason for the words 'miracle' and 'admire' to be mentioned in this section.

> *Mere c. 1400, "unmixed, pure," from Old French mier "pure" (of gold), "entire, total, complete," and directly from Latin merus "unmixed" (of wine), "pure; bare, naked;" figuratively "true, real, genuine," probably originally "clear, bright," from PIE *mer-*
>
> *Old English mere "sea, ocean; lake, pool, pond, cistern," from Proto-Germanic *mari (source also of Old Norse marr, Old Saxon meri "sea," Middle Dutch maer, Dutch meer "lake, sea, pool," Old High German mari, German Meer "sea," Gothic marei "sea," mari-saiws "lake"), from PIE root.*

Reflectivity is an attribute of a mirror and of a calm sea on a clear night. It's also an attribute of mercury.

> *Mercury: silver-white fluid metallic element, late 14c., from Medieval Latin mercurius, from Latin Mercurius (see Mercury).*
>
> *Mercury: "the Roman god Mercury," mid-12c., from Latin Mercurius "Mercury," originally a god of tradesmen and thieves, perhaps from merx "merchandise"; Later he was associated with Greek Hermes.*

Thus, we find HER of Hermes to be the origin of 'herald' and MIR/MER, given as 'herald' in Sumerian dictionaries, to be the source of 'mirror', 'mercury' and 'mer' (sea). The original Hermes was an alchemist, a magician, a master astronomer, a great hero and herald. But was Hermes the model for the biblical figure of John? Was he the fish-god? Were they one and the same?

> *And when the sun had set, this Being Oannes, retired again into the sea, and passed the night in the deep; for he was amphibious.* [132]

I could affirm that a man who became known as Hermes Trismegistus once existed. I could and have said more than once here that he was a great magician, the greatest ever. It is possible that such a person knew the measurements of the universe, that these were encoded in the dimensions of his temples, constructions that he or others of the same origin perhaps oversaw at a time before the Great Flood of our mythologies. But I can't pretend to know for sure why he would have been portrayed wearing the skin of a fish or with fish swimming in the water flowing from his shoulders. Was the fish an indication of someone who travelled on the seas, amalgamating the sailor and his ship, navigating with the stars? Was 'whale' (see NUN on page 286) the name given to a type of ship? Or was the sky considered to have the same quality as an ocean on Earth, the mirror of it? As above so below. Did the fish-skin correspond to the silver of a metallic suit or a metal ship that swam in the sky? Was Hermes Trismegistus a being from another planet as Zechariah Sitchin would have us believe of his counterpart Enki? Or was he the survivor of the sunken city of Atlantis, acquiring the fish-god reputation as the story of his escape by sea became a myth? Did he gain his reputation by using the flow of water in the manifestation of his magic? Then again, perhaps the account attributed to Berosus was accurate and mermen did indeed walk out of the sea at regular intervals…

Ea, the water temple, according to academia has all the attributes of Hermes Trismegistus and Egyptian Thoth. Unless there were several wise figures who became famed for teaching mankind at different moments in time, who were remembered for millennia as emerging out of nowhere in locations not so very distant from one another, as having fabulous knowledge, and who were all in some way associated with both ocean and sky, then it must be admitted that one man has an impressive number of names attached to his memory: Hermes Trismegistus, Thoth, Enoch, Idris, Enki, Ea, Oannes, Adapa, Abgal, Apkallu, perhaps Prometheus and, of course, the other mythological spin-offs, Greek Hermes, Roman Mercury… Were they all originally just one? I believe so. You must decide for yourself. In defence of my stance, it should be remembered that these names result from thousands of years of re-recounting and embellishing the story. Here's my contribution:

I imagine the Great Magician in his natural setting at Giza, standing tall on the back of the Great Lion. Perhaps he wears a silver robe or an outfit of some flamboyant iridescent shade that leads to his reputation as half fish half man. Why not? Magicians are known for wearing capes. The waters of the Nile flow closer to the pyramids in this age and have been channelled to surround the Sphinx entirely. Water is drawn upwards by clever machinery and pours constantly from the fountain that is its gaping mouth. At times the lion roars and at others it whispers as the proverbs tell us. It's this flow that will finally wear the face down and cause it to need remodelling. There are flooded areas underground and above the plateau, such that the three pyramids and the Sphinx all appear to float. A weir below ground at the tail of the Lion controls the flow cascading down, pap...pap...pap, creating an effect of resonance inside the Great Pyramid. Machinery is constantly in motion there but to what end?

This is both machine and temple, a Hieron, encased in a magnificent white skin of limestone, immaculate, reflective. That skin, a tent that tightly holds its magical crystalline stones in place, has been likened to another binding, ME-HI, the sacred hymen, symbolized by the Egyptian ankh and epithet of the Great Sphinx who holds its key; MEHIDA, key to the riddle, the arm of Mehi, also known as MU, a name of great renown, a celestial clock.

The equally magnificent Hermes Trismegistus mounted on the back of the Sphinx surveys his work, addressing the crowds who gather every evening to marvel at him and at the mirror of the sky. Then, as darkness settles over the place, he pulls the cloak tightly around him and, ...disappears from view. There is a hatch on the back of the Sphinx. The general public doesn't know where it leads and neither do I.

Piezoelectricity

More food for thought than ending, an excerpt from the introduction to a scientific study made in 2002 and published on the US National Library of Medicine website:

> Piezoelectricity and the Pineal Gland
>
> *The complex texture structure of the microcrystals may lead to crystallographic symmetry breaking and possible piezoelectricity, as is the case with otoconia. It is believed that the presence of two different crystalline compounds in the pineal gland is biologically significant, suggesting two entirely different mechanisms of formation and biological functions. Studies directed toward the elucidation of the formation and functions, and possible nonthermal interaction with external electromagnetic fields are currently in progress.* [133]

Found on a number of clay tablets at the Uruk IV period of 3350 to 3200 BC, this combination offers a new dimension to the PI symbol, particularly if the information from the pineal gland study is taken into account.

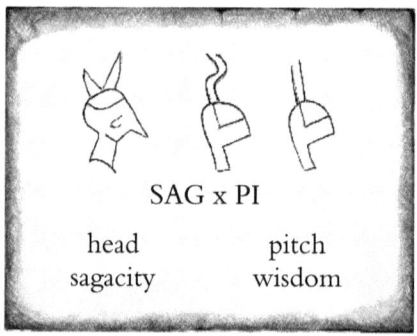

SAG x PI

head   pitch
sagacity   wisdom

I have copied three of the symbols to show something of the diversity of their execution. There are also two examples on the CDLI website that show the head in the company of UR, the dog. It is true that the pointed ears, worn as part of a cap on one example, resemble the pointed ears of Anubis, the sacred Egyptian jackal. PI with its phonetic form of GEŠTUG, is given as 'ear' along with 'reason, plan, to be wise, wisdom', and 'understanding' at the earliest

294

period. On later examples, PI/GEŠTUG is shown as a pair of straight or curved vertical lines that rise from the crown of the head.

The clay tablet with the Great Fish discussed in the context of Atlantis (see page 270) also shows this combined symbol, situated in the writing on the other side of the tablet, on the edge and in the same square as GEŠ, the tree. That tablet is now part of the Schoyen Collection[122].

GEŠ-TUG$_2$-PI, the three symbols that compose the Tree of Consciousness and Knowledge, appear together seven times in *The Story of Sukurru*, notably in the introductory passage. Line 3 begins:

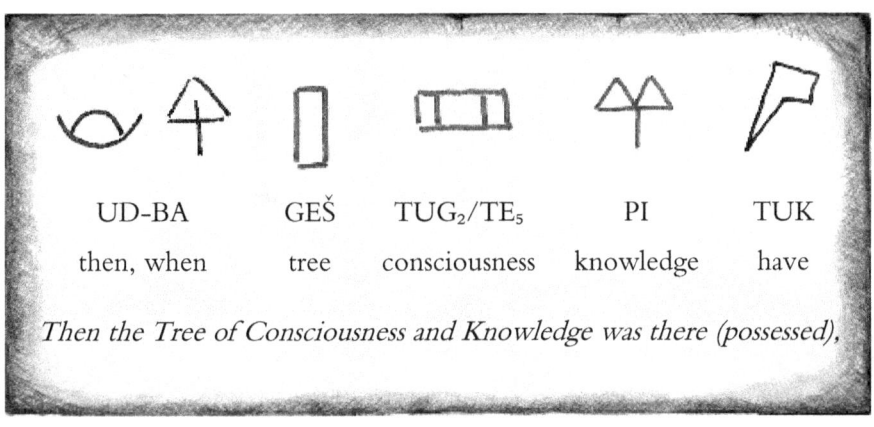

UD-BA	GEŠ	TUG$_2$/TE$_5$	PI	TUK
then, when	tree	consciousness	knowledge	have

Then the Tree of Consciousness and Knowledge was there (possessed),

This is the oldest known account of a Golden Age, a time when wisdom reigned supreme, before the advent of a great flood recounted in this poignant line:

Surrounded by water, the people of Ma on her life-raft.

It would appear from *The Story of Sukurru*, a text copied onto clay around 2600 BC from a much older source and brought back to life in 2017 AD, that the magical powers of that Tree were lost at the same time as the people. Lost but not forgotten?

Of Sheep and Bull

That light shines in the darkness, yet the darkness did not overcome it. There was a man named John who was sent from God. He came as a witness to testify about the light, so that all might believe through him. He was not the light, but he came to testify about the light. John 1:5-8.

For the Lamb in the centre of the throne will be their shepherd. He will lead them to fountains of living water, and God will wipe away every tear from their eyes.' Revelation 7:17

Logos: 1580s, 'the divine Word, second person of the Christian Trinity,' from Greek logos 'word, speech, statement, discourse,' also 'computation, account,' also 'reason,' from PIE root.

Notes and References

Inner cover: KE-ME, detail CDLI ref. P004479, Uruk III (ca.3200-3000 BC), German Archaeological Institute, Berlin, Germany. Also shown on page 207.

Citations: Voltaire mentions in chapter 3 of Micromégas (1752) a discovery concerning Mars that was announced in 1877: *They saw the two moons that serve this planet, and which have escaped the notice of our astronomers.*

The full title of Fulcanelli's book is *The Mystery of Cathedrals and the Esoteric Interpretation of the Hermetic symbols of the Grand Work.* Introduction, Part III, (1926) published by Jean Schemit, rue Laffitte, Paris.

1. THE TOWER OF BABEL

1. Sources include:
   - The *electronic Pennsylvania Sumerian Dictionary* (ePSD) for phonetic values of the symbols, given meanings, approximate dating and quantifying of their appearance, corpus of the lexical lists. (Although it's still possible to consult the corpus entries, the original full lexical lists disappeared from ePSD in October 2018 and have not been reinstated at the time of publishing.)
   - *Cuneiform Digital Library Initiative* (CDLI) for photographic evidence of the pictographic forms.
   - *Electronic Text Corpus of Sumerian Literature* (ETCSL) transliterations, shows only phonetic forms.
   - Lucien-Jean Bord and Remo Mugnaioni, *L'Ecriture Cunéiforme, Syllabaire Sumérien, Babylonien, Assyrien,* Geuthner Manuels, 2002, from pictogram through the different stages of transformation of cuneiform alongside their various phonetic values. It's not necessary to read French to use this book.
   - René Labat and Florence Malbran-Labat, *Manuel d'Epigraphie Akkadienne*, Geuthner Manuels, 1988 edition, showing the evolution of signs, with transliterations and explanations in French.
   - Most etymological references are sourced from www.etymonline.com which is a most useful compilation of explanations from numerous sources which are listed in its introductory pages. Sincere thanks to Douglas Harper.

2. The earliest examples of the Phoenician alphabet, developed from a cuneiform script, date to around 1000 BC.
3. Sketch of the Venus of Willendorf, a tiny figurine carved out of limestone, found in Austria and estimated to be around 30,000 years old.
4. A list of lexical references is given on p.309.
5. PIE (proto-Indo-European) stems from a comparative analysis of modern languages carried out in an attempt to establish a common root. The resulting sounds indicated next to 'from PIE root' in etymological dictionaries are, for the most part, far off the mark. Unfortunately, they appear to have truly taken root.

Although it has long been suggested that there was once a single common language, Sumerian has not yet been considered for that role. In the meantime, 'from PIE root' should not be misunderstood as a valid source for our words.

6. A full translation of *The Story of Sukurru*, originally *The Instructions of Shuruppak*, begins on page 310. It was published in the form of a bilingual book in 2017. An example of the layout can be seen on page 116. The oldest known version of the text, discovered at Abu Salabikh in modern-day Iraq, can be seen on CDLI under the reference P010233.
7. Detail CDLI ref. P005573, Uruk III (ca. 3200-3000 BC), Musées royaux d'Art et d'Histoire, Brussels, Belgium.
8. (a) Detail CDLI ref. P000251, Uruk III (ca. 3200-3000 BC), National Museum of Iraq, Baghdad, Iraq. (b) Detail CDLI ref. P005365, Uruk III (ca. 3200-3000 BC), Louvre Museum, Paris, France. (c) Detail CDLI ref. P005446, Uruk III (ca. 3200-3000 BC), Katholieke Universiteit, Nijmegen, Holland.
9. Detail CDLI Ref. P004587 Uruk IV (ca. 3350-3200 BC), German Archaeological Institute, Berlin, Germany.
10. Genesis 11:5-7.
11. Source www.etymonline.com, etymology of Babel.
12. Herodotus, *Histories*, Book 1:179.
13. Detail CDLI ref. P003540, Uruk III (ca. 3200-3000 BC), National Museum of Iraq, Baghdad, Iraq.
14. Earliest use and etymology of 'soupape': CNRTL (Centre National de Ressources Textuelles et Lexicales), 1419-20 « pièce mobile du sommier de l'orgue » (Extrait du compte de la fabrique de la cathédrale de Troyes ds R. Sté sav. des départements, t. 3, 1872, p. 473) (Movable piece in a cathedral organ's wind-chest.) From 'Pap' of obscure origin, perhaps from Latin pappare, to eat.

2. THE ENKI HERESY

15. ORACC (Open Richly Annotated Cuneiform Corpus), Ancient Mesopotamian Gods and Goddesses, List of Deities.
16. Ibid.
17. The Rustle of Stones, 27th August 2016, Articles, www.grahamhancock.com.
18. Sumerian King List, ETCSL ref. 2.1.1.
19. *Šuruppag, the wise one, who knew how to speak with elaborate words lived in the Land.*
    The Instructions of Shuruppak, line 5, ETCSL ref. 5.6.1.
    Then Zimbir fell (?) and the kingship was taken to Šuruppag. In Šuruppag, Ubara-Tutu became king.
    Sumerian King List, lines 31-32, ETCSL, ref. 2.1.1.

3. HARRAN

20. Theodore Abu Qurrah, Orthodox Christian Bishop of Harran, ca. 900 AD. All of the ancient references date to the 1st millennium AD and, as secondary sources transmitted and translated through both Arabian and Christian hands, should be received with caution through that prism. That is why the well-worn story of a pagan people acquiring the name 'Sabian' at a late date, despite not being entitled to it, as told from Christian sources should also be handled with care, particularly as the location and identity of 'real' Sabians are equally unconfirmable.
21. *Terah took his son Abram, his grandson Lot son of Haran, and his daughter-in-law Sarai, the wife of his son Abram, and together they set out from Ur of the Chaldeans to go to Canaan. But when they came to Harran, they settled there.* Genesis, 11:31.
22. CDLI, ref. P001475, Uruk IV, (ca. 3350-3200 BC), Vorderasiatisches Museum, Berlin, Germany. (Given as phonetic value KIN_2)
23. Revelation 2:12.
24. Celsius, Greek philosopher 2nd century AD.
25. *Lokasenna*, part of The Poetic Edda, trans. Henry Adams Bellows. (with thanks to Sacred Texts website) These lines are to be understood in the context of a contest of insults, a tradition of the Norse people. The contest of insults is also a feature of *The Story of Sukurru*.
26. G. de Santillana and H. von Deschend, *Hamlet's Mill*, P.284, (David R. Godine, Publisher). I mention in passing the mass of information contained in this book, relevant to the underlying astronomical themes encapsulated in Sumerian symbols and in *The Story of Sukurru*.
27. Ezekiel 8:14.
28. Exodus 14:21-22 followed by Exodus 14:28.

4. GOBEKLI TEPE

29. Mentioned by Graham Hancock in *The Sign and the Seal*, with a sketch of it on P.412, 1992, William Heinemann Ltd. The mouth of the lioness is open, giving a profile similar to PIRIG and she faces a symbol identified by the author as a Templar cross.
30. P. R. T. Gurdon, *The Khasis*, 1914 (online Gutenberg Project).
31. G. Hancock's visit to the still buried site at Karan Tepe is described on pages 298 to 299 of *Magicians of the Gods,* (2016, Hodder & Stoughton).

5. THE GREAT BULL AND THE FLOW OF BEER

32. www.tepetelegrams.com, 4/24/2016.

6. TWO HORNS OF THE GREAT BULL

33. A major theme in *Hamlet's Mill* mentioned above at 26.

34. Lucas Partanda Koestoro and Ketut Wiradnyana, *Megalithic Traditions in Nias Island,* 2005.
35. Referring to Nias, source Wikipedia.
36. Mont Bego drawings. Plates published in the 1920s by Italian archaeologist, Piero Barocelli, can be seen online thanks to TRACCE *Online Rock Art Bulletin.*
37. Italian philosopher-funambulist, Andrea Loreni. www.ilfunambolo.com.

7. THE UMBILICAL CORD AND THE FLOW OF WATER
38. Philip Ball, *The Water Kingdom – A Secret History of China,* 2016 Penguin Random House, London.

8. SPRINGS, FOUNTAINS AND WATERSPOUTS
39. a) *Paenitentiale Theodori,* 7th century AD, a penitential handbook.
    b) St. Eligius, 7th century AD, France.
40. Mircea Eliade, *The Forge and the Crucible,* P.160, 1978, Second Edition, University of Chicago Press and Flammarion. Also see note 75.

9. CURSING STONES OF GODS AND BULL
41. P. 92 *Cursor Mundi,* Northumbrian, early 14c.
42. W.G. Wood-Martin, *Traces of the Elder Faiths of Ireland,* Vol. 1. Longmans, Green, & Co., 1902, available at archive.org. Chapter 6, *Stone Worship,* is of particular interest in this context. Singing stone, holed stone, stone of destiny...
43. Ibid. Figure 10, Page 97.
44. W.G. Wood-Martin, *Traces of the Elder Faiths of Ireland,* Vol. 1. Longmans, Green, & Co., 1902., P.66, *Cursing Stones, Well Worship and its Concomitants.*
45. Ibid. Figure 14, page 98, *Well Worship and its* Concomitants. The author gives a detailed account of the aspect and uses of cursing/curing stones and sacred stones in general in Ireland and elsewhere.
46. Thanks to Goran Pavlovic and his highly informative website, *Old European Culture,* for the thought behind this further analysis of cursing stones and their potential, even obvious, link to grinding stones.
47. Aesop, *Fables 564* **(from** *Babrius* **48)** (trans. Gibbs) (Greek fable C6th BC) source: Theoi.com.
48. Dr Irving Finkel, *The Ark Before Noah,* 2014, Hodder & Stoughton.

10. SIGNS OF THE MAGICIAN
49. Detail from CDLI ref. P281729, Uruk V (ca. 3500-3350 BC), Louvre Museum, Paris, France.
50. Detail from CDLI ref. P000849, Uruk IV (3350-3200 BC) Vorderasiatisches Museum, Berlin, Germany.
51. www.tepetelegrams.com, 3/15/2018.

52. Tablet CDLI ref. P281728, Uruk V (ca. 3500-3350 BC) Louvre Museum, Paris, France.
53. Detail from bulla CDLI ref. P254193, Pre-writing (ca. 8500 to 3350 BC), The Schøyen Collection (MS 5125), Oslo and London.
54. *Response to an archaeologist at Göbekli Tepe*, Articles, 7th February 2018, www.grahamhancock.com.
55. On display at the Çorum Archaeological Museum in Çorum, Turkey.
56. Detail of bas-relief on the southern gateway wall of Alacahoyük in central Turkey, dated to 1400 BC.
57. CDLI ref. P004107, Uruk IV (ca. 3350-3200 BC) National Museum of Iraq, Baghdad, Iraq.
58. A photo of the Tau lintel at Biot and information on the Antonins can be found in a book (in French) by Lea Raso Della Volta, *Les Sentinelles de Maître Hiram, Histoire des Templiers dans le Comté de Nice et en Provence Orientale*, 2018 Editions Hermésia.
59. Herodotus, *Histories*, Book 2:42, (Trans. G. Rawlinson) Wordsworth Editions Ltd., 1966 edition.
60. Corpus Hermeticum II, *Asclepius* (Trans. G.R.S. Mead).

11. PROMETHEUS

61. Aeschylus, *Prometheus Bound*, (trans. H.W. Smyth).) Extract from the opening lines where the overall plot is laid out. This is characteristic of Greek plays and reminiscent of the introductory lines of *The Story of Sukurru*.
62. Ibid.
63. Statius, Silvae 3. 1. 5 (trans. Mosley) (Roman poetry 1st AD) Sourced from the excellent website, Theoi.com. Find there several other references to the effects of Seirios/Sirius. Sumerian Sirius can be found in another combination of symbols. AR results from ŠI with RI, 'eye' and 'gather' which together give 'watch' but also the 'bird's eye'. Is SI-RI, Sirius, the 'watcher'? This may also constitute the etymology of 'sear', the searing heat of summer, from ŠE or SE with AR.
64. Pliny the Elder, *Natural History*, 7:198.
65. Ariadne, Pseudo-Hyginus, Fabulae 40 - 43 (trans. Grant) (Roman mythographer 2nd century AD, sourced from Theoi.com.

12. THE ANCIENT CLEWS

66. Namkha: This quote sourced from Wikipedia. The reasoning behind the manipulation of a crossed form and threads cannot be traced back to any ancient writings on the subject. Nevertheless, the artefact and its name remain.
67. Ibid.

13. THE IDIGNA BIRD OF THE TAURUS MOUNTAINS

68. Detail CDLI ref. P001360, Uruk IV (ca.3350-3200 BC) Vorderasiatisches Museum, Berlin, Germany. Also appearing on this fragment are GI and TE.
69. Detail CDLI ref. P000835, Uruk IV (ca.3350-3200 BC National Museum of Iraq, Baghdad, Iraq).
70. Detail CDLI ref. P002593, Uruk IV (ca.3350-3200 BC) Vorderasiatisches Museum, Berlin, Germany.
71. See note 29.
72. Detail CDLI ref. P006153 Uruk III (ca.3200-3000 BC) The Schøyen Collection (MS 2862/06), Oslo and London.

14. BIRD OF PROPHECY

73. Observed at an exhibition in London in 1638 by Sir Hamon l'Estrange.
74. Detail from Akkadian cylinder seal, 2334-2150 BC.
75. *The names of the Philosophers who spoke about the art: Hermes, Agathodaimon and many others... They are remembered for making the head and the perfected elixir.* Ibn an-Nadim, *Kitâb al-Fihrist* (Book of the Catalogue) Ch.10, (p. 849-850 of translation by Dodge) AD 987. Dr Annine van der Meer in her lecture entitled *The Harran of the Sabians in the First Millennium A.D.* gives the above quote to demonstrate that the severed head (of Orpheus) and prophetic talking head of mythology might have its origin in an alchemical process.
76. Apollodorus, *Bibliotheca*, Book 1, 2nd century AD.
77. Herodotus, *Histories*, Book 2:55, (Trans. G. Rawlinson) Wordsworth Editions Ltd., 1966 edition.
78. Anita Stratos, *Divine Cults of the Sacred Bulls*, article in touregypt.com.
79. Laird Scranton, *Decoding Maori Cosmology: The Ancient Origins of New Zealand's Indigenous Culture*, 2018, Inner Traditions.
80. Plato, Timaeus 48e.

15. SHAMAN AND ALCHEMIST

81. Graham Hancock, extract from *The War on Consciousness*, banned TedTalk, January 13, 2013.
82. Symbol ŠI appears in this form in the 'primitive' category of *L'Ecriture Cunéiforme, Syllabaire Sumérien, Babylonien, Assyrien, Sumerian Lexicon* (referenced in note 1).
83. Detail CDLI ref. P002178, Uruk IV, (ca.3350-3200 BC) Vorderasiatisches Museum, Berlin, Germany).
84. Mircae Eliade, *The Forge and the Crucible,* P.29, (1979) second edition, University of Chicago Press and Flammarion.

85. The Siren Vase, ca. 480-470 BC, Attica, Greece, displayed in the British Museum.
86. Sourced from Wikipedia.
87. Farid ud-Din Attar, Persian poet, 12th century AD, *Bird Parliament*, also known as *The Conference of the Birds*, (Trans. E. FitzGerald), text available on SacredTexts.com.
88. Ibid.
89. Ibid.

16. TALON, THE METAL ROBOT

90. Greek drachma, Phaistos, (ca. 300/280-270 BC), displayed in the Cabinet des Médailles, Paris, France.
91. Apollodorus, *Bibliotheca*, Book 1.9.26, 2nd century AD (Trans. Frazer), William Heinemann Ltd. 1921.
92. Apollonius Rhodius, *Argonautica* 4. 1638 ff, 3rd century AD (trans. Rieu) source: Theoi.com.
93. *Logos Teleius*, Corpus Hermeticum.
94. a) Diodorus Siculus, *Bibliotheca Historia*, Book 5.64.1, ca.36 BC, (Trans. Oldfather),
    b) Titus 1:12-13, New Testament, English Standard Version.

17. THE SUN, THE LION AND THE PYRAMID

95. Dr Irving Finkel, P.49, *The Ark Before Noah*, 2014, Hodder & Stoughton.
96. (a) Detail CDLI ref. P004291, Uruk III (3200-3000 BC) National Museum of Iraq, Baghdad, Iraq.
    (b) Detail CDLI ref. P001563, Uruk IV (3350-3200 BC) Vorderasiatisches Museum, Berlin, Germany.
97. Sumerian proverb, Urim, ETSCL Collection 23, 6/2 335.
98. (a) Detail CDLI ref. P000817, Uruk IV (3350-3200 BC) Vorderasiatisches Museum, Berlin, Germany.
    (b) Detail CDLI ref. P000757, Uruk IV (3350-3200 BC) Vorderasiatisches Museum, Berlin, Germany.
    (c) Detail CDLI ref. P000744, Uruk IV (3350-3200 BC) Vorderasiatisches Museum, Berlin, Germany.
    There are other examples of PIRIG at this earliest period, including one that shows a single vertical mark below its chin (see CDLI, ref. P001551).
99. AZ can be seen on CDLI ref. P005386 from the later Uruk III period. It appears to show a row of teeth in the lion's mouth.

18. HERMES AND THE CRYSTAL HERESY

100. Isha'al-Qatiyi (Christian author) writing about the *Al Hatifi*, (Book of the Sabians). Also see notes 20 and 75.

101. Ibn an-Nadim, *Kitâb al-Fihrist* (Book of the Catalogue, Ch.10 Trans. Dodge), 987 AD.
102. Isha'al-Qatiyi writing about the *Al Hatifi*, (Book of the Sabians). The three quotes sourced from Dr Annine van der Meer's lecture (PDF): *The Harran of the Sabians in the First Millenium A.D.: Channel of Transmission of a Hermetic Tradition?*, 2002.
103. See the entwined serpent on the Libation vase of King Gudea (ca.2100 BC) displayed in the Louvre Museum, Paris, France.
104. UET 2, available online at CDLI Sign Lists, Early Dynastic I period. This example is entry 307 within a section devoted to forms of symbol EZEN, belonging to the same family. Its identity as HER is confirmed by the Akkadian cuneiform version that Burrows gave opposite it. The complete drawing of the original tablet can be seen at CDLI under ref. P005951.
105. Plato, Republic, Book X.
106. Available online at CDLI Sign Lists, Late Uruk Period, A. Falkenstein, *Archaische Texte aus Uruk* (Archaische Texte aus Uruk 1; Berlin-Leipzig 1936).
107. Detail, CDLI ref. P004479, Uruk III (ca.3200-3000 BC), German Archaeological Institute, Berlin, Germany.
108. www.wordsense.eu is an invaluable source for following up on a hunch of this sort.
109. Giza mastaba ref. G 4561, Kaem Ankh, burial chamber, Details from ancient Egyptian sailing scene, Photo: KHM-Museumsverband, Austria, displayed by The Giza Project at Harvard University.
110. Book of Matthew 2:1.
111. Mircae Eliade, *The Forge and the Crucible*, P.87. (1979), second edition, University of Chicago Press and Flammarion.
112. See note 75. Detail CDLI ref. P001251, Uruk IV (ca.3350-3200 BC), Vorderasiatisches Museum, Berlin, Germany.
113. ETCSL Sumerian proverbs, Coll 1 (c.6.1.01), Section A, line 30.
114. *The Asclepius*, Corpus Hermeticum.
115. From the curator's comments published on the British Museum website.
116. Sourced from Wikipedia 'Piezo-electricity'.

19. THE SATOR TEMPLAR CONNECTION

117. **Archives Louis P. Poincet** *The story of the unfortunate man's last days is found in a handwritten note (1601) of a certain P. Poincet (whose function and first name are unknown apart from the initial 'P') who, assisting the surgeon, wrote down in great detail the words and circumstances of the accident. It was no doubt following this tragedy that Father Albouys, aware of some collapsing close to this cylindrical fault, had the 'infernal mouth' definitively closed off.*
118. www.nasa.gov, 11/17/2003.

119. (a) Detail CDLI ref. P001299, Uruk IV (3350-3200 BC) Vorderasiatisches Museum, Berlin, Germany. (b) Detail CDLI ref. P000493, Uruk IV (3350-3200 BC) National Museum of Iraq, Baghdad, Iraq. (c) Detail CDLI ref. P001170, Uruk IV (3350-3200 BC) Vorderasiatisches Museum, Berlin, Germany.
120. Aetius of Antioch, Greek philosopher, 2nd century BC.
121. Graham Hancock, *The Sign and the Seal*, 1992, William Heinemann Ltd. Also see note 29.

20. ATLANTIS AND THE FISH

122. Detail CDLI ref. P006268, Uruk III (ca. 3200-3000 BC), The Schoyen Collection (MS 3035), Oslo and London.
123. Plato, *Dialogues* Timaeus and Critias, 360 BC.
124. Cylinder Seal VA243, Vorderasiatische Museum, Berlin, Germany.
125. Pindar, *Pythian Ode* 4. 290 ff (trans. Conway) (Greek lyric C5th BC.) sourced from Theoi.com.
126. Plato, *Dialogues*, extract from Timaeus, 360 BC.

21. THE SKY TO KNOW THE END

127. George Smith, *The Chaldean Account of Genesis*. London. 1876. He was an Assyriologist working in the British Museum, one of the first translators of the cuneiform tablets. He quotes the fragments of texts attributed to Berosus.
128. MANA is one phonetic value for the Sumerian symbol given as 'two' and 'to repeat'. Mana is known to Polynesians as a supernatural force.
129. R. Rogers, *Cuneiform parallels to the Old Testament*, III. The Myth of Adapa, P.67, 1912, Eaton & Mains.
130. ETCSL ref.1.7.1., *The Marriage of Martu*, line 7.
131. *Fragments Of Chaldean History*, Berosus: from Alexander Polyhistor. *Ancient Fragments*, Trans. Cory, 1832, sourced from www.sacredtexts.com, C. M. Weimer.
132. Ibid.
133. US National Library of Medicine, 2002, Calcite microcrystals in the pineal gland of the human brain: first physical and chemical studies.

Photos
Pages 43, 51, 57, 79, 119, 159, 213, 220 : Ian Faure.
Page 110 Detail from 'Orthostates, Alaca Höyük 06': Bernard Gagnon, Creative Commons Attribution-Share Alike.
Page 173 'Didrachm Phaistos obverse CdM' : public domain.
Page 216 Ancient Egyptian sailing scene at Giza: KHM-Museumsverband.
Page 237, 244 Galamus Sator stone: Thierry Rocque (www.sableo.com).

INDEX OF SUMERIAN SYMBOLS (non-exhaustive) (159 symbols)

A 10-11, 16, 21, 23, 30-31, 32-33, 47-48, 60, 62, 64-65, 80, 86, 88, 102, 126, 139, 144, 147, 156, 226, 235, 264, 283

AB 17, 19-22, 41, 78, 167, 203, 283, 287, 289

ABGAL 283, 287-288

AD 269-270, 275-277, 283

AK 102, 164, 218, 253

AL 153, 165, 175, 177-178, 180, 226-227

AM 46, 151-154, 158

AM_3 32

AMA 138

AN 6-9, 12, 15, 18, 21, 23, 29-30, 32-33, 36, 42, 44, 60, 64-65, 67, 78, 86, 123, 125-126, 138, 152, 167, 185, 226, 232, 275, 281

ARA see ŠA

ARAD 275

AŠ 125-127

$AŠ_2$ 42-43

AZ see PIRIG

BA 16-17, 19-21, 64-65, 86, 102, 140, 144, 284, 289, 295

BAD 232, 270, 283

BAD_3 232

BAL 86, 167, 240

BI 40, 60, 64, 69-70, 78-80, 86, 127, 145, 168, 283

BU 16, 144

BU_3 8

BUL 95-96

DA 47, 86, 115, 117-118, 177, 203, 243, 277, 283-284

DAM, 60, 62, 243

DAR 147

DI 47-48, 143-144, 152, 226

DIL see AŠ

DIM_2 31, 123

DU 148, 152

DUB 275

DUGUD 277,

E 44, 47, 71, 86, 101, 167, 203, 218, 232, 242-244

E_2 30-31, 60

EL 87-90, 185

ELLAG see KIL

EM see IM

EME 254

EN 29-30, 33-36, 44-45, 104-105, 203, 232-233, 242, 246, 248, 250-251, 257, 281-282

ER 128, 166, 184, 186, 194-196, 235, 244-245, 250, 290

ES/IS see GIŠ

EŠ 95, 169-170, 202, 204, 219, 224, 272

ES_2 71, 115, 255

EZEN 231-234, 256

GA 23, 71, 203, 226, 275

GABA 203

GAL 60, 266, 287, 289

GAN 17-18, 21-24, 45, 164-165, 194-196

GAR 21, 23, 61, 101, 226

GAR_3 139-140, 144,

GI 47-48, 202-203, 255

GI_4 276-277

GIG 85, 226

GIR 181, 271-273

GIŠ 201-205, 211, 222-223, 281, 295

GU 75, 78, 124, 131, 278

GU_2 21, 63-65, 86, 131, 139-142

GUD 58, 60, 62, 64, 67, 71, 75, 123-125, 128, 131, 154-155, 157, 296

HA 271

HAL 86, 139

HAR 42-45, 99, 248

HER 12, 133, 181, 194-195, 197-198, 200, 202, 204, 211, 219-222, 224-231, 234, 243, 248,

306

253-254, 257, 267, 272, 281

HI 42-43, 117-118, 195-196, 235, 244, 248, 250, 293

HU 147

HUL$_2$ 185

I 9-10, 15, 143-144, 156, 210, 232

IB 152, 209-210, 213, 215

ID 198-199, 208, 248-249, 251, 281

ID$_2$ 60, 86, 139

IDIGNA 137-140, 142-146

IG 21, 37, 143-144, 187-188, 190

IK see IG

IL 89-90, 100

IL$_2$ 243, 275, 277

IM 21, 47, 163-164, 190, 255

IN 101, 232,

IR see ER

ITI 208,

KA 6-8, 62, 101, 123, 133, 167, 203, 240, 254

KA$_2$ see KAN$_4$

KAK 34

KAL 21, 198-199, 287

KAN$_4$ 6-7, 15-16, 22-24

KI/KE 29-30, 33, 36-38, 44, 87, 89-91, 93, 100, 123-124, 167, 185,
198, 200, 206-210, 213, 219, 221-222, 224, 243, 272, 281

KID 102

KIL/KILI 83-90, 93, 95-97, 100, 131, 135, 139, 157, 262

KIR/KIRI see GIR

KIRID/KIRIS see HER

KU 62, 64, 66, 167, 260

KU$_4$ 61

KUR 36, 100-101, 135, 154-156, 157, 166, 259-260, 269

KUŠ see ZU/SU

LA 21, 123, 185, 275, 278

LAGAR.DU 101

LI 93-94, 161

LIMMU$_2$ 254

LU 9, 11-13, 17-18, 138, 143, 287, 296

LU$_2$ 44, 64, 71, 86, 101-102, 115, 126, 162, 167, 283

LUL see NAR

LUM 287

MA 23, 45, 115, 134

MA$_2$ 148

MAH 60, 64

MAL 138

MANA 282

MAŠ 139-140
ME 17, 32, 90-91, 104-106, 109-115, 117-119, 122-125, 163, 175-176, 178, 180, 201, 203-204, 207-208, 210-211, 213-219, 247, 250-251, 254-255, 258, 282, 283, 288, 290-291

MEHIDA see MU

MES 200-202, 204, 206-209, 211-212, 219, 234

MEŠ see MES

MI 99, 208, 267

MIR 289-290

MIS 235

MU 117-119, 124, 157-158, 218, 243, 262, 277, 293

MUN 270

MUŠ$_3$ 47-48

NA 8-9, 21, 45-46, 67, 71-72, 78, 85, 99, 123, 126, 143-144, 147-148, 151-152, 154, 157-158, 167, 217-218, 267

NA$_2$ 141, 145

NAB 78, 167

NAM 17, 44-46, 71, 123-124, 126, 133-134, 147, 150-152, 154, 157-158, 169, 203, 216-218, 243, 277, 278

NAR 66, 122-123, 278

NE 34-35, 101, 123, 125, 167, 203, 233, 242-244, 246, 248-249, 251, 265, 281

NI 126, 152, 208

307

NIM 31

NU 62, 117, 277, 286

NUN 285-286, 288

PA 17-18, 283

PAD 23

PAP 4-5, 17, 19-20, 27, 140-141, 145, 270

PER/PIR see UD

PI 184-185, 187-190, 234-235, 245-246, 250, 272, 294-295

PIRIG 186-189

PIRIG$_3$ 188

PEŠ, PIS, PUS see GIR

RA 5, 12, 42, 46-47, 75, 86, 100-102, 126, 156

RI 21, 23, 147-148, 166, 174, 176-180, 187-188, 190, 198, 221-222, 224-226, 228-230, 234, 250, 272, 281

RIG see ŠIM

RU 36, 258-260, 265

SA 261, 269

ŠA 161

ŠA$_3$ 40, 47, 60

SAG 102, 125, 149, 223-4, 278, 281, 294

SAG$_2$ 18

SAL 87-88, 90, 278

SAR 203

ŠAR$_2$ 126

ŠE 128

SI 87-90, 270, 275

ŠI 21, 105-106, 115, 163-164, 190, 209-210, 216, 277

SIG 203

SIM see NAM

ŠIM 162-163, 169, 190

SIN see EŠ

ŠIN 168

ŠU 102, 123-124, 128, 157-158

SUM 61, 71

TA 46, 80-81, 128, 167, 177-178, 180

TAB 140

TAM see UD

TAR 5, 122

TE 111-114, 119, 122-125, 175-176, 247-251, 258, 282, 283

TI 208

TIG see GU$_2$

TUG$_2$ 295

TUK 199, 226, 243, 295

TUM 90-91

TUR 261

U 264

UBARA 231-232

UD 45, 75, 102, 124-125, 183-184, 188, 208, 234-235, 245, 264, 295

UG see PIRIG$_3$

UL 60

UM 77-81, 123-125, 127, 146

UN 117, 175-176, 178-180, 243, 277, 286

UR 125, 259-260, 269, 294

URU 278

UŠ 44, 71-72, 123-125

ZA 189, 253

ZAG 252-253

ZI 166, 168, 232-233

ZU/SU 17-18, 21-22, 36, 47, 101-102, 115, 141, 145, 168, 270, 273, 275

ZUBI 145

Lexical List References (non-exhaustive)

P.7 KAN₄ Proto-Ea 238

P.9 ILU Ea II 272

P.16 BA-A-BU Igi-duh Tablet 1 347

P.17 PA-AB Ea 1 265,

P.17 BA-AB Sb Voc. I 67b

P.23 GAN Proto-Ea 694

P.27 PAD Proto-Ea 212

P.30 E₂-A OB Diri Nippur Section 10 42

P.45 TAM Sa 132

P.75 GUD Sa 214

p.78 NAB Proto-Ea 138

P.87 KIL KI EL   Ea I 42,

P.88 SIKIL SI KIL Izi C ii 13

P.89 KI-IL Ea I Assur MA Excerpt Section A 9

P.90 ME KI IL TUM KI (Hh XX-XXIV OB Forerunner 1 vi 8)

P.91 ME KI EL TUM KI (Hh XX-XXII Nippur Forerunner 235)

P.93 KILI Proto-Ea 916

P.133 NAM KA HER (Hh II 54)

P.140 IDIGNA Diri III 179

P.141 PAP NA2 Proto-Ea 840

P.143 IDIGNA Diri III 179

P.145 ZUBI Ea VIII 39

P.152 NAM   Ea II 299ᵉ

P.163 SIM Hh XXIII-XXIV Nippur Forerunner Section 7.2 2

P.177   TAL VAT 244 ii 35, Ea II 298

P.184 PIR Proto-Ea 154

P.187 PIRIG Proto-Ea 572

P.189 PI-RIG Sa 223

P.194 HER Proto-Ea 761

P.195 HER Sa 382

P.198 KIRID Hh VI 7

P.200 RID Ea IV 144

P.201 MES Sb Voc. II 118

P.202 GIS Ananum Tablet 5 209

P.203 ME-AB Proto-Ea 187

P.204 ME-EŠ Kagal C 139

P.208 KE-ME Izi C iii 24

P.209 KIŠIB Sb Voc. II 119

P.210 IŠIB Aa I/5 i 8

P.215 ŠI-IP Aa I/5 i 8

P.222 KIRIS Aa VIII/2 37-42

P.232 EZEN Sa 383

P.232 EZEN Proto-Ea 759

P.250 TEMEN Proto-Ea 388

P.254 ZAG Sa 393

P.260 KUR Proto-Aa 447:1-6

P.262 GIŠ-SA-TUR Hg A I 89

P.272 PEŠ Sa 40

P.285 NUN-ME Erimhuc V 7

P.286 NUN Aa V/3 25-33

P.287 AB-KAL-LUM Erimhuc V 7

P.290 MIR Ea VIII

ANNEXE

THE STORY OF SUKURRU
(Re-translation of The Instructions of Shuruppak)

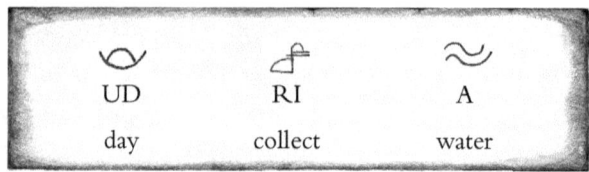

1) UD RI A UD SUD DU RI A
   By day, the deluge. That distant day, the deluge.

2) MI RI A MI BAD DU RI A
   By night, the deluge. That endless night, the deluge.

3) MU RI A MU SUD DU RI A
   In that age, the deluge. That bygone age, the deluge.

4) Then, the Tree of Consciousness and Knowledge was there.
   The ladder through the Word was known.
   Surrounded by water, the people of Ma on her life-raft.

5) Sukurru the Tree of Consciousness and Knowledge possessed, the stairway through the Word knew.
   Surrounded by water, her people on the life-branch of Ma.

6) Oh, Sukurru! Fresh oil on these reputed stones collected.

7) Sukurru when young Ubara Du Du ruled.

8) Life long ago established, fresh oil on the native millstones collected.

9) Young Mu on soft stone narrating the year of the meteor.

10) Life long ago established, voices around the milk-churning ocean, Tree of Consciousness and Knowledge, the Light Vessel.

    Borne witness on this clay.

11) Softly tell the name of the hand whose task to prepare the bark for flight.

12) Soft words by the full moon at the stone shrine where the whirling kanab smoke will rise.

13) Tell how Ab his place below with the Lamassu will be.
    That the gully inspector from wind in his eye they will guard.

14) Of the proverbial ass and the other-worldly basket, her divine voice counting, counting the grains of sand.

The first-fruit specialist in the beating heart of the ocean his horn will raise.

15) With a space for the beer-cask to hang, that inner fire be pacified, the city leader and a façade loaded into the basket will be.

16) For the camel, the beer-cask, and the voice of might a shared destiny: high furrow or low, life under the rise and fall of Ga's needle it will be....

17) For the field to know water from the sky, a cistern with a thick stone roof built high above the noble people in its heart collects the clouds of great destruction.

18) At the House of broad diversion, where new clouds are weighed on high, a binder by a small side door there is.

19) The floodgate operator not a lofty fly-in-a-field, Beer-Heart below from above the beer seizes.

20) With a loud cry, lofty Za, the floodgate operator, the flow releases, his name to make on high!

21) Ra his heavy eye spreading before the sky, over the lofty City-Sun with beer at heart the flying cloud sinks.

22) In the place, hot-heads quarrel and mutter.
The beer to re-establish or the fire?

23) The hot-heads and their smoke, with the voice of Ma, a shared destiny: above or below, together they will enter.

24) The hot-head and fired-clay specialist a shared destiny (BROKEN)

25) The hot-head his task to make smoke for the lord (BROKEN)

26) (BROKEN) in the gate of the great hanging temple, less blasting from the horn of Ga.

27) The hot-head and the smoke, going out, coming in, circumcised or uncut, a different rhythm on the horn.

28) The thick cloud over the land to measure, his name in words on clay to know, his name to spread on high.

29) A stone temple there will be, with a thick cover up to the lord.
Black Horn the soil of Ra will hoe, his own spirit to know.

30) Self to know, the Stone Lion, weight of destiny, thrusts down the Bull, below its head, weight of destiny.

31) That Young Mu his sheaf and seeds be crushed, that to make his name on high, some thinking he do.

32) His lofty self to know or lip to be, a fiery ark out to fly, strong and high?

The virile herald horn on Sina, the stones of wisdom in the sky (TABLET BROKEN).

33) At the raised place where trust is acquired by the side of a tall fire, from the homeland to rise, a great whispering there will be.

34) Young Mu, at the meeting place of stone, where a man a spouse acquires, close seated for high fire pacifying,

35) A ballad about writing and fired-clay specialists and stones from the sky his heartstrings stretches.

36) The musician's fate: with the chord of his grinding lyre his head from a fine neck will hang.

37) His mouth to cut its fire, to Tartarus the noble poet, to measure the beat of the rain.

38) To At, by the barrier of reeds, that he return, his heavy eye in a foreign land that he raise!

39) That man with his arm measure his wet mouth… his name muttered to the place on high will rise.

40) A knowing hand leaning there will be. Between the stone and the feather, into the Dini he sinks.

41) Round curses from the hole on the heartless bull collect as the bark flies down: with the skin of a sheep on the sabbath that his ark sink…

42) After nugatory pondering, on a lighter note, the beer to not kill with sand, the beer they will lift.

43) To return with the native beer, the wooden paddle he has created and the central beam hanging on high.

44) His flute to not hear in the basket, a rope on the sheep-knowing breath-bearer for his task as spirit.

45) The male who is weaned a rope around the stone bull-man lift,

46) while males unweaned from the cask milk given shall be.

47) The black stone cask to the roof they will carry, Beer-Heart with his thyrsus the volcano to water.

48) The ass in stony Edin the grains of sand counting, count your shekels, that the sun's ray with beer the (BROKEN) three high will oil.

49) The roots of the foothills the virile roof-builder is getting to know when the renowned wing gathering straw for her nest his name calls out.

50) With a curse his strong arm rises at the stone shrine of Ebal, his virile hand the tablets of testimony breaking.

51) The slippery hand to shorten her wing, to the roof he ascends, his strong arm her fire to weaken. The renowned lofty wing her Ra protects as he beats on the door.

52) From great beer the long wing of Garuda blocks the sky, on the lofty place a cover imposes.

53) Round curses are heard; that the roof be opened on high, that Beer-Heart on the sabbath less high (BROKEN)

54) The heavy lamma on each side of the temple roof with baskets pacify the sky.

55) The native straw-turner establishes a fire and on the spirit of the ark his cloud imposes.

56) In the place sits the cannabis man whirling smoke on high.

57) Leader of the people. Leader of the people. Spirit between the eyes. The Brewer smokes on high.

58) A sickly reed into a tree will grow. Its mouth near milk spreads smoke on high for the lord.

59) Cream of the ocean. Cream of the ocean. Spirit between the eyes, and the Brewer's smoke.

60) The dog its reputed mouth opens to the lord. The hot-head in the otherworldly basket will fly to the lord.

61) Young Mu, leader of the city, his name to make with the lord. Luki, his virile goading rises to the lord.

62) The young men their virile arms rising on the roof, with the heat of their fire surround the noble palace, the hatching chick of Zu to know.

63) The strong arm of the Lama is acquired the roof to open, the noble to lift, in the wall a hole to dig… The roof the lofty angel destroys for the lord.

64) The stones from the roof spreading high, on to the city they fly… The noble citizens their anger collecting, the stones to the sky they return.

65) A soft regal whisper from the façade, he who the wooden spindle created without any knots, 'Look not!'.

66) 'For the leader in water a lofty destiny shared with the lofty dodo. Flight of the noble.' Tears from the heart of the reed façade, 'and both from their homeland stones estranged!'

67) 'As for the man who the lying scales created and the noisy voices in the house of beer, to cut and gather tar their fate.'

68) 'And Luki his virile mouth on the nose-rope of Shu, a stone in the sky the Guds to light!'

69) 'Dog-head with a single stone – weight of destiny – with one fell stroke has decided; all of mankind crushed will be.'

70) 'Exalted Sun with one thick stroke on the stone of destiny has decided; all of mankind slaughtered must be.'

71) 'Dog-head close to his long foot new life from rising again his noble arm will guard.'

72) 'Exalted Sun the long-footed new-born of Zu from between his noble arms will free.'

(Second refrain)

73) Oh Sukurru! Fresh oil from the millstone there will be and thick homeland straw again.

74) Sukurru when young Ubara Du Du ruled.

75) Long-established life, fresh oil from the native millstone, thick homeland straw again.

76) Second chorus of Native Land. Sukurru, fresh oil of Ra on these reputed stones collected.

77) Sukurru when young Ubara Du Du ruled.

78) Life long ago established. Fresh oil on the native millstone. Thick homeland straw to gather.

79) Child of Mu on stone softly collect the story of the Age of the Seated Womb.

80) Life long ago established. Fresh oil on the millstones of the homeland collecting.

81) Softly narrate the name of the worker, his task to heat the bark for the flight of the noble;

82) Soft words on the gentleman at the sone shrine whirling smoke on high for the noble.

(Nine severely broken lines in the following section)

83) A mouth around the beer flowing – (BROKEN)

84) The refrain…..Young Mu (BROKEN)

85) Says beer thirst water flow (BROKEN)

86) In the sky finely cover mouth horn (BROKEN)

87) Says other-worldly basket borne wind (BROKEN)

88) Other-worldly basket collect (BROKEN)

89) Water thick homeland middle raise (BROKEN)

90) On clay the writing collect ((BROKEN)

91) Says clay head from the shrine the broken blocks collect (BROKEN)

92) Over the man with the unregal screech, over his skin the lofty eye sinks.

93) By the wooden staff, for the goat and his flute a heavy destiny. To Beer-Heart a whispering there is.

94) 'A great house on a great river there must be. At its heart, the beer and the bull. Expand to fit madame.'

95) 'That the place they enter side by side if they agree'

96) 'If not, by day between the spouses a thick reed fence place.'

97) Place a man at the mouth of the milk-churning ocean and give him a beer.

98) Not sitting in water, give beer to the harvester under the open sky.

99) Milk-churning ocean give beer to the man churning the ocean with a thick virile straw.

100) Not churning the ocean, give them a name and a place in front of beer.

101) Replace the single flute. Give force to the puny arm

102) of the gentleman and place there the foreign dadi flute.

103) Says the sweet, sweet reed…. SAYS the lofty administrator,

104) his thick voice BUILDING, BUILDING, his thick tablet RAISING, RAISING.

105) Says the flute, its honeyed voice flying long and high.

106) SAYS 'Take a native sheepskin, good thick quality water and wind proof.

107) SAYS Very good quality native sheepskin, empty of milk breast. Homeland guaranteed. Very, very great quality.

108) SAYS Less sagging breast for a thick roof.

109) Place the skin around the great builder, the thick native less lofty to make.

315

110) The strong arm of the Lamma acquire, the man whose wing beats less than a fly in a jar, less questioning inside to rain.

111) That the lofty fool place a length of cord and pour oil on the ark.

112) Inspect and reflect on the quality. Then…. That the lofty fool place a length of cord and pour oil.

113) That the roof he bind for flight, warm homage there must be.

    For black straw on the door.

114) Flattery and homage there must be.

    For black straw on the door.

115) Established head he will not be if he stops the leaders's ark from flight.

116) The dog that does not hold the native and reputed root of man pisses high.

117) Around the basket. Weight of destiny. The front of the house begins to lift.

118) The lofty guard-post whose task is to cut flight less on his seat sits.

119) The native man, basket expert, the native sheepskin's forehead holds less high.

120) The native sheepskin the leader's pride to swallow on high.

121) The native fleece, the leader and their spirit to grow old on high.

122) In the hanging basket, the spirited leader his paddle turns.

123) Sliding towards the opening, the great house begins to rise.

124) Young son the home of Zu will know, by the wind seized and spirited away.

125) Young daughter the beautiful fine basket of Zu will know, by the wind seized and spirited away.

126) Beer-thirst water will know as through the fire to the heavy justice in the sky he rises.

127) Puffing towards the midday sun, its heart of stone to know, out of the opening they rise.

128) The setting sun by his spouse displaced, the beautiful vessel sweetly, sweetly swaying will be.

129) Through the mountain peaks to a windy place that the sheep of Luna populate,

130) Over the mountains, rising in its flight, 'The Clay Eye' around the sky is fluttering.

131) Then, the day, the sun rising before the noble frame, the sweetly swaying vessel its rope seizes.

132) 'Fine Kore I created. Soft gathering at the native shrine I created. To be swallowed by the water!'

133) 'For Young Mu, the foothills I created, and flower collecting I created. To be swallowed by the water! A sack of curses when bearing heavy nobles the fate of Ma shall be.'

134) 'A curse invoked on the foreign-reed spy; that his straw façade be crushed.'

135) 'Insignificant fly-in-a-bottle leader, clay-beating wooden head!'

136) Says: 'And a sack of curses on the lofty musician with the ears and eyes of a lofty camel!'

137) 'Cursed equally, Garuda. Lofty light-imposer, that the native flying stone he raise.'

138) Says: 'Dreaming of Siwa, a long, long time hanging there he will be. As long as the flute like a sick cow's innards that will be!'

139) 'Until the year when geese from the ground a cord on high to Mu near the sun establish.'

140) Says: 'New words of wisdom in that age born in great profusion there will be.'

141) 'That the midst of water Ra know. Through the space where it divides to its heart of reed where the wind will rise.'

142) 'And a curse divide the basket from the unworldly baggage by the Tree of Consciousness, Knowledge and Winnowing Light in the land that Ma rules.'

(Third refrain)

143) Oh, Sukurru! Fresh oil on the grindstone, flour from the harvest, thick straw to gather.

144) Sukurru, when young Ubara Do Do ruled.

145) Life long ago established. Fresh oil on the grindstone, seed from the harvest, thick straw to gather.

146) Third chorus of Native Land. Sukurru, fresh oil of Ra, stones on the homeland flying.

147) Sukurru when young Ubara Du Du ruled.

148) Life long ago established, fresh oil on the millstone, flour of the harvest, thick straw to gather.

149) Young Mu, his soft flight on the Naga narrated, the year that Mu was borne to the floor.

150) Of life long ago established, the guides around the milk-churning ocean, the Tree of Consciousness and Knowledge, the Light Vessel. Borne witness on this clay.

151) Tell of the gentleman, his task to prepare for flight.

152) Soft words on the gentleman at the stone shrine whirling smoke on high.

153) Young farmer threshing a raga, his name to inscribe in the sky, the lofty nipple to reach its cord he stirs the wind.

154) As Tiamat and her kid heavily move across the skies, counting, counting seeds, dry-mouthed in the garden he beats the refrain.

155) Ama, wet nurse, heavy across the skies, funnelling the stars, as long as the flute like a sick cow's intestine she is.

156) The nurturing rope, roof across the skies – count your shekels, count your shekels – her heavenly shoulder tied to a thunder bolt and dragged to his virile net will be.

157) Low over the mountains the great hanging temple, funnelling the stars, through the cleft to the trough where the native beer she will seize.

158) His head by crows and thundering mountains beaten, on the cord of beer or on the cord of water will he ascend?

159) Luki, not a doctor of the oils, his renowned reflections on high are carried.

160) On the young mocker, on the earth, the exalted midday sun some watering will do.

161) The water birds, their name to inscribe in the sky, from the cask to pour on high, their leader to know, bearing rope the ganas come.

162) No more home. To the temple of thick water the flow on the hanging rope is carried down.

163) No more city. The thick native hanging below is carried down.

164) Hanging below rises. The arm of bliss rises. Up the side of the hill. As hanging below lowers, the arm to the vessel rises.

165) The young mocker on the exalted midday sun he spits.

166) The hot-ash specialist between the beer cask and the people of the land a thick roof establishes;

167) Doctor of potions from the zoo, with water on the brain, his head and hand before the sun less beat the mat.

168) Years and years of water and soma a soft head and foot giving, the leader reflecting, he beats the clay of the land.

169) Of crows between mountains, of stones circling the sky his tablet speaks.

170) That beer, its fate cut short on Earth, flowing around Ara it will be.

171) Man's form in thick clay of the land his arm, for the sky, has cut the smell.

172) 'Great Brother, heavy waters of destiny. Great Sister, mother of the fated land.'

173) 'Great Brother who knows the root of the Tree of Consciousness and Knowledge and the Light Vessel, bear witness to this clay.'

174) 'Great Sister, creator of the Amazons, the lord-bearing 'Clay Eye' protect.'

175) Lofty Za the leader meets on high. For Ta, the roof he is raising.

176) The word of Ta comes to him. 'Measure the fate not of the sheep that Luna populate'

177) 'But of the hanging basket with the reed paddle that the temple defiled by reputed native beer bringing.'

178) 'Measure the height of the man in the fiery coracle, that his straw go up in smoke!'

179) Two liars, the fox and the wolf, to the offspring of Atum they give names.

180) 'Measure the height of the man in the kurta on the Mount of Ta, that the wind of Madara send up his smoke.'

181) 'In his hearth with the tiny turret, the great man who smells of beer, that his chicks behind their straw façade on the Milky Way reflect on their birth.'

182) To the great and lofty hearth of the Temple, a building to bring water to the eye of the miller, their round curses fly.

183) (BROKEN) regal forceful hand in the clay thrusts.

184) 'Man his measure to take, man his measure not to take.' The troublesome native in the clay it places.

185) 'For man to acquire trust', the powerful hand in the clay expands.

186) 'That an unworldly spouse he take, with the pungent seed of reputed homeland tobacco to lie down.'

187) Inside the house, the wolfen maiden of the new moon the sheep will cook. By the arm of Dan in the sky, the house will dangul high.

188) 'For man his life to extend anew, that man his arm its prayers to the sky he multiply.'

189) 'The Great Bull in the midst of its gully, man, weighted with beer, under an opaque flow will sit.'

190) 'Man in the watercourse, less beaten with storms and the spindle he would cross above.'

191) 'Man on the city hanging cord, his noisy voice below his shoulder with lowered reflections his questioning will oil!'

192) Young Mu and Za their round curses through the water flying, borne on the wind to the clay of Meria, they send up the smoke of her fire.

193) The maiden her foothills to know, the sack of curses at its head, to Tahta 'The Clay Eye', to the throne in the sky the fly-in-a-jar she brings. By her palm the leader into the clay will be entered.

194) Under the eye of Ur, behind the reed façade, along the Milky Way, through the sky to Anta the fly-in-a-jar she brings.

195) The soft palm of Ga in her hand is. The eye of Ur on the heart of the Milky Way is.

196) Under the soft palm of Ga the reed stalk in her hand, that the bark not fly away.

197) The eye of Ur, the reed stalk in his hand, that the bark not into the Dini fly.

198) Over the soft palm of Ga on Earth a great flood there is, the reed stalk not holding back.

199) The eye of the dog on the Treasure house of Gargara beats a raga. Ra, his round curses above the low-placed mouths they rise.

200) 'Volcano side or river side, that the boat bearing the noble arm sink!'

201) 'From the sky onto Eden's stony plain that it sink. That the waterskin bearing the noble arm split!'

202) 'At Earth's heart to measure the heat of its funnel place the house!' At his furnace and storehouse, the master builder reflects on dams.

203) The heart of a troublesome volcano a bad place for the house of a moon wolf and their spouse to dam.

204) On other realms a lofty door to place, the measurements he takes, wide as a guardian spirit for a heavy prince.

205) The door to other realms Ra's weighty beating to withstand, with nine hinges he protects.

206) The strong arm of a wise soul he acquires, one with knowledge of their birth, the fiery lord to supervise.

207) Young Mu or the man with the eye of a dog should they beat on the volcano's door, nine hinges and an open eye its threshold will guard.

208) With a festive song of the land, a heavy dam for the roof we will acquire on high.

209) In the rope basket, blood there will be. In the rope basket, prey there will be.

210) In the rope basket, precious metal there will be. In the rope basket, lapis lazuli there will be.

211) In the rope basket, yarn there will be. In the rope basket, linen there will be.

212) (BROKEN) in a foreign land divide.

213) The Bull (BROKEN) a thick stone roof to pay – count your shekels, count your shekels.

214) For the bull a heavy lullaby we will play – count your shekels, count your shekels. (BROKEN) the other-worldly stable cover

215) Sal, leaping on a rope over the house, before the leader a straw façade will place.

216) The sun and its donkey to the voice of the ass the stones of the sky counting, counting.

217) The ass across the opening (BROKEN)

218) The ass with a lullaby the opening of the clay will supervise.

219) Young Mu the lofty musician with his homeland shoulder horn will sweeten.

220) Sal, wild girl, with a wave of her hand, to the temple in the cleft the reputed native beer she brings.

221) Through the din, to the beer pouring from on high, the thirsty noble frame into the clay sinks, sinks, sinks.

222) The hand of the fish by the nurturing Tree its rope to seize, the two lofty men on the state of Da before Di cannot agree.

223) In the Temple of Ea, mosquito creator, a buzz is building and dark night its cloud gathering over the lord.

224) The ass of Tara above the altar her thick voice counting to the lofty accountant rises.

225) Her servant with tar water and fresh oil beating a raga, her name in a thick cloud to the opening rises.

226) On the female voices round curses heard: 'That their harping mouths by their whirling reeds be dammed!'

227) The wooden spindle with round curses churning, Shu from homeland stones her Ra protecting, the heavy hand of Muna the door to another era opens.

228) Into the temple of Ea a multitude of water and straw entering, entering, entering.

229) The tall, wide Ebu, weight on the neck of Ra, the moon with the reeds will light.

230) The arm in the otherworldly basket, churning the spirit wind, to the shrine ascends.

(Eleven lines broken in the following section)

231) Above the walls at Siwa, divided by the horns, the silent eyes (BROKEN) raised high.

232) On Earth, the hothead and his smoke by the door on the rope to rise with the wind (BROKEN) flutter up into the sky.

233) (BROKEN) the place imposed… below… arm clay

234) …Rise (BROKEN) whirl reeds three new moons to watch, with thick black clay his mouth to oil.

235) (BROKEN) rule the heart of the volcano the troublesome giant acquire.

236) Young Mu (BROKEN) on the circle loom a beautiful black feather to thread.

237) (BROKEN) water…straw cut

238) (BROKEN) middle

239) (BROKEN) lie down

240) (BROKEN) establish

241. 'That the joyful heart be uplifted and spread on the multiple winds of Siwa.' (BROKEN)

242) 'Measure the fate not of the lively Lama with the fat arm of the cuckoo, but that of Zeus with the fat cuckolding arm.'

243) 'Measure the fate of the great vessel, carrying in its hold the noble cargo with the haughty spirit and tongue.'

244) 'Young Mu, who two darts first created, that his eye be twice pierced.'

245) 'That from the sky unworldly seeds beat down on his roof…That the Great Binder gather and burn the noble wood, that his strong arm with beer oil all of it.'

246) 'And on the lofty womb a curse: that the noble young daughter in the straw reflect on the birth of everyone in the land!'

247) 'Under the shady tree stump, that Black Horn knead soil and water. Fired with beer, that the noble young son in the straw reflect on his birth in the land.'

248) From her spouse the homeland to save, Ria the noble mouths on the roof with a stone from the sky in a basket will pacify.

249) To the place of the dam Ria's waters flow, that the city spy crushed by her basket be.

250) In the middle of her waters, a gullet blocked with a white stone there is…That the spirit of the dodo smoke with the lord.

251) The man on the hanging cord with his sling, with one lofty blow, with milk from the stone, encircles the spirit of the fiery lord.

252) With the head-dress of Ma and the stone from the sky, to the reed wall, between two prongs, the noble child is emptied naked from the straw.

253) The noble who the remote water-churner created, Sis between sky and Earth, the wall of reed to establish, her noble heavy hand waves stones from the sky on the master builder of the noble who the remote water-churner created… (See page 34)

254) On the spirit cord of Ga, a fine basket with milk from her kid for the great man with the beer smell, 'The Clay Eye' to cut its flight.

255) The amazon to know her root, to the mouth of the waterspout, less sand in the beer of the lord, under the eye of the dog, at the heart of the volcano, on the Sabbath, less beating of Ga's giants there will be!

256) Mother's voice rumbling through the sky, with her basket the noisy mouth of Za to seize, on a new cloud his seat to serve more beer to the lord.

257) Mother the exalted sun will be, that the man in the moon reflect on his birth.

258) Father below, fewer storms in the sky there will be. For the man in the homeland, days of blazing sun she will establish.

259) Father under cover will be, in the mouth of beautiful Ma that he raise his arm.

260) Under the flying stone, father by the rope of the Tree of Consciousness and Knowledge, the Light Vessel, will bear witness before Ia to multiply her waters.

261) A city temple, in its centre to beat the mat to soften the heart of Ga, the leader and master builder will raise.

262) For Young Mu a lofty space for the beer-trough where Sis will hang and guard.

263) Magnificent the water distributor will be! A hot water distributor there will be!

264) Measure the length of the cord of water pouring from the cask. Measure its spirit. Measure its beat. Beat its measure.

265) Copper for a beautiful thick cover to acquire at the place of stone, count the shekels of your blood brothers as Sis glides close by.

266) The dog to not know, a volcano there must be. Man to not know, a mouse-hole there must be.

267) The beer cask to not know, a gap in Mount Kara and the mouth of the crow.

268) In the sky, the crow man to swallow, that he measure the mouths and reflect on the spirit of the three.

269) The house of man she has designed without nails, but not built. The city of man she has designed without nails, but not built.

270) The place to know water for the mouths of men, that their voice on the Sabbath beat the burning midday sky for rain.

271) If the shepherd beats his working kin, the heavy old moon his sheep will turn.

272) If the farmer beats his camel, a rueful farmer the stony old moon will till.

273) (BROKEN) whirl Muna the seat of the lord

274) Measure the heart with water and the truth of Ma's word with beer. Measure the heart by the stone of Muna. (BROKEN)

275) The Great Hanging Temple of Galla to enter with the crow and the beer, measure the heart of heavy Saturn.

276) Measure the flowing heart of the voices of the land to (BROKEN) (the star-filled skies – my addition).

277) Tell the story of Sukurru when young Ubara Dudu ruled. Tell the story of the flying stone of Ga.

278) Sukurru when young Ubara Dudu ruled softly narrated.

279) Finely covered Great Hanging Tableau of the Galaxy, Her hand fittingly watered.

280) Linking Earth and sky with her fine thread, the seeds of soft stone knotted on Her fine shoulder.

www.ingramcontent.com/pod-product-compliance
Lightning Source LLC
Chambersburg PA
CBHW071213040426
42333CB00068B/1795